Quam tibi Cisterci placeat ſanctiſſimuſ ordo.
Hęc nobis pmum oſtenſio facta probat:
Ergo tuo maneat ſemp ſub nūmine tutus.
Deditus ante alios Virgo beata tibi.

Mary, Patroness of the Cistercian Order.
Woodcut from the Book of Cistercian Privileges, 1491.

The White Monks

A HISTORY OF THE CISTERCIAN ORDER

by

LOUIS J. LEKAI, Ph.D.
S.O.Cist.

CISTERCIAN FATHERS

OUR LADY OF SPRING BANK, OKAUCHEE, WIS.

1953

Permissu Superiorum Ordinis.

Imprimi potest.

Festo S.P.N. Roberti, A.D. 1953.

Raimundus Molnar, S.T.D.
Prior Monasterii B.M.V. de Spring Bank.

Nihil obstat.
L. F. Sharkey,
Censor Librorum.

Die 30a Aprilis, 1953.

Imprimatur.
✠ Josephus Aloisius,
Episcopus Buffalensis.

Library of Congress Catalog Card Number: 53-7711

PRINTED IN THE UNITED STATES OF AMERICA

Contents

Part I

A HISTORICAL SURVEY

Part II

CISTERCIAN CULTURE

Appendices

Illustrations

PART I

A Historical Survey

1. Western Monasticism

The monks of the West, however eagerly they fled the world, remained always a part of contemporary society and thus participants of its development, subjects of its history. The truth of Revelation is timeless, but each generation developed a distinctly different approach to its exalted ideals. The monks, in their persistent striving after perfection, truly reflected the changing mind of new ages. Moreover, it was through monasticism that religion exercised a direct formative influence on the unfolding character of Christian civilization.

The religious life, broadly interpreted, is as old as mankind itself. In all ages, in every great civilization, there have been men and women who dedicated their lives to the service of God either by living in retirement from worldly affairs or by spending themselves in works of charity. Christianity did not create a new type of life by its monastic institutions. Rather, it breathed a new soul into an old structure. Its program of asceticism was based upon the solid foundation of the evangelical counsels—voluntary poverty, chastity, and obedience.

In the very first Christian centuries, thousands of hermits and anchorites abandoned a pagan and hostile civilization for the solitary life in the deserts of Egypt and Syria. Through severe penances and continuous meditation they mapped out a daily schedule for fighting the allurements of the evil spirit and conquering the temptations of the flesh. Many grouped themselves around such strong personalities as St. Paul of Thebais or St. Anthony, and started a form of community life. St. Pachomius (296-346) further added to this development by building the first monasteries and giving to his cenobites the first monastic rule.

By the end of the fourth century, Eastern monasticism was profoundly influenced by St. Basil (330-379) and his rule. Instead of the strange austerities emphasized by the Desert Fathers, Basil stressed the practice of basic Christian virtues, the value of community life, and the importance of regular work. Basilian monasteries mushroomed throughout Asia Minor and Palestine, and his spirit is still perpetuated in Greek and Slavonic monasticism.

After its conversion, the West also embraced the eremitical life of the East. St. Martin of Tours, and especially Cassian (360-420) by his *Institutes* and *Collations,* contributed substantially to this development; yet, it was soon proven that neither climate nor the western character was in accordance with such an austere eastern pattern. Except for Ireland, the eremitical system never took deep root in Europe, and at the end of the fifth century the early establishments were in full decline.

St. Benedict

St. Benedict (480-547), who not only detected the troubles but basically reorganized religious life, became the real founder and father of Western Monasticism. He was a noble Roman in birth and mind; and his work, the Rule, was a classical masterpiece of a dying civilization and a splendid synthesis of the best in Roman and Christian traditions. He definitely turned his back to the extravagant individualism of the Eastern hermits. His religious community followed the model of a well ordered Roman family. There was one head, the father of the monastery, the Abbot, having an unlimited authority, while the members of the community were obliged to carry out his commands in perfect obedience and discipline. Yet this severity was always tempered by the abbot's fatherly love and his deep understanding of human nature with all its needs and weaknesses. St. Benedict's practical mind permeated the smallest details of the daily schedule and arranged everything by the use of his favorite phrase, "reasonably and with right measure." Corresponding to western mentality, there was a sound balance between prayer and work, the former including the recitation of the Divine Office and spiritual reading, the latter involving physical or mental occupation. Obviously, St. Benedict's Rule was not given for a select group of perfect monks ready to practice the virtues in a heroic manner; rather, he considered it as the least of rules, written for beginners, for everyone who truly seeks God, presupposing all kinds of shortcomings and transgressions. In his keen sense for legal justice, there were strict punishments too; but the holy author could state with full sincerity in the Prologue, that he was about to establish a school of the service of God, in which he hoped he would ordain nothing rigorous or burdensome.

The superiority and practical value of the Rule of St. Benedict was proven by the fact that within two hundred years it conquered the whole West, supplanting the Celtic monasticism and the latter's more severe Rule of St. Columban (540-615). The quick spread of Benedictine life was greatly promoted by Pope St. Gregory the Great (540-604), who committed to the Benedictines the mission of converting the still pagan people of England. After achieving splendid success in this field, they extended their activities into Germany, Scandinavia and farther east among the Slavic peoples, converting them not only by preaching the Gospel, but by the example of Christian life in their well ordered monasteries.

Although, during the three centuries following St. Benedict's death, no considerable change took place in the observance of the Rule or in the religious ideals, yet the monastic establishments north of the Alps gave quite a different picture from the modest beginnings of the early sixth century. The original "schools of the Lord's service," far from the proud centers of contemporary civilization and established for a limited number of God-seeking souls, gradually became the hub of an economic, social, and intellectual revival for a whole new society longing for higher learning. Charlemagne (768-814) entrusted his magnificent educational program to the monasteries recently reorganized by himself; moreover, his most influential advisers, the eminent representatives of the so-called "Carolingian Renaissance," were all Benedictines.

With the monks' expansion north of the Alps, the new duties and colder climate produced unimportant modifications in the daily schedule, food, and clothing; but far more important changes were imminent, because the newly born society and civilization, nurtured by the Church, was basically different from that of St. Benedict. Although the British, French, and German monasteries did their best to transplant elements of the antique culture together with the rudiments of Christian faith into the minds of their new pupils, the result was essentially influenced by a third element, namely the native culture and historic tradition of these one-time barbaric nations. On this triple integration of antiquity, Christianity, and national traditions, hinged the new civilization of the Middle Ages. This new world was soon strong enough to assimilate all the institutions inherited from past antiquity. The medieval Papacy, with its constantly growing influence, the reborn Empire, and the cities rebuilt upon Roman ruins are the best examples of how the new society transformed the antique heritage. For the same reason, it is understandable how the Rule of St. Benedict and his monastic ideals—as another product of the late Roman civilization—sooner or later was to face a procedure of adaptation to the requirements of the changed world.

The human ideal of these young and vigorous peoples was the fearless warrior; the virtue they most admired, heroism; and the only vocation they thought fitting to free men was that of the soldier and the knight. Upon such a mentality a smoothly running monastery, with its classical gravity and monotonous daily schedule under a mild Rule, in which nothing harsh or rigorous was legislated, made not too deep an impression. At the same time, far more appealing was the heroic life and example of the Desert Fathers engaged in a continuous battle against legions of demons and whose miraculous stories and legends were available in every monastic library. For these overzealous converts, the Rule hardly offered any opportunity to prove their individual heroism in severe ascetism; consequently, their growing discontent led to a long period of crisis in monastic history, created by a gap existing between new needs and desires on the one hand, and the immense authority of St. Benedict and his Rule on the other. The solution was not easy, because open alteration in the monastic Rule was out of question. Even disregarding the traditional veneration of the Rule and its author, there was no word more detested in the Middle Ages than "innovation." The only way to find a satisfactory compromise between the two vital factors, tradition and life, was the re-interpretation of the silent letters of the Rule according to the new ideals. Its unfoldment from the first attempt toward a final solution presented by the Cistercians, constitutes the most interesting pages of the history of the European mind, and runs parallel with the evolution of other medieval institutions which reached their culmination in the twelfth century. It is needless to emphasize that the real monastic "reforms" in the future ebullitions of the forthcoming centuries did not presuppose necessarily low moral standards or decline, and never meant certain simple measures for extirpating some abuses to restore the ancient discipline. On the contrary, the "reforms" were repeated attempts to find a new formula and way of living, in which the old and new could melt into one harmonious synthesis.

St. Benedict of Aniane

The first definite challenge of the new ideals was represented in the life and reform activities of St. Benedict of Aniane (d.821). He received a traditional Benedictine training, but soon left the community. With his devoted disciples, he started a life of extreme simplicity and austerity, openly declaring that the Rule was for beginners only, while the imitation of the Desert Fathers was meant to lead to perfection. For the West, this program was still premature. As soon as he realized the unfavorable reaction, Benedict yielded to a compromise, without losing his determination to carry out his plans with the effective backing and commitment of Louis the Pious. Assuming the position of reformer of all the monasteries of the Empire, Benedict called together in 817, under the auspices of the Emperor, a general meeting of abbots at Aachen, where they passed a series of regulations, the *Capitula,* concerning monastic reform. The Rule was kept as a basis, but the indefatigable reformer succeeded in putting into practice some of his original ideals, such as perfect seclusion from the world and the increase of time spent in prayer. Consequently, the *Capitula* prohibited the maintenance of schools in the monastery, discontinued the agricultural work of the monks, and recognized liturgical prayer as almost the only monastic occupation.

St. Benedict of Aniane was doubtless a strong revolutionary character and an excellent organizer; but, since he had built his work upon the support of the Emperor, instead of upon the understanding sympathy of his fellow abbots, his work was reduced to nothing after the collapse of the Carolingian Monarchy.

The following troublesome decades of the "Dark Ages" weighed heavily upon monasticism everywhere in Europe without any hope for a sound revival. In the foundation of Cluny in 910, however, the program of Benedict of Aniane was resumed with such success that this time the reform changed the standard of monastic life entirely and permanently influenced Benedictine spirituality. Besides the observance of the Rule according to the interpretation of the Aachen *Capitula,* Cluny's principal achievement was the securing of complete independence from any secular interference of all the monasteries and churches belonging to the congregation. In this endeavor the monks met the aims of the renewed Papacy and exempted from the authority of the local bishops, enjoyed the full protection of Rome. To secure the perfect uniformity of rite and discipline—putting aside the Rule's original thought concerning the independency of every single monastery—the Abbot of Cluny exercised a direct and unlimited power over the whole Congregation. The growth and influence of Cluny reached its peak during the long regime of Abbot Hugh (1049-1109), who controlled about 1300 monasteries.

Although the vast majority of the legally incorporated houses were in France, Cluny's influence extended all over Christian Europe. It was particularly strong in Spain, where the first crusade against the Arabs (after 1063) had been started with the full support of Cluny. In Flanders and Lorraine, Gerhard of Brogne (d.959) reformed about twenty houses in the spirit of Cluny and after a short interval his work was continued in the first half of the eleventh century by Richard of Verdun (d.1046). Richard was particularly persistent in eliminating every kind of secular influence from his monasteries and, in behalf of preserving the unity of the congregation, proposed an annual meeting of abbots.

The reform of almost 70 monasteries goes back to John of Gorze, who, in the middle of the tenth century, insisted on the literal interpretation of the Rule, introducing an extremely severe penitential discipline. William of Dijon (d.1031) reformed the Benedictines of Normandy, and, after the Norman Conquest, his monks also reorganized the English monastic life. Although Cluny's direct influence in Germany was negligible, the customs of the largest congregation—with about one hundred houses, headed by Hirsau—were nothing but a modification of the regulations of Cluny.

The Eleventh Century Reforms

Cluny's importance in the formation of Western monasticism cannot be overestimated. The movement, in close cooperation with the Papacy, helped to restore the independence and dignity of the Church and raised the reputation and moral standards of the religious vocation to a higher level than had ever existed. Yet it is difficult to deny that the well organized life in the magnificent monasteries, the artistically developed daily liturgical service, the splendor of the romanesque churches, the active role in feudal politics were in open contradiction with the reformatory ideals of simplicity and austerity of Benedict of Aniane. At the same time, the vision of the asceticism of the Desert Fathers did not lose its challenging power. On the contrary, the attraction of the eremitical life had been revived with a stronger impulse than ever before, especially in Southern Italy, around the year 1000. During the Middle Ages, the peninsula was always a link between East and West, and, though under varying political control, it yielded a steady Byzantine and Oriental cultural infiltration. Communication with Eastern Christianity was particularly increased when the Turkish invasion of Asia Minor compelled large numbers of priests and monks to seek refuge in Italy, and the hills of Calabria were populated once again with hermits and anchorites.

One of the first to revive the memory of the pre-Benedictine asceticism in Italy was St. Nilus (d.1005), the founder of a Basilian monastery. A more conscious reformer was St. Romuald of Ravenna (d.1027). Dissatisfied with the Cluniac discipline of his monastery at Ravenna, he left the community and with his disciples founded several hermitages, among them one at Camaldoli. Inspired by the reading of the lives of the Desert Fathers, he wished to restore the monastic life according to the earliest tradition of solitude and austerity. Except for liturgical prayer in common, his monks lived a solitary life of perpetual silence and severe fasting in small huts. Romuald himself did not compose a separate rule, but characteristically enough maintained the Rule of St. Benedict although his interpretation was obviously opposed to its real spirit.

The life and activity of St. John Gualbert of Florence (d.1073) followed a similar pattern. Leaving his Benedictine monastery, he joined for a time the Camaldolese; ultimately, however, he abandoned the eremitical life and founded a cenobite monastery at Vallombrosa, near Florence. He also kept the Rule of St. Benedict, interpreting it in the scope of a purely contemplative life. In addition to requiring the strictest silence and enclosure, he forbade manual work, which was given over together with the other administrative duties to lay brothers.

In far-reaching influence and authority, both Romuald and John Gualbert were surpassed by St. Peter Damian (1007-1072) whose role and activity in the eleventh century was similar to St. Bernard's a century later. After his "conversion," Damian joined a group of hermits at Fonte Avellana, founded by a disciple of St. Romuald. Soon becoming the leader of the hermits, he composed a rule which was based on the Rule of St. Benedict, supplying it with the necessary instructions for the eremitical life. He—like St. Benedict of Aniane—contended that St. Benedict's Rule was meant only for beginners in the spiritual life, being but a preparation for the more perfect life of the hermits. Having this conviction, he felt himself perfectly justified in arguing that he and his fellow-hermits were just as true Benedictines as the cenobites. He propagated successfully his views on asceticism through his pamphlets and letters which were full of erudition and cast in a style of splendid Latinity. Later his position as a cardinal and an intimate adviser of the Popes gave his teaching additional prestige.

The monastic reform in Italy during the eleventh century aroused little echo elsewhere, and the Orders of Camaldoli and

Vallombrosa never gained ground north of the Alps. Further decisive steps toward a reformed religious life, sweeping throughout the whole Latin Christianity, were made again in France, in the same Burgundy whence the Cluniac reform started its victorious campaign two centuries earlier. This movement received a valiant and unexpected impetus from the First Crusade (1096), which aroused an unparalleled religious enthusiasm in millions of souls. Just as hundreds of thousands received the cross eager to die for Christ, legions of noble souls swarmed into the reformed monasteries, filled with the same heroic spirit, to embrace the cross of a life of incredible severity.

One of the early centers of this monastic renewal—though not the most successful one—was Molesme, founded for a group of hermits in 1075 by the same St. Robert who was later to lead the first Cistercians. The undertaking, at first promising, attracted St. Bruno of Cologne (d.1101) who, after a short time, left the monastery and around 1084 founded a hermitage with his followers in the valley of Chartreuse, near Grenoble. Their Rule was that of St. Benedict according to the interpretation of the Camaldolese, with more emphasis on contemplation, simplicity, and austerity. In 1098 Robert himself, the Abbot of Molesme, abandoned the troubled place with disappointed hermits, heading into the forests of Cîteaux.

Another meeting place of monastic reformers was the forest of Craon, near the border line of Normandy and Brittany. Inhabited by a number of hermits living in scattered huts, it was called significantly in contemporary sources "a new Egypt." At the close of the eleventh century, these hermits were organized under the leadership of Vitalis of Mortain (d.1122). Other prominent members of the assembly were Robert of Arbrissel, a celebrated itinerant preacher, and Bernard of Tiron (d.1117), formerly a Benedictine monk of St. Cyprian at Poitiers. Although, basically, all recognized the authority of the Rule of St. Benedict, except for a common program of strict asceticism, their views on monastic reform varied considerably. In succession, each of the leading figures established independent communities for their faithful disciples.

Robert of Arbrissel founded c.1100 a community on the model of the Apostolic Church at Fontevrault in Anjou. A phenomenal success, it became a fully organized order with three groups of members—the contemplative nuns, the lay sisters, and priests who served as chaplains. The abbess of Fontevrault had jurisdiction over the whole organization.

Vitalis of Mortain, in search of greater solitude, retired in 1105 to the forest of Savigny. The life of the new establishment, with special emphasis on agricultural work with the assistance of lay brothers, as well as a system of visitation and general chapters resembled closely the organization of Cîteaux. The fusion of the flourishing congregation of Savigny with the Cistercians in 1147 was effectuated as a direct result of their common endeavor.

The fervor of discipline and simplicity animated Bernard in the foundation of Tiron in 1109. The return of this group to manual labor and to the original simplicity of liturgical services in accordance with the prescriptions of the Rule of St. Benedict safely supports the assumption that Bernard was quite familiar with the reform of Cîteaux. His monks, however, besides doing agricultural labor, practiced all the arts and crafts without the employment of lay brothers.

A strictly eremitical community was founded c.1100 by Stephen of Muret (d.1124) at Grandmont near Limoges, after the fashion of the Camaldolese and the Carthusians. Personally impressed by the hermits of Calabria, he carried the same idea which secured the brilliant success for the Cistercians to its extreme logical limit. In the love of poverty and simplicity, Stephen rejected every kind of fixed revenue including lands and animals, while for the sake of undisturbed contemplation he committed the administration of his whole plantation to lay brothers with almost full responsibility.

Direct Cistercian influence was working in England in the reform of Gilbert of Sempringham, involving communities for both men and women. In 1147, the founder himself proposed the fusion of his growing congregation with the Cistercians. Cîteaux, however, opposed to the establishment of any legal connection with convents, declined the offer.

Cistercian ideas inspired the reformer of the Augustinian Canons, St. Norbert (d.1134), a personal friend of St. Bernard of Clairvaux. The admirable success and quick growth of the Premonstratensians which was begun at Prémontré near Reims, the mother house, almost equaled that of the Cistercians.

The heroic spirit of reform was not restricted to the monastic orders; it penetrated the whole society, especially the populations of the growing cities. The desire for a reformed church with a reformed clergy increased with such impetus that the movement could not be stifled. While the religious communities with their well instructed and disciplined membership never escaped the direction of legal authorities, those half-cultured city crowds swung toward revolutionary extremes. What the Rule was for monastic reform, the Gospel was for the lay movement; and, as the monks were inspired by the example of the Desert Fathers, the popular preachers idealized the life of the Apostolic Church, especially in its poverty and simplicity. They supported their demands concerning the absolute poverty of the clergy and a perfect detachment of the Church from every secular implication by the literal interpretation of the Gospel. Their background of extremely austere asceticism was nothing more than a revived form of Manicheism. In their belief that matter and the body originated from the principle of evil, they condemned marriage, refused to eat meat, and fasted until starvation. This movement, as an anticlerical heresy, also had the political result of revolting against the bishops' authority and of achieving a free municipal autonomy by the elected communes. The best known and most talented representative of all these doctrines was Arnold of Brescia (d.1155), the founder of the famed Roman Republic, a lifelong adversary of St. Bernard of Clairvaux. This popular heretical revolution found its stronghold in Southern France, particularly at Languedoc, with Toulouse and Albi as its centers, hence the name Albigenses. These disturbances endured for a century. As an organized movement, it was crushed by the bloody crusade of Simon of Montfort; but the heresy survived, although greatly weakened, through the preaching of the newly established Mendicant Friars.

Succinctly told, this is the story of religious reform in the West from the ninth until the twelfth century, leading from the failures of Benedict of Aniane to the phenomenal success of the Cistercians. The early attempts, lacking the solid support of a legal framework, could not survive; the well balanced program of traditional and modern ideas adapted to the spiritual needs of a new civilization, together with a smoothly working constitution, explain the lasting prosperity of the Cistercians and made them the first real Order of the medieval West.

2. Cistercian Beginnings

Early Cistercian history is intimately connected with a previous attempt at monastic reform, namely that of St. Robert of Molesme. Robert's career and character are rather enigmatic. He was born about the year 1028 in Champagne, France. At the age of 15, he entered the Benedictine monastery of Moutier de Celle; but, like many of his contemporaries, in his quest for perfect discipline and zeal for reform, he soon left the monastery. First as an elected prior or abbot, then as a simple monk, he successively joined a score of other communities, though, in his disappointment, he spent a considerable time in solitary retirement as a hermit. Although his frequent changes of habitation earned him a reputation for fickleness, his persistent efforts, good will, and saintly life gained him sincere honor and respect.

Molesme

After many discouraging experiments, Robert finally accepted the leadership of a group of hermits in the woodland of Colan, near Langres. He moved his new community to Molesme, and there, in 1075, they started a life somewhat resembling that of the Camaldolesians. In extreme poverty and hard manual labor, they lived in small huts made of boughs. Partly his reputation for holiness and partly the convenient location of the new settlement, close to the main road connecting Paris with Lyons and leading to Italy, attracted numerous visitors. Among them were St. Bruno and later Stephen Harding, who had just returned from a pilgrimage to Rome. Bruno, the future founder of the Carthusians, did not spend much time at Molesme, but Stephen joined the community and became the key figure of its future development. The increase in members and in reputation was followed by rich donations, and Molesme, in a surprisingly short time, developed into a center of a new monastic congregation. By grants, a great number of parishes and churches were placed under its care, and some monasteries also subjugated themselves to its jurisdiction; moreover, the growth of personnel made possible the foundation of new houses.

But the quick growth caused serious disturbances within the community. The group of founding hermits was soon outnumbered by newcomers and they lost control of discipline. Differences developed to a regrettable degree between the two parties and continued for years with the usual bitterness of religious controversies. Nevertheless, it would be a gross mistake to suspect a decline of religious fervor or even moral deterioration among the members of the major party. Behind the quarrels, there was the basic antagonism of old and new; the overwhelming influence of the widely accepted and honored discipline of Cluny was sharply contrasted to the new ideals of the small revolting group of former hermits who in their heroism regarded the standard regulations of the former as utterly unsatisfactory and obsolete. During these turbulent years, two of the basic features of the future Cistercian program were crystallized: one, on the positive side, manifests a cleverly selected slogan sounding almost like a battle cry, "back to the letters of the Rule"; on the negative side, there appeared a spontaneous antagonism against Cluny, her customs and traditions. The former furnished legal justification for the cause of the fighting hermits; the latter kept their uncompromising determination in constant tension.

Robert, their Abbot, unable to master the situation, left his monks in disgust and retired to a hermitage, where he was followed by some of the persecuted hermits, among them Alberic, the Prior, and Stephen Harding. This sudden secession of the Abbot and the most zealous members of the community threatened the high reputation of the monastery. Therefore, the abandoned monks turned to Rome, and Urban II, considering their grievances, ordered Robert back to Molesme. The Abbot obeyed; but since there was no possibility of a compromise between the opponents nothing was solved by his return. As a result, the plan to leave the turbulent monastery emerged again, but this time Robert and his faithful flock proceeded with utmost circumspection. First of all, they secured the enthusiastic backing of Archbishop Hugh of Lyons, Apostolic Legate of France, a former monk and ardent promoter of Gregorian reform. The Archbishop recommended them to Odo, Duke of Burgundy, who with his progeny proved to be the most devoted and generous friend of the new foundation. The site of a monastery was donated by his vassal Raynald, Viscount of Beaune, in whose diocese of Châlons, Bishop Walter also showed his good will toward the proposition.

In the meantime, within the very walls of Molesme, the propaganda and recruiting efforts of Robert and his companions measured to such success that altogether twenty-one monks, inspired with the highest ideals of monastic perfection, prepared themselves to assume the hardships of a new foundation.

Cîteaux

Life at the "New Monastery," Cîteaux, a "place of horrors and vast solitude" south of Dijon, began on March 21, 1098—significantly on the feast of St. Benedict. Except for the added emphasis on eremitical seclusion, both the setting and program were very much like Molesme of a quarter of a century before; and, if Robert had had a chance to lead the new monastery for a longer period of time, most likely it would have become nothing more than a reformed house of the Benedictines. But, in the meantime, the persistent community of

Molesme, in order to save its shaken reputation, mobilized all available connections in Rome, and succeeded in obtaining a new Papal decree returning to them their Abbot. Robert, after having spent about a year in the "New Monastery," reassumed the government at Molesme, taking with him some monks of Cîteaux, who were more attached to the person of the Abbot than to the high ideals of Cîteaux. Robert died at Molesme in 1111, without having been able to witness the successful realization of his dearly cherished dreams.

The most difficult times for Cîteaux were still in the future. Alberic, the former Prior, was elected Abbot in Robert's place. He was one of the founding hermits of Molesme, and an intrepid warrior of the reform, who in the time of the most passionate debates had been beaten and imprisoned. His small community had already suffered from the departure of their widely respected founder and his followers; but now the unceasing jealousy of Molesme and some neighboring monasteries, their calumnies and attempts to interfere, seriously threatened the very existence of the new establishment. In this distressed position, Alberic, with the recommendation of the Apostolic Delegate and the Bishop of Châlons, took refuge in the Holy See. Pope Paschal III, who succeeded Urban II, appreciated the applicant's holy endeavor, and, in his letter dated April 18, 1100, addressed to Alberic, took the "New Monastery" under immediate Papal protection. Although the letter cannot be regarded as exempting the monastery from diocesan jurisdiction, the formal Papal approval finally secured the peaceful and quiet development of the community.

Surrounded by rival Benedictine houses, and exposed to their criticism, there gradually developed in Cîteaux a certain self-consciousness based upon its different discipline and peculiar way of living—the psychological element traced in the foundations of every new order. The first definite step in that direction was made when Alberic composed the first Statutes of Cîteaux. These few lines are rather negative comments on Cluniac discipline; yet, a special stress on simplicity and poverty, as well as his idea of introducing lay brothers into the community, became firm cornerstones of future Cistercian legislation. According to tradition, the adoption of the white habit, instead of the black used by Benedictines everywhere, occurred during his regime. After completing almost ten years in office, Alberic died in 1109. His successor was found in the former Prior, Stephen Harding, who, from the earliest years of Molesme, played a decisive role in the further development of the foundation. He is the first personality in the history of Cîteaux whom we have to recognize as a genius. Born before 1066, and of noble Anglo-Saxon blood, he received his first education in the monastery of Sherborne in Dorsetshire. During the troubled years following the Norman Conquest, he fled together with the monks to Scotland. In his pursuit of higher learning, Stephen went to Paris and later, as a pilgrim, he visited Rome, where he was assured of his monastic vocation. When, on his way back, his attention was called to the promising new venture of Molesme, he possessed all the learning and experience the era could furnish him. He had been educated in the atmosphere of English monasticism, still rich in Celtic traditions and recently reformed by St. Dunstan according to Cluniac and Lotharingian models. Paris certainly had been the best place not only for studies but for his acquaintance with the general problems of monastic and ecclesiastical life. Moreover, during his Italian journey, he must have been greatly influenced by the prevailing spirit of St. Peter Damian and impressed by the living example of Camaldoli and Vallombrosa. After joining Molesme, he had the opportunity to learn both the power and weakness of the ruling Cluniac system and to witness sorrowfully the breakdown of the original ideals of the founders through poor internal organization and external force. Now, invested with the responsibilities of Abbot of Cîteaux, he exerted all his energies toward putting into practice the results of his long experience and silent meditations. This gave him an opportunity to employ his exceptional abilities as an organizer, and forced his keen legal mind to give shape to a foundation whose existence had, until then, been foundering in its effort to seek its own place in a revolutionized monastic world.

Yet there was neither opportunity nor time for any large scale activity. Cîteaux was still so poor that at times of meager harvest the community was close to starvation. A contagious disease severely decimated their number; but most alarming of all was a serious dearth of vocations. This unexpected difficulty cannot be explained by the extraordinarily austere life at Cîteaux; its main cause was presumably the influence of their jealous monastic neighbors who were eager to spread false and distorted stories about the life of those eccentric monks who dared to break with age-old traditions. The collapse of the "New Monastery" seemed inevitable and imminent, and the Abbot with his discouraged brethren "besought the Lord, weeping day and night and were on the verge of desperation."

They did not pray in vain. A sudden change in fortune came when in 1112 the youthful Bernard knocked on the gate of the abbey with his thirty companions. The example and irresistible personality of this brilliant young man reversed the problem. From now on, the greatest difficulty developed from the fact that in a matter of years thousands of applicants would be accepted and a score of new monasteries founded. Because of these unforeseen eventualities, there was immediate necessity to establish a form of central government in order to safeguard the unity of the rapidly growing Order and to secure the original spirit and discipline. The historic meeting of these two geniuses, Abbot Stephen and Bernard, brought about the erection of an organization and spirituality, exemplary from every respect for centuries, which satisfactorily solved the problems facing them.

The first daughter-house of Cîteaux, La Ferté, was founded in the very next year, 1113, near Châlons, less than twenty miles from Cluny. In the following year, Pontigny was erected north of Auxerre, and, in 1115, the twenty-five year old Bernard was placed in charge of a new community of twelve monks, including his four brothers, his uncle and two cousins. The monastery which Bernard and his companions established was Clairvaux, located in a deep valley on the left bank of the Aube, between Langres and Troyes. In the same year, and in the same diocese, Morimond was founded, the fourth filiation of Cîteaux.

During the following three years, new foundations were made, while Abbot Stephen was preparing the outline of a new monastic constitution. Before the final draft, he twice convoked the abbots of the first four daughter-houses to discuss the matter, although beyond any doubt the constitution's basic ideas were his own. The result, the *Charter of Charity* is a rare masterpiece of medieval legislation and certainly one of the most important documents of monastic history. Within a few pages, it defined the machinery of a great order with such simplicity and clarity that no essential additions were ever needed in its sequel. In 1119, the *Charter of Charity* was presented to Pope Callixtus II for final approval, together with a documented account of the early history of Cîteaux, the so-called *Exordium Parvum* by the same Abbot Stephen. On December 23 of the same year the Pope sanctioned the documents and therewith the canonical existence of the Cistercian Order was acknowledged, thus closing the first chapter of its development.

3. Rule and Constitution

The documents of early Cistercian history—besides facts and dates concerning outside events—contain sufficient information to reconstruct the ideological evolution of the reform, its basic principles, and final goal. The sources to be consulted for a complete study are above all the *Exordium Parvum* and the *Charter of Charity,* both composed simultaneously and attributed to St. Stephen Harding; the book of *Consuetudines* or "Usages," a collection of regulations concerning liturgical duties and daily monastic life which was gradually developing during the first half century following Cîteaux's foundation; and finally the *Instituta Generalis Capituli apud Cistercium,* the first code of Cistercian law, compiled by the General Chapter of 1134, which, however, contained former decisions and became further supplemented until about 1180, when the *Instituta* was published in its present final shape in order to secure a uniform discipline.

In the process of evolution, three stages are quite clearly distinguishable.

In the first, during Abbot Robert's regime in Molesme and later in Cîteaux, the founders hardly realized that their beginnings were that of a new order. It seems that Robert's program did not exceed generalities, but merely encompassed an austere discipline and strict poverty which had belonged to every contemporary reform. Even the more characteristically Cistercian emphasis on agricultural labor and literal interpretation of the Rule had their precedents in Camaldoli and in the reform program of John of Gorze. This rather vaguely defined conception was responsible for the initial failure of Molesme under the pressing influence of the minutely elaborated Cluniac regulations.

In the second phase, under Alberic's leadership, no essential change was made in the original scheme; however, in a defense against the same Cluniac attack, every point of the program received its definite form, meaning, and motivation. Thus, return to the original purity of the Rule meant for the early Cistercians the omission of all those customs and allowances added and interpreted by Cluny, which were not to be found literally in the Rule, especially those concerning clothing, bedding, and food. Likewise, appealing to the Rule, Cîteaux rejected the whole system of feudal administration of monastic property practiced by Cluny, renouncing the management and possession of manorial bakeries, mills, fairs, courts and serfs. For a similar reason, they gave up all income of ecclesiastical origin, such as possession of churches, advowsons, rights to customary offerings, altar and burial dues, and all tithes. Consequently, as a further antithesis of the Cluniac system, the only permissible source of income for Cistercians was hard manual labor in their fields with the help of lay brothers, an institution already started at Vallombrosa. To safeguard the purity of these ideals, Alberic emphasized—alluding to St. Benedict's example—that the monasteries must be established far from every human settlement, in perfect seclusion from the world.

In the third stage, during St. Stephen's regime, the same principles were extended to every detail of monastic life, and thus there came into existence a new code of "Usages," already characteristically Cistercian and uniformly compulsory for the whole Order. St. Stephen's first act, shortly after his election was to intensify the Rule of seclusion by informing Duke Hugh of Burgundy, the greatest benefactor of the Order, that his visits to Cîteaux were no longer desirable, since such occasions greatly disturbed the silence and peace of the monastery. The ideas of poverty and simplicity were strictly applied in church building, furnishing and liturgical equipment, tangibly repudiating the splendor and exuberance of Cluniac churches and liturgy. Thus the use of precious metals, silk or any superfluous decoration was strictly forbidden, and copes, dalmatics, and tunics were banished. Crucifixes were to be painted wood, candelabra of iron, thuribles of copper, vestments of linen, and only the chalices were permitted to be of silver.

The book of "Usages" regulated the daily schedule, liturgical life, and various works and duties of Cistercian houses. Although, in its details, the book appears to be a rather complicated and overdone system for the modern reader, in fact, it is a drastic simplification and shortening of Cluniac customs and ritual. Since the Cistercians, following the Rule of St. Benedict, spent considerable time in manual labor and spiritual reading, it was obvious that they could not imitate Cluny in its endless service in the church, with all the accretions of centuries to the *Opus Dei.* Except for a daily Conventual Mass and a short Office of the Dead, the special offices, litanies, processions, visits to altars, and recitation of additional psalms were simply omitted at Cîteaux. These necessary changes not only restored the original sound balance of the Rule between prayer and work, but gave ample time for the development of a new spirituality, in which individual devotion played an essential part. In order to maintain an absolute uniformity, every monastery was supposed to copy carefully the original liturgical books and ritual of Cîteaux, and follow them without any alteration. The same tendency of universal conformity inspired the famous Bible of St. Stephen, an early attempt at a new and critically revised edition of the Vulgate.

The *Instituta* shows in further detail how the first General Chapters continued the work of practical application of the original thought. It describes accurately how the site of a future monastery should be selected, and regulates the work on the fields, the organization of agricultural units, the granges, and the life of lay brothers living in them. It strictly prohibits trade for profit, since the products exceeding the needs of the monastery should be given to the poor or used for the upkeep of hired workmen. If there is a serious need to attend fairs and markets, the conduct of the brethren authorized to do business is also precisely circumscribed, because living outside of the cloister is strictly forbidden to the monks.

The *Instituta* contains new regulations concerning the novitiate, an institution almost forgotten at Cluny, and renders an opportunity for fugitive monks to join the Order under certain circumstances. Conducting schools for boys or for the education of oblates, even inside the monastery—despite a massive Benedictine tradition—was definitely prohibited. No one under fifteen years of age could be admitted into the novitiate. The precepts of silence and simplicity in clothing were repeatedly emphasized.

The *Instituta* did not oppose the election of a monk to the diocesan episcopate if he possessed the approval of his abbot and the General Chapter, but it did insist that elected bishops remain under the obligation to observe the Cistercian customs in food, clothing, and the breviary. Finally, the same document forbade any pastoral functions for monks, including the abbot, except in the case of an emergency.

The Charter of Charity

Though it is evident that neither the basic Cistercian principles nor the majority of the above listed regulations were entirely new, yet the system as a whole was a revolutionary innovation, especially in Burgundy, the stronghold of Cluniac domination. Since the rule of such a powerful majority presented a continuous challenge to the White Monks, they were forced to protect their new life against any extraneous influence by strong central government and control. This was achieved by the *Charter of Charity* with remarkable success.

According to this Constitution, Cîteaux is the heart and center of the Order, and its representative head is the abbot of

Cîteaux. But, in sharp contrast to the Cluniac system, he personally is not entitled to exercise the governmental powers that are committed to the annually convoked General Chapter. This Chapter is an assembly of the abbots of all Cistercian houses, meeting traditionally around the feast of the Exaltation of the Holy Cross, September 14th, and the abbot of Cîteaux merely acts as president. The Chapter's duty is the maintenance of a uniform discipline. This is performed by additional legislation for curbing abuses of major importance and punishing delinquents. The organ of execution and control is the annual visitation of each abbey by the abbot of the founding house. Cîteaux was to be visited by the abbots of her first four daughter-houses simultaneously. Despite multiple controls, however, the authority of both Chapter and Visitor is so limited, that every house enjoyed a considerable degree of autonomy. Besides these significant institutions, there are contained in the *Charter* instructions concerning abbatial elections and abdications, regulations of precedence, hospitality, mutual help in times of material need, and emergency measures against unworthy or rebellious abbots.

Here again, the single elements of this admirable document of medieval legislation are not entirely new. The system of visitation had been practiced long and successfully as a means of control in the congregation of Cluny. Even the idea of regular chapters emerged here and there, as for example in the reform movement of Richard of Verdun about a century before. But the Cistercian *Chapter* as a whole, with all its perfectly coherent elements, was the timely work of a highly comprehensive brain, ideally fitting a contemporary social environment. As has been frequently stated, it reflects the gradual subordination of feudal society; but instead of old customs and personal dependencies, this relationship is founded now on a positive, written law. The time had, in fact, come when, under the increasing influence of Roman Law, both civil and ecclesiastical legislation were reborn, replacing traditional and primitive customary regulations by charters and constitutions. A deep respect given to local autonomy, a corporative form of legislative body, and the mutual help of neighboring monasteries represent new ideas of greatest importance, vigorously working in the contemporary communes of Italian and French cities.

Cluny, Cîteaux and the Rule

It is impossible here to discuss in detail the social and cultural implications of the Cistercian reform; nevertheless, the internal structure of the movement would not be fully understood without a short analysis of its two powerful factors: a reaction against Cluny and a peculiar interpretation of the Rule.

Without denying the historical importance of Cluny and its achievements, it is easy to detect at the beginning of the twelfth century certain obvious symptoms of enervation. Cluny's overgrown organization was losing its general appeal, its expansion stopped, and criticism against its administration became more vocal and more frequent. Oddly enough, there is no proof of any noticeable relaxation or change in the original discipline; on the contrary, the long administration of Abbot Hugh the Great (1049-1109) is rightfully regarded as the climax of Cluny's glory. We must approach the problem from the opposite side: Cluny remained unchanged, but the world about her had changed so greatly that, for the early Cistercians, Cluny became the symbol of obsoleteness. And it was not only the Cistercians who criticized Cluny. The French secular clergy, who were almost helpless against Cluny's extensive Papal privileges and exemption, watched with growing uneasiness the territorial expansion of the Black Monks. In the provincial synod at Reims in 1119, the convened bishops, in a very stormy session, condemned Cluny's feudal politics.

Against the abbot's autocratic power the resistance gained ground even within the Order. Endeavor for independence became quite common in the more influential abbeys; moreover, there were frequent cases of open resistance against the priors imposed upon these communities by Cluny. The once so devotedly admired Cluniac liturgy, now immoderately prolonged, was also losing its appeal. When St. Peter Damian visited the abbey in 1063, he coolly reported that the services took such a long time that he could hardly find half an hour in a whole day to talk over the matter of his mission.

The immediate ground of Cistercian criticism was the unfortunate abbatial succession after the death of Hugh, and a subsequent series of grave scandals which made world-wide publicity. The young Abbot, Pontius de Melgueil, a splendor-loving noble of the South whose character reminds us of a renaissance prince, was expelled from Cluny in 1120 after years of quarreling with his own subjects. His own monks accused him before Pope Callixtus II of being passionate, harsh in his administration, and wasting the monastic revenue in useless litigation. In the meantime, Pontius organized a private army, attacked and captured his abbey, and plundered its fabulous treasury. His victory did not last long, and the unworthy man died in exile in 1126, but his successor, the able Peter the Venerable, had a difficult time remedying the disastrous results of a total financial and moral collapse. These events sufficiently explain and justify the hostile Cistercian attitude toward Cluny, the program of sharp reaction against her, and St. Bernard's later acid criticism.

Another no less significant factor in the development of Cistercian life was the founders' interpretation of the Rule. There is no other point in the earliest documents of Cîteaux so persistently emphasized as their unflinching will to return to the very letter of the Rule. In the eyes of contemporary critics this was the most conspicuous characteristic of the White Monks and the primary target of opposition. Peter the Venerable branded them as *sillabarum discussores;* according to Ordericus Vitalis, they adhered as much to the letter of the Rule as the Jews to the Mosaic law. The comparison obviously insinuated the conclusion that as the Jews had lost the real meaning of the Law, so were the Cistercians losing the spirit of the Rule by their hair-splitting interpretation. For us, however, a far more interesting subject of study is the method employed by the Cistercians to support their austerity program, which was inspired largely by the pre-Benedictine ideals of the East, through a Rule which was conceived originally in an open opposition to oriental asceticism.

In many instances the literal exposition of the Rule seemed to support the ambition to create a life of extraordinary austerity. For instance, the prescriptions regarding food, clothing and work, which in St. Benedict's time roughly corresponded to the general standards of the common Italian people, meant a real burden for the young Bernard and his noble knights in the shivering cold of Burgundian winters.

In weeding out accretions and "mitigation" of the Rule, especially the customs of Cluny, the text of the Rule again furnished an excellent weapon. Since in the original document there are no allusions to the correlation of a feudal society and monastic community, the Cistercians used successfully the *argumentum ex silentio* against the over-complicated administration of Cluny in favor of the original simplicity of the early Benedictine life. The restoration of the initial pattern, however, was impossible as long as the monastery remained in close contact with the world, consequently the retirement into the solitude of the woods presented for the reformers the only logical alternative.

There were, of course, in the earliest regulations of Cîteaux a number of items not detailed in the Rule, e.g. the minute prescriptions regarding liturgical vestments and equipment. In these cases the Founding Fathers of Cîteaux interpreted the Rule according to the strict ideals of poverty of contemporary reformers in the firm belief that their procedure necessarily fulfilled St. Benedict's intention. Most characteristic of their way of thinking was the motivation of a very significant innovation without any allusion to it in the Rule, namely the institution of lay brotherhood. As the *Exordium Parvum* stated, they received lay brothers into their community "because without their help they were unable to fulfill perfectly the precepts of the Rule, day and night," failing to realize that if regular life was such a burden for the monks of St. Benedict, perhaps the holy lawgiver himself would have employed lay brothers.

The same mentality may explain why they cast out a momentous institution of the Rule, the reception of children into the community for monastic education; the presence and the care of the boys might disturb the atmosphere of eremitical solitude which in their opinion was a cornerstone of the Rule. The provisions of the *Charter of Charity* as a whole lay outside the framework of the Rule; moreover, the strict centralization scarcely favored the unlimited authority of each abbot, which was emphatically stressed in the Rule. Yet, the system of full control found a perfect justification in the eyes of the early Cistercians, because without such measures the precise fulfillment of the Rule eventually might be endangered. In other words—paradoxically though it may sound to us—Cîteaux did not shrink from conspicuous innovations in monastic life, if such measures promoted closer observation of the Rule.

The real, though unconscious, motive behind this peculiar interpretation was the heroic zeal for establishing a life full of sacrifices. In this endeavor Cîteaux spontaneously focused her attention upon the hardships of regular observance, overlooking the poignantly indulgent character of the Rule. There are indications that besides the irresistible sway of a rigorous monastic piety of the era, in the formation of Cistercian spirituality the direct influence of the example of the Desert Fathers was by no means negligible.

The contemporary Benedictine author of the *Historia Ecclesiastica,* Ordericus Vitalis (d.1142), related in a rather detailed manner the strife between Robert and his monks at Molesme in the form of a dialogue. There, while Abbot Robert explicitly and repeatedly referred to the example of the Egyptian Fathers, the monks retorted with a surprisingly keen historical analysis of the Rule's passages concerned. Although the wording of the debate was certainly the author's own, there is no reason to doubt that its points covered the real issues of the dissension.

As to an even more striking evidence of the same trend, reference can be made to the *Dialogue between a Cluniac and a Cistercian,* a long scholarly debate written in the second half of the twelfth century. Since the document, according to its very nature, seems only to resume the arguments of the heated controversy of the previous generation, it certainly reflects the mind of the Founding Fathers. The chief weapon of the Cistercian debater against the Cluniac was not the Rule, but almost invariably Cassian with his stories and maxims of the Desert Fathers. When the Cistercian repeatedly referred to the Rules of Serapion, Paphnutius and Macarius in support of his opinions, the Cluniac questioned why he should accept their authority. The Cistercian replied: "Well, it means much to us; for St. Benedict told us that upon any point of the Rule in which he was silent, we were to enquire in other books, and especially in the Institutes of the holy fathers." Then, the Cistercian continued interpreting with an instinctive but obvious tendency the seventy-third chapter of the Rule, where St. Benedict simply recommended the reading of these books for edification.

Beyond doubt the founders of Cîteaux in their own interpretation of the Rule proceeded with the best faith and never doubted that the monastic life they inaugurated was anything but the true reconstruction of St. Benedict's genuine ideals. If they failed to realize that their firm belief was not fully supported by historical facts, it was no sign of poor judgment. For the medieval man, completely unaware of the tremendous differences between the late Roman and their own civilization, any closer approach to the original pattern of Benedictine life was utterly impossible. Nevertheless, the Cistercians rendered an invaluable service in the preservation of St. Benedict's concept of monastic life in an era when the resurgent spirit of the eastern hermits seriously challenged the foundations of traditional Benedictine monasticism. The Cistercian Order not only saved the basic institutions of cenobitic life but definitely reaffirmed the shaken authority of St. Benedict and his Rule, while refreshing the old structure through a youthful blend of contemporary religious reform.

4. St. Bernard and the Expansion

There was little doubt that despite the hard beginning, a great future was awaiting Cîteaux. Her program, organization, and St. Stephen's wisdom carried the guarantee of a success presumably on a much larger scale than that of Grandmont or the Carthusians, who also made progress with less favorable auspices for prosperity. The phenomenal advance of the Cistercians—so far unparalleled in monastic history—cannot be explained properly without taking into consideration the personal influence of the "man of the twelfth century," St. Bernard of Clairvaux. When he entered the novitiate at Cîteaux in 1112, there was hardly more than a small desperately struggling community; yet when he died in 1153, the Order possessed 343 houses all over Europe, with a respect and influence no other religious body enjoyed.

Bernard was born in 1090, of noble Burgundian stock at Fontaines, near Dijon. After being educated in the midst of a deeply religious family he was sent to Châtillon for formal studies at the school of the Canons of St. Vorles. Returning home, he lived the normal life of the contemporary youth together with his older brothers, although the silent and reserved boy soon realized that his place was in Cîteaux, with its rigorous life so well known in the neighborhood. As soon as he became certain of his own vocation, he convinced all his brothers, his closest relatives and friends to join him in his holy endeavor. This was the first occasion which proved him to be a man born to be a leader, with an unwavering will and irresistible personal appeal. The austere religious training in Cîteaux did not change his character, but deepened and sanctified it. Abbot Stephen understood and admired his docile and humble pupil, and in 1115 the young man of twenty-five became the Abbot of Clairvaux. The trials and hardships of the founders of Cîteaux were reiterated during the first years of Clairvaux, but Bernard's faith and determination remained unbroken. The heroic spirit of the Abbot attracted hundreds, so that in three years Clairvaux was able to found her first daughter house at Trois-Fontaines.

The fame of Bernard's holiness, wisdom and miracles soon spread all over France, and, although he never cared for publicity, he soon found himself in the spotlight of an era desperately searching for able and competent leadership. It was a time of political and intellectual turmoil. With the death of Emperor Henry V, the Salian house was extinguished and the Emperor's successors, involved in internal troubles, were unable to maintain their international supremacy. Similar disturbances broke out in England after the reign of Henry I, while in France the boy king, Louis VII, was still too young and inexperienced to take over his father's role. Meanwhile in Italy, the powerful cities and the most influential families, utilizing the impotency of their northern neighbors, started anew their bloody rivalries. In Rome, the Papacy again fell victim of the fighting parties, thus causing the most dangerous schism in the Church. When Honorius II died at Rome in 1130, the two opponent parties elected on the same day two popes, Innocent II and Anacletus II. The befuddled Christian world was at the moment utterly helpless to deal with the problem; the only power able to restore order in Rome would have been Roger II of Sicily, who, however, used the occasion to extend the territory of his new kingdom.

The convention of the French clergy and nobility at Étampes committed the decision in this crucial question to St. Bernard, who took his stand with Innocent II. Much more difficult to solve were the political problems resulting from the dual election; namely, convincing the opponent powers to acknowledge Innocent unanimously and driving out the usurper from his Roman stronghold. It took all of St. Bernard's skill, authority, and energy plus eight years of tedious travelings, conferences, personal meetings, and hundreds of letters to achieve the goal. During these years, St. Bernard stood literally in the center of European politics, yet he never acted merely as a diplomat. He never yielded nor used threat of force, nor compromised. The secret of his success was his moral superiority, his unselfish good will, and the magic of his personal appearance. On the other hand, the fact that the whole world obeyed the poor and humble Abbot of Clairvaux is the greatest praise of an era when moral ideals still prevailed over brutal violence.

The zenith of St. Bernard's earthly career was the moment when his pupil, a former monk of Clairvaux, Eugenius III (1145-1153) was elected Pope. On the latter's order, the Saint launched the Second Crusade in 1147. By his preaching, he moved hundreds of thousands of people even in places where they could not understand his language. His powerful words and irresistible personality worked wonders in another field of his activity—among the heretics of France. The South was at the edge of an open revolt against the Church; nevertheless, St. Bernard, in his strong belief that "faith is a matter of persuasion, not of compulsion," refused to take violent measures against them. Though his mission had only temporary effects, his sermons and miracles proved to be much more successful than Simon of Montfort's army a half century later. Not so much by his eloquence as by his penetrating mind and deep erudition, he fought victoriously against doctrinal heretics like his famous contemporary, Abelard, and later, Gilbert de la Porée.

The Expansion

St. Bernard's public activity was not limited to the above mentioned issues of greatest importance. For about thirty years, he and his letters, written in a masterly Latinity, were present everywhere, when peace, justice, or the interest of the Church demanded his intervention. Together with his fame and popularity, the Cistercian Order grew and expanded. His flaming example attracted thousands to the Order. Clairvaux alone, during the abbacy of St. Bernard, erected 65 daughter houses. Meanwhile, despite the new foundations year after year, the total personnel of Clairvaux counted about 700 monks, and there were a considerable number of other abbeys not far behind this figure. This almost incredible number of new monasteries does not necessarily mean that they were all new foundations. Parallel with the decline of Cluny and the increasing reputation of the Cistercians, numerous Benedictine houses, even whole congregations, joined the Order. Thus, for example, in 1147 when 51 new houses were recorded, 28 among them belonged to the flourishing Benedictine congregation of Savigny, and three to another small group of monasteries reformed previously by St. Stephen Obazine.

The time soon arrived when the White Monks appeared almost everywhere in Christian Europe. Former monastic reforms, including Cluny, never spread beyond the borders of the country of their origin to any great extent because their programs were either too narrow for general acceptance, or there was no system available to control a great number of distant foundations. But now, in the twelfth century, with the final achievement of the admirable unity of Western Christianity, the Cistercians possessed all the requirements and advantages for an international dispersion. St. Bernard became the symbol of the unity of Christian nations. The same ideas which bore the Cistercian reform swept over the whole continent with the Second Crusade, and the constitution of the Order, the *Charter of Charity,* was firm enough to carry an international organization.

As early as 1120, monks from La Ferté crossed the Alps and founded Civitacula (later Tiglieto) in Italy; in 1123 Morimond built Camp, the first Cistercian house in Germany; the first monastery in England was founded in 1128 at Waverley in Hampshire, followed four years later by Rievaulx in Yorkshire, established by Clairvaux; Austria received the first group of Cistercians in 1130, who settled in Rein; in 1132, the White Monks crossed the Pyrenées and in the same year they founded their first house in Belgium. In 1133, the Cistercians appeared in Switzerland, in 1134 in Savoy, in 1136 in Scotland, in 1138 in Portugal, in 1142 in Hungary and Ireland, in 1143 in Poland, Sweden and Bohemia, in 1144 in Denmark, in 1146 in Norway. Outside of France, the Cistercians grew to be the strongest order both in number and influence in Great Britain and Ireland with a record of 122 houses. In Italy, they had 88 monasteries; in Spain 56; in Portugal 13; in Belgium 20; in German territories, over 100; with no fewer in Eastern and Northern Europe. After the death of St. Bernard, particularly after the start of the Mendicant Friars, the expansion slowed down, though it did not stop altogether. The greatest number of Cistercian houses in the middle of the seventeenth century surpassed 1500, among them nearly 700 houses for monks and 900 for Cistercian nuns. France alone recorded 241 monasteries for men. The total number of Cistercian establishments, together with those suppressed during the course of time, is even higher.

The large number of rapidly developing Cistercian foundations all over the European continent indicated the universal appeal of Cistercian ideals, affecting the whole of contemporary society; yet, among the vocations, a surprisingly large number came from the intellectual elite. During the early years of Clairvaux, the famous school of Châlons was almost emptied because students, together with their professors, followed the call of the young Bernard. Similar cases repeatedly occurred wherever the Abbot happened to be preaching, particularly in Reims, Liège and Paris. According to Ernaldus, one of the first biographers of the Saint, Clairvaux was the monastery where men of learning, masters of rhetoric and philosophy, studied the theory of divine virtues. The reason why the young scholastic generation preferred the Cistercians can scarcely be attributed to St. Bernard's impressive personality alone, since many spent their lives in other monasteries than Clairvaux. The decisive factor in the vocation of those intellectuals must have been the novelty of Cistercian spirituality, a highly original system of mystical theology, a school of the love of God, inaugurated and developed by St. Bernard.

In his widely circulated and famous sermons on the *Canticle of Canticles,* in his treatises and letters, the Saint presented a satisfactory solution of a much discussed problem, the importance of love in human life. Since the middle of the eleventh century, there was behind the increasingly vigorous intellectual movements a definite tendency toward emotionalism, with a specific emphasis on the motive of love. However, since neither the adequate form of expression nor its moral imputability was yet clarified, the problem caused considerable confusion in public opinion as well as among men of literature and theology. The extremists were represented by two heretical movements. The Manicheistic doctrine of the Albigensians maintained that the flesh and carnal desires, consequently love and marriage, are works of evil, therefore altogether detestable. On the other side, the protagonists of a revolutionary new poetry, the troubadours, elevated the woman upon a pedestal, a move unparalleled in Christian traditions, and in their worship of femininity, ignored the principles of Christian morality. The ruling Cluniac spirituality, unprepared and unable to match the problem, took its stand on the negative side. Above the portals of their lavishly decorated churches appeared scenes of the last judgment with horrendous punishments for those who sinned in sensuality. Among the symbolic figures there frequently stood a skillfully carved likeness of a woman, *La femme aux Serpents,* her body covered with frogs and snakes. At the same time, the Cluniac Bernard of Morlais, published his great metrical composition, *De Contemptu Mundi,* which contained the darkest and most pessimistic presentation of love and womanhood in medieval literature.

St. Bernard, with the heart of a troubadour himself, placed the motive of love in the center of his mystical theology, teaching that affectionate love of God was the only way of approaching the final goal of Christian perfection, the union of the human soul with its Creator. Although the Cistercians were more strict than the Cluniacs in keeping women away from the neighborhood of their monasteries, the contemporary admiration of womanhood found its most sublime and delicate form in a devotion to the Blessed Virgin as Queen of Heaven. Her medieval cult flourished wherever Cistercians lived and always found inspiration in the deeply poetical writings of St. Bernard. The intellectual elite of the century understood, admired and eagerly followed St. Bernard in his way of perfection, thus starting an unbroken succession of great mystics, whose influence greatly affected Christian spirituality for centuries to come.

The Problems of the Expansion

What would have been the fate of Cîteaux without St. Bernard is certainly an idle question. Nevertheless, his personal influence upon the evolution of the Order was a factor of great importance. Beyond doubt, the program of the Founding Fathers of Cîteaux was a purely contemplative one, animated by an admirable zeal for heroic asceticism. The young Bernard wholeheartedly and sincerely embraced the life of Cîteaux as it was, and under the direction of Abbot Stephen, he himself became one of the greatest contemplatives of all times. He was, however, a unique and universal genius with a providential mission for leadership. It was impossible for him to hide for long within the walls of Clairvaux; but even during the years of feverish public activity, he remained basically the same Cistercian ascetic and contemplative. The greater his faith in Cistercian ideals grew, the more devotedly he worked to propagate it. He never concealed his firm conviction that the Cistercian rule was the surest way to secure one's salvation, and he never hesitated to accept anybody into Clairvaux, from public criminals to royal princes, from fugitive monks to bishops. The prodigious increase of the Order during the first half of the twelfth century would have been impossible without St. Bernard, and therefore, though only indirectly, he was largely responsible for its consequences.

To this overgrowth must be ascribed an advancing antagonism between quality and quantity within the Order. While the twelfth century proved to be an exceptionally appropriate era to beget and foster contemplative vocations, it remained true that contemplation, according to its nature, never could concern the masses. It is therefore, *a priori,* quite unlikely that those hundreds of new foundations all harbored true contemplative souls. As early as 1135, Ordericus Vitalis, a chronicler of the Black Monks, remarked that despite a fervent spirit of religion there were many hypocrites, like tares among the wheat, among the members of the new Order. The problem became even more acute when the Order reached its widest expansion, but shortly thereafter the spirit of the approaching Renaissance reduced the number of monastic vocations considerably, especially those of the strictest contemplatives. In the meantime, the machinery of the General Chapter functioned with exemplary earnestness. The visitors reported year by year the smallest deviations from the common discipline, and the delinquents always received severe punishments. But the Chapter's desperate struggle was directed only against the symptoms, and was, of course, unable to control the real cause, the changing European mind. The Order was too large a body to resist successfully the contrary elements.

Otherwise, it is amazing how well aware the Chapter Fathers were of the dangers behind that spectacular expansion even at the very beginning. Far from being dazzled by their own success, they proceeded with an increasing cautiousness in matters of new foundations or incorporations into the Order of already existing monasteries. The excessively reverent Cistercian posterity carefully abolished the traces of dissension among the members of the General Chapter during these glorious years. Nevertheless, there are some signs that upon the point of too hasty foundations opinions were far from being unanimous. It is indeed hard to believe that the only reason for Abbot Stephen's abdication in 1133 was his old age. Other considerations certainly were ensconced in the background, since his withdrawal caused a serious crisis. His immediate successor, Guido, the former Abbot of Trois-Fontaines, was deposed shortly after his election and his name was even blotted from the list of the abbots without any indication of the reason. Thereafter, Raynald, a monk of Clairvaux and a close friend of St. Bernard, took over the supreme government of the Order. His term was an era of the most vigorous expansion. When he died in 1150, Goswin, the Abbot of Bonnevaux (an affiliation of Cîteaux) succeeded him in his high office. The General Chapter turned immediately against the former policy, and in 1152 categorically prohibited the foundation or incorporation of new houses in the future. Though these facts cannot safely support far reaching conclusions, they sufficiently prove that the problem of rapid growth was continually evident. The above mentioned decision reversed the dearly cherished ambitions of St. Bernard who at that time lay fatally ill at Clairvaux and who died in the following year. Evidently, the prohibition of new foundations was never interpreted too strictly. At the climax of its popularity, the growth of the Order could not have stopped altogether, although the tempo of expansion slowed considerably.

To meet the challenge of a changing civilization, theoretically, there were only two possible procedures: the first would be to reduce systematically and proportionately to the decreasing contemplative vocations the number of houses and their membership, in order to attempt to secure as far as possible the primitive spirit and discipline; the second would be to maintain the preeminent position of the Order in the Church and society in its full extent, providing the whole organization with the necessary vocations by a compromise, namely, the adaptation of the Rule to the contemporary religious needs and desires. Since the first course was practically impossible and in fact, never happened in monastic history, there was no real choice but to take the second alternative. The fate of the Cistercians and their vocation was by no means a singular phenomenon. Those great religious orders of the Middle Ages which survived the crisis of Renaissance and Reformation, underwent a similar process of transformation, while smaller congregations, with the single exception of the Carthusians, simply vanished from the stage of history.

A natural and inevitable consequence of the large scale expansion was the increasing prestige, power and activity of the Order in the public life of the Church. The abbot of Clairvaux was the first to answer the call of the distressed Church, and he, the great contemplative, played an unrivaled role in the directing of European politics for three long decades. His example presented an irresistible challenge for the Cistercian posterity, all the more because both the highest ecclesiastical and secular authorities hopefully expected that the Order with its immense moral potentiality, would continue to stay at their service as champions of peace, justice, and order among Christian nations. Undoubtedly, the accepted role of the trouble-shooters of the Church was far from the ideals of the Founding Fathers of Cîteaux who sought a life of perfect silence in an absolute retirement from worldly affairs. Nevertheless, to refuse the challenge and to withdraw again into solitude was just as impossible as it was to reduce the number of their overgrown membership.

The new school of mysticism, the policy of vigorous expansion and active participation in the affairs of the Church, however, represented only partially St. Bernard's influence upon the development of the Order. The year of 1134 was a significant milestone in Cistercian history not only because of the crisis caused by St. Stephen's abdication and prolonged by a disputed election but because it was the year when the last members of the old guard of the Founding Fathers were relieved by the more radical second generation under St. Bernard's spiritual leadership with a program of increased emphasis on monastic simplicity. Thus, the General Chapter passed in the same year the first collection of laws known as the *Instituta* with its new restrictions regarding monastic art and other intellectual activities. This was about the time of the first revision of the *Charter of Charity,* when the privileges of the proto-abbots were extended to the Abbot of Morimond and when a commission was working under St. Bernard's direction in further purification of Gregorian chant. It is not surprising, however, that after the departure of the great Abbot's commanding personality the second half of the twelfth century witnessed a reaction and a gradual eclipse of his puritanical ideals.

Taking together the single components of our short survey, it becomes manifest that even the first half century of Cistercian life presents a picture full of dynamic energy where the laws of development were just as essential as in any other field of human history.

Characteristic of future Cistercian centuries were unceasingly repeated but not always successful attempts to maintain the state of balance between the genuine spirit of the first founders and the justified demands of successive new generations, which urged a more intensive participation in the intellectual and spiritual movements of contemporary Church and society.

5. The Vanguard of the Church

The decades which elapsed between the death of St. Bernard and the Fourth Lateran Council (1215) did not result in any significant changes in the discipline or organization of the Order; but the series of challenges which confronted the Order imposed upon her a remarkably active role within the public life of the Church. Such activity was not entirely new, since it had been inaugurated by St. Bernard himself, and his successors' energy was restricted exactly in those fields where Bernard achieved his greatest victories.

Participation in the Crusades

Disregarding the fact that the founders of Cîteaux themselves were inspired by the heroic zeal of the first crusades, as early as 1124 a serious attempt was made to extend the activity of the Order toward the Holy Land. Arnold, the first Abbot of Morimond, deserted his post with the best of his monks without the authorization of the General Chapter, firmly resolved to found a house in Palestine; only his early death prevented him from carrying out his plans. Although St. Bernard vehemently opposed the adventurous idea, he encouraged the Premonstratensians in their similar endeavors and gave his enthusiastic support to the Knights of the Order of the Temple, and addressed to them his famous treatise entitled *In Praise of the New Warfare* (*De Laude Novae Militiae*).

St. Bernard's example encouraged Raymond, the Abbot of Fitero, to found a new military order in the western battlefield of Christian resistance against the Mohammedans in Spain. Upon the suggestion of a former knight, Diego Velasquez, now a simple monk of that Cistercian community, Raymond offered his services to Alfonso VII, King of Castile, in order to organize the defense of castle Calatrava (1157). In the beginning, lay brothers were employed for active military duties; after the death of Raymond in 1163, the choir monks left Calatrava while the fighting brethren remained and elected their first Grand Master, thus founding the Order of the Knights of Calatrava. This somewhat revolutionary arrangement was approved by the General Chapter of Cîteaux, and in 1187, the Chapter Fathers worked out for them a Rule modeled upon the Cistercian customs for lay brothers. However, the Knights were not directly subject to Cîteaux but to Morimond, the mother house of Fitero, from which Calatrava had sprung. The Abbot of Morimond exercised the right of visitation, and the highest ecclesiastical dignity of the Order, that of the Grand Prior, could be held only by a monk of Morimond. During the following centuries, the Knights growing steadily in wealth, number, and reputation, rendered an invaluable service to their country in consistent fights against the Moors. At the end of the fifteenth century, they had about 2000 knights in 56 commanderies and 16 priories; but after the expulsion of the Arabs from the Peninsula, they lost their original spirit and religious character. As a mere political factor, however, they continued to play an important role until the general secularization of their possessions in 1838. A thirteenth century offspring of the Knights of Calatrava was the similarly organized military Order of Alcantara, although the latter was in less direct contact with the Cistercians. The Portuguese Order, known from 1181 as the Knights of Avis, and later the Valencian Knights of Montesa, together with several others of lesser importance were also under Cistercian visitation.

The fate of the Holy Land and the events of the Third and Fourth Crusade aroused a significant echo within the Order. Although the General Chapter repeatedly forbade pilgrimage to the holy places for the members of the Order, the organization of the Third Crusade (1184-1192) was largely the work of the Cistercian prelates with the moral backing of the whole Order. In Italy, the Cistercian Archbishop of Ravenna, Gerard, as Papal Legate was in charge of the preaching and recruiting. Henry, Cardinal of Albano, the former Abbot of Clairvaux, acted under a similar appointment in France and Germany, while Baldwin, Archbishop of Canterbury, formerly Abbot of Ford, propagandized the crusade in England. A number of abbots and monks followed the armies to the East. Archbishop Gerard fell in battle under the walls of Akkon; Archbishop Baldwin and Henry, Bishop of Basel, died from diseases. When some years later the Fourth Crusade (1201) was about to be launched, the General Chapter agreed upon Papal request, that Abbot Guy of Vaux de Cerney with three other abbots and a large number of monks should join the armies as preachers and chaplains. The same Chapter solicited the wealthier abbeys for a considerable sum of money for the support of the crusaders.

The same crusader spirit animated those Cistercians who, against St. Bernard's cautious hints, hurriedly established monasteries in the East. In the second half of the twelfth century, there are records of six abbeys in Syria, in the diocese of Tripoli and Antioch; but these houses soon vanished without trace after the crusader states fell victim of the Turkish expansion. A longer future awaited those monasteries erected shortly after the Fourth Crusade in the newly organized Latine Empire. The best known among them was the abbey of St. Mary of Daphne, near Athens. Two centuries later, the ruin of the Empire completed its fate. The last known Abbot, Peter, significantly preferred to be buried in the Parthenon on the Acropolis, instead of his monastery (1412).

Cistercians as Diplomats

Prominent representatives of the Order followed in St. Bernard's footsteps as diplomats and mediators in negotiations between the Papacy and secular powers. In the strife between Emperor Frederick Barbarossa and Pope Alexander III (1159-1181), the former abbot of La Ferté, Peter, Archbishop of Tarentaise, promoted the cause of the lawfully elected Alexander against Barbarossa's anti-popes. During these troublesome two decades, until the Treaty of Venice (1177), the General Chapter and a score of the most influential abbots were working on an agreement acceptable to both parties, and the final negotiations were carried out by two Cistercians, Bishop Pontius of Clermont, and Abbot Hugh of Bonnevaux. The Pope acknowledged the excellent services of the Order by the solemn canonization of St. Bernard of Clairvaux, January 18, 1174.

The differences between Pope and emperor were renewed under Frederick II (1215-1250), when three Cistercian Cardinals, Conrad of Urach, Jacob of Pecoraria, and Rainier of Viterbo served the Pope, Honorius III, and his successor, Gregory IX. The Cistercian Order was also involved in the conflict between Pope Boniface VIII (1294-1303) and Philip the Fair, King of France. The Pope and John of Pontoise, Abbot of Cîteaux, fought side by side against a ruthless violence. As a reward, the Pope granted to Abbot John the use of the white pontifical seal with his likeness in a sitting posture; the Pope explained, "you alone stood by me, so you alone are privileged to sit with me." Nevertheless, this time their fearless resistance did not result in anything but early death for the Pontiff and imprisonment for the Abbot.

Missions

While the occasional crusading and political activity of the Order thus far concerned only the most eminent prelates and abbots, St. Bernard's missionary bequest among contemporary heretics and pagans developed into an organized sideline of the Cistercian vocation, at least until the arrival of the mendicant friars. The Cistercians did not seek that appointment either; but their poverty, rigorous asceticism, and general respect qualified them for the evangelization of southern France which was then facing the ever growing Albigensian menace, and thus they were unable to decline the Papal commitment. Alexander III entrusted a general mission in the South to Peter Cardinal of San Chrysogone with two Cistercians on his staff, Garin, Archbishop of Bourges and former Abbot of Pontigny and Henry, Abbot of Clairvaux. In 1180, the whole mission, both military and apostolic, was taken over by Abbot Henry, who at the same time was appointed Cardinal Bishop of Albano. He fulfilled his task with remarkable success and soon after his death in 1198 Innocent III created another Cistercian commission headed by two monks of Cîteaux, Rainier and Guy. After Rainier fell ill, the Pope replaced him by Master Peter of Castelnau, Archdeacon of Maguellone, who almost immediately made his profession in the Cistercian monastery of Fontfroide near Narbonne. In 1203, Peter was appointed Legate of the Holy See with the assistance of another monk of Fontfroide, Raoul. Finally, in order to emphasize that the undertaking was entrusted to the whole Order, the Pope conferred the supreme direction of the Albigensian mission on Arnold Amaury, Abbot of Cîteaux, who played an important role in the subsequent crusade of Simon of Montfort. The extraordinary difficulties of the undertaking among the rebellious crowds, distrustful nobility, and tepid prelates seemed to exhaust Peter's energies, and he begged the Pope to allow him to retire to the solitude of Fontfroide. The permission was not granted. "Stay where you are," wrote Innocent, "At this hour, action is better than contemplation." However, this work soon called for effective help and the Pontiff instructed Diego, Bishop of Osma and his young Canon Dominic to assist the Cistercians. It was at the side of the devoted Cistercians that Dominic conceived the idea of founding the Order of Preachers. On January 15, 1208, St. Peter of Castelnau was assassinated and public opinion attributed the murder to Count Raymond VI of Toulouse, chief promoter of the Albigensian cause. The following bloody crusade (1209-1229) against the Count and his associates, with its evident political implications, hardly resulted in anything for the Church until the intensive pastoral activity of the Franciscans and Dominicans eliminated the heresy itself. During these critical years, the recalcitrant bishops of the South were replaced mostly by Cistercians. One of them, Fulco, Bishop of Toulouse, a former troubadour, became St. Dominic's strongest support in establishing his order, and the new successful institutions of his diocese served as models for certain canons of the Fourth Lateran Council.

Another territory where missionary activities were directed and carried out largely by Cistercians was Prussia and the Baltic provinces. There too, as among the Albigensians, preaching constituted only one part of the task; the conversion of hostile and barbarous tribes required clever diplomacy, sometimes able military leadership.

The first Bishop of Livonia, Meinhard, employed the Swedish Cistercians of Gutvalla (on the island of Gotland) in converting the people. After his death (1196), a Cistercian, Berthold, Abbot of Loccum was elected his successor. Berthold successfully organized a crusade against the constantly revolting pagans, but he himself fell in battle in 1198. His work was continued by Dietrich of Thoreida who founded the monastery of Dünamünde (near Riga) in 1205, as a basis of the following large scale missionary activities, and he became its first abbot. In 1211 he was appointed as the first Bishop of Estonia. Dietrich's closest associate was Peter of Koblenz, a monk of Himmerod, the "Apostle of Livonia." In that stage of the mission the cross and sword went side by side, and Dietrich too was killed in battle against the pagans in 1219. His successor at Dünamünde was another warrior-monk, Bernard of Lippe, a former knight who later became the first Bishop of Semgalien (1218, Southern Latvia) while the Cistercian Godfrey of Pforte occupied the seat of the newly organized bishopric of

Ösel (Saaremaa island in the Gulf of Riga) where Frederick, a monk of Altzelle suffered martyrdom in 1215. Bishop Bernard's successor in Semgalian was Baldwin of Alna, who later acted as Apostolic Legate in the Baltic provinces. The last known Cistercian personality in Livonian missions was Abbot Nicholas of Dargaun around 1240; from the middle of the century the unfinished work was taken over and completed by the Dominicans.

In Prussia, Abbot Godfrey of Lekno began his preaching tours in 1206, accompanied by a monk of his abbey, Philip. Here the monastery of Oliva was used as a basis of the missions. At this time a young monk, Christian, joined the community; he soon took over the direction of the whole work, and in 1215 became the first Bishop of Prussia. This territory, however, proved to be even more unyielding than Livonia; and for military support of the missions the Knights of Calatrava were summoned from Spain. Philip died as a martyr at the hands of the revolting people. Neither did Bishop Christian shrink from the use of force of arms in defense of his converts but the final success was delayed by political rivalries until the Teutonic Knights broke the resistance of the defiant Prussians.

For several years, prior to 1238, Cistercians operated a missionary station for Ruthenia at Opatow near Sandomierz. Abbot Gerald of Opatow, who was still living in 1254, had held, since 1232, the title of Bishop of the Latins in Russia.

All these new duties placed such a heavy burden upon the Order that the General Chapter of 1211 ordered the Abbot of Cîteaux to contact the Pope, asking him to excuse at least priors, sub-priors, and cellarers from outside commissions. Nevertheless, in his urgent need for further help, Innocent again turned to the Chapter of 1212, which appointed the Abbot of Morimond to investigate the situation and work out a satisfactory solution so that both the wish of the Pontiff and the monastic life and discipline could be upheld. Innocent's successor, Honorius III (1216-1227), even after the successful start of the

Mendicants, in 1220 in a circular letter to the bishops of the eastern European countries asked them to organize in their dioceses missionary groups of able preachers, preferably Cistercians. At the same time, the Pope, referring to their previous merits in similar activities, ordered the Cistercian Abbey of Flora in Calabria to cooperate with the Dominicans in the ministry of the word of God.

Exemption

The large number of Cistercian cardinals and bishops attests to the high esteem in which the Order was held by the people as well as the highest civil and ecclesiastical authorities. The Holy See was also ready to acknowledge and reward the excellent services and prominent position of the Order by granting privileges, which gradually amounted to a complete exemption of the Order from diocesan jurisdiction. Although the Founding Fathers of Cîteaux, together with St. Bernard, sharply condemned the Cluniac tendency to accumulate privileges, they themselves gratefully accepted in 1130 from Innocent II the exemption from tithes, since the first years of expansion meant a tremendous financial stress upon the Order. But this privilege, so favorable for the Cistercians, seriously affected the diocesan revenues because the growing estates of the Order, in the same proportion, reduced the bishops' steadiest incomes. Alexander III reaffirmed this tax exemption against repeated attacks of the secular clergy; but the General Chapter, realizing the dangers of a continuous tension, in 1180 restrained future application of the much debated immunity concerning new acquisitions. The exemption was further enlarged by a decision of Alexander III, freeing Cistercian abbots from their obedience toward diocesan bishops, and completed by a bull of Lucius III, issued in 1184, which prohibited the bishops from inflicting any ecclesiastical punishments upon houses or individuals belonging to the Order.

The culmination of the universal reputation and influence of the Cistercian Order coincided with the most glorious era of the medieval Church under the great Innocent III. The Fourth Lateran Council held in 1215, in a general reform of monastic constitution, pointed to the Cistercian Order as a model of perfect organization. The twelfth canon directs that the Benedictines in each province of a kingdom shall hold a chapter of abbots and priors every three years. Since they were unacquainted with the method of holding such meetings, it was suggested that two Cistercian abbots of the neighborhood be invited to give counsel and help in matters of procedure. For, as the canon states, "The Cistercians have long been accustomed to the holding of such chapters." These chapters also were ordered to establish a system of regular visitations with clear allusion to the Cistercian pattern. The general satisfaction with the latest improvements of monastic life went so far that the thirteenth canon declared, "Lest too great a diversity of religious Orders lead to serious confusion in the Church of God, we strictly forbid anyone in the future to found a new Order. Whoever is desirous of entering an Order, let him choose one already approved." Nevertheless, that was the time when the two great Orders of the late Middle Ages, Franciscan and Dominican, were about to emerge from their cradles in order to imprint their characteristics upon the whole of Christianity and thus also upon the Cistercians.

6. The Impact of Scholasticism

The early twelfth century, the era of Cistercian reform, witnessed the dawn of an admirable development of medieval civilization. The promises of its fresh and vigorous beginning were soon fulfilled, yet the panorama of the thirteenth century exhibited a picture vastly different from that of a century before. Due to developing industry and trade, the center of economic life shifted from the large rural estates to the cities with an ever growing population, power, and wealth. In the pursuit of profit and domination, however, the nobility also wanted to secure its share; consequently the former social order lost its stability, while the gap between riches and poverty grew wider steadily. Together with the material progress the intellectual horizon widened; nevertheless, the old centers of learning, cathedrals and monasteries, lost their importance to the rising universities, which were possessed with an authority and influence unparalleled in history. Meanwhile, the once so impressive unity of Christian nations was breaking up into strong national states, each endowed with their own political aspirations, increasingly centralized government and advanced bureaucracy. The enthusiasm for crusades vanished and the Papacy, in the crossfire of conflicting national ambitions, was unable to organize unified action. The Church herself, in order to keep her spiritual supremacy and to fulfill her universal mission, was also in urgent need of internal reform and wanted men filled with apostolic zeal whose approach to a new assignment might secure for the Church the loyalty and genuine Christian spirit of subsequent generations. Neither the hierarchy nor the old monastic orders were sufficiently adjusted to meet the problems; they were solved by the foundation of two new religious communities, those of the Dominicans and Franciscans.

St. Francis of Assisi's (1182-1226) spiritual demands from his followers, such as absolute poverty, refusal of ecclesiastical privileges, and renunciation of human learning, to a certain degree also belonged to the program of the early Cistercians; but the declaration that his Friars as a body had the vocation of preaching and consequently the abolition of monastic stability and even of a permanent residence were revolutionary new features in the history of western religious orders. St. Dominic (1170-1221), working side by side with the Cistercians started his community during the Albigensian mission. He adopted a similar program to that of the Franciscans; but Dominic insisted on the necessity of higher learning and established an elaborate scheme of central government, which was hastily appropriated by the poorly organized Franciscans. The Mendicant Friars of both orders swarmed over the whole continent in a matter of years, quickly surpassed the Cistercians in popularity, and took over the initiative in all ecclesiastical public activities. As the Cistercians had done previously, the Mendicants made their influence felt among the older religious orders; and their highly advanced central administration as well as their quest for higher theological education inspired important changes in the Cistercian constitution and customs. These changes, however, were not merely superficial imitations of a heterogenous system: they had deep roots in Cistercian history.

The Constitution of Clement IV

The ground of constitutional development lay in certain ambiguous statements of the *Charter of Charity* concerning the legal position of the Abbot of Cîteaux, manifested through a controversial interpretation of its paragraphs about jurisdiction and authority. In fact, the presently adopted text of the *Charter,* as we have stated above, is already a modified transcription of the original. The alteration, made somewhat before 1152, defined the right of visitation of Cîteaux to be exercised by the four proto-abbots, established their decisive role in the General Chapter in case of disagreements, and strengthened the influence of father-abbots over their affiliations in abbatial elections. This was the first sign of an unfortunate rivalry for power between the Abbot of Cîteaux and the abbots of his first daughter-abbeys. The prominent position of the Abbot of Cîteaux was effectively emphasized by the fact that both the highest ecclesiastical and civil authorities respected him as a real general superior of the whole Order; but on the other hand his mighty daughter houses, especially Clairvaux, were always able to rely on the effective backing of their own affiliations in General Chapters against Cîteaux. At the turn of the twelfth century the quarrels became more and more frequent and embittered, and, as a result, the authority of the real organ of supreme government, that of the General Chapter, suffered seriously. The strife culminated at the election of Jacob II, Abbot of Cîteaux, in 1262, when his predecessor, Guy II, was promoted to the cardinalate. The party of the proto-abbots, under the leadership of Abbot Philip of Clairvaux, declared the election null and void because of certain formal defects in the procedure. The intervention of both Pope Urban IV and King St. Louis of France failed to reconcile the opponents. At the time of the approaching General Chapter of 1264, Philip called together the abbots of his party to Clairvaux, while those faithful to Cîteaux opened the regular Chapter there. Since the events tended toward an irreparable schism within the Order, in 1265, the recently elected Pope Clement IV, referring to his supreme jurisdiction, after careful deliberation, issued a new constitution for the Order, the *Parvus Fons,* or as Cistercian historians call it, the *Clementina.*

The *Parvus Fons,* despite its authoritative character, having been composed after long consultations with the parties concerned and inspired by Cardinal Guy, is a precise interpretation and supplement of the *Charter of Charity* and as such an organic part of Cistercian constitutional development. In order to remedy the ominous rivalry, its basic idea was to limit the redundant influence of the proto-abbots and to re-establish the General Chapter's shaken authority. The *Clementina,* therefore, restricted the rights of visitors in cases of major abuses, especially in those involving the deposition of abbots, which became reserved for the General Chapter. The supreme authority and smooth function of the General Chapter was supported by the creation of a consultative body of 25 abbots, the *Definitorium.* It was composed of the abbot of Cîteaux and the four proto-abbots; each of them nominated four other abbots from his own affiliation.

Doubtless, the *Definitorium* as a constitutional organ was a novelty inspired by a similar institution of the Dominicans, yet it had its Cistercian foundations. The second version of the *Charter of Charity* already referred to a private council of the Abbot of Cîteaux which was to decide disputes between equal parties in the Chapter. The word *Definitores,* meaning the same council, was first used in a decree of the Chapter of 1197. From 1223 the *Definitorium* seemed to be a regularly elected administrative body at the Chapters, and this character was not changed by the *Clementina,* wherein it was clearly emphasized that their suggestions were of no legal force without the consent of the full Chapter. The future decisive importance of the *Definitorium* was a result of the fact that in later centuries the number of attending abbots in the Chapter was reduced so enormously, that the members of the *Definitorium* always represented a numerical majority and consequently their standpoint became automatically that of the Chapters. On the other hand, it is true that the rising, and in a certain respect usurped or misunderstood authority of the *Definitorium,* soon undermined the prestige of the General Chapter, and thus further discouraged the abbots from attending. Nevertheless, this unfortunate development at the time of the *Clementina's* composition could not be foreseen; its effects for the rest of the thirteenth century were certainly beneficial.

The Dominican influence in the *Parvus Fons* is easily explicable from the close connection of the two orders in the first half of the thirteenth century and from the fact that in the Papal committee for the elaboration of the new constitution, there were successively two distinguished Dominicans, Godfrey of Beaulieu and Humbert de Romans. Moreover, before the *Clementina,* the development of the Cistercian *Definitorium* as a regular institution closely followed the final formation of the Dominican constitution in 1220, where the *Definitores,* as representatives of the single provinces, played a decisive role in the general chapters. Although the centralization was a universal phenomenon during the thirteenth century, the restriction of the authority of father-abbots and a new stress on the power of the General Chapter can be also regarded as another item of Dominican influence.

Another form of centralization appeared in the introduction of official representatives of the Order in the capitol of Christendom at Rome. In 1220 two secular clerics occupied themselves with the legal affairs of the Order which were handled through the Holy See. A decision of the General Chapter of 1303 speaks about a Procurator General as a permanent delegate in Rome and orders the abbeys to proceed with all their cases through him. His duty was also to keep a watchful eye on the rights and privileges of the Order and to secure and defend them if necessary. His office was under the control of the General Chapter and was supported by the contributions of the whole Order. Similar reasons led to the appointment of a Cardinal Protector, as another evident proof of Franciscan influence. The title *Protector Ordinis* emerged at first in 1260, concerning Cardinal John of Toledo. As long as members of the Order were successively among the Cardinals, they were the most competent representatives of Cistercian causes; but when the cardinalate became a rarely granted honor for Cistercians, the office of the Cardinal Protector developed into a significant institution, especially when after the Reformation the Protectors effectively helped the Order in its efforts to restore regular life and discipline.

The College of St. Bernard

More conspicuous and substantial was the impact of the victorious scholasticism upon Cistercian tradition concerning education and learning through the immediate example of the Mendicants. Except for a strict ascetic training there were no signs of any educational program or organized studies at Cîteaux during the early years of its existence. However, in all probability, the Founding Fathers did not belittle learning altogether. The *Exordium Parvum* proudly remarked about Abbot Alberic that he was a man of letters, well educated both in divine and human sciences. It was St. Bernard again who, by his passionate debates against representatives of early scholasticism, created an air of suspicion and aversion toward the new way of theology based upon philosophic speculations rather than Scripture and tradition. Hence it is understandable that the faithful disciples of his mystical theology and ascetic simplicity failed to realize the importance of the revival of Greek philosophy and its revolutionary effects on the Christian mind and theology. During the second half of the twelfth century the Church itself adopted a very cautious attitude toward the unexpected advance of the recently translated writings of Aristotle in the University of Paris; but as soon as it had been proven that Aristotelianism was not only reconcilable with traditional patristic theology but could be adopted as an outstanding tool in its precise exposition, scholastic philosophy became an indispensable part of routine theological education. The third (1179) and fourth (1215) Lateran Councils wholeheartedly recommended academic studies for the clergy; but the real movement did not start until the Dominicans organized their first *Studium Generale* in connection with the University of Paris in 1229.

They shared the glory of a miraculous progress in scholastic theology with the Franciscans, and in St. Thomas Aquinas (1225-1274) and St. Bonaventure (1221-1274) both schools reached the climax of their achievements.

It was a sign of unbroken vigor and alertness of Cistercian spirit how soon and successfully they adopted the idea of higher learning, despite contrary tradition and internal opposition, while in the meantime the still wealthy and influential Black Monks failed in their similar endeavors. As early as 1227 Clairvaux possessed a house in Paris, and the General Chapter of 1237 acceded to the proposal of Abbot Evrard of Clairvaux to keep monks there for the sake of academic studies. At the beginning, Cistercian students apparently studied under Mendicant professors; but the appeal of the new way of living and teaching was so strong that several Cistercian members of their audience together with hundreds of others changed their habits to those of the Friars. The General Chapter of 1242 protested to the Dominican and Franciscan superiors against their admission, but a more successful remedy was applied by another Englishman of clear sight and strong determination, Stephen Lexington, Abbot of Clairvaux (1242-1257). Himself a former student of Oxford, Stephen developed his abbey's property in Paris into a *Studium Generale,* which, as the College of St. Bernard, was acknowledged by a bull of Pope Innocent IV in 1245, who granted the same rights and privileges to the institution which the Mendicants already enjoyed. Furthermore, the Pope ordered the General Chapter to make arrangements necessary to keep in the new College a sufficient number of students from each abbey; whereupon the Chapter Fathers decided to promote secondary education in every monastery.

Meanwhile Abbot Lexington purchased a new property in the district of Chardonnet and the construction of a new college was begun in 1249. A large scale collection to cover the expenses was supported by the members of the French hierarchy, who granted indulgences to those contributing to the worthy cause.

On the other hand, the influence of the conservative opposition prevailed in the decision that the abbots remain free to refuse to send students to Paris, and in the fact that the General Chapter refrained from taking over for the whole Order the College which was maintained and directed by Clairvaux alone. Moreover, Abbot Stephen's person became the target of bitter attacks, so that finally the worthy prelate resigned his office in 1257; he died three years later.

The developments of the near future, however, perfectly justified his stand. Shortly after the start of the *Bernardinum* at Paris, the Abbey of Valmagne founded a similar house at Montpellier, in Southern France, in 1252; in 1281, the English Cistercians began their house of studies, Rawley Abbey, which was connected with the University of Oxford. The Abbey of Grandselve opened its institution in the same year in Toulouse; the German Abbey of Ebrach, in 1284, in Würzburg; and one year later the Abbey of Camp, in Cologne. The General Chapter of 1281 obliged the abbeys with more than 80 members to organize their own home courses of liberal arts and theology. Such studies were generally made compulsory for every religious order by a canon of the Council of Vienne, 1311. Finally in 1321, the General Chapter proceeded with more determination in the matter of the College of St. Bernard at Paris, and declared the institution to be the property and general study-house of the whole Order under the direction and supervision of the Chapter, which in the following year circumscribed in detail its organization, course of studies, and discipline.

The Constitution of Benedict XII

The triumphant spirit of scholasticism imprinted its character also on an important document of Cistercian history, the constitution *Fulgens Sicut Stella Matutina,* or briefly *Benedictina,* issued in 1335 by the second Cistercian Pope, Benedict XII (1334-1342), former abbot of Fontfroide, and a graduate of the College of St. Bernard. He regulated the studies within the whole Order, and in particular, the life and function of the College at Paris. Monasteries with more than 40 members were obliged to send at least two talented students to Paris, while those with 30 to 40 members were to send one. Other houses with a membership between 18 and 30, were to send one student to any other college of the Order. He confirmed the already existing colleges at Oxford, Toulouse and Montpellier, transferred the college of the Spanish Estella to Salamanca and ordered the establishment of two new *studium generale;* one at Bologna for Italians, another at Metz for Germans.

The major part of the constitution fitted into a general scheme of religious legislation sponsored by the Pope. Within four years he issued similar constitutions for the Black Monks, the Mendicants and the Augustinian Canons; all were conceived in the spirit of a highly advanced bureaucratic centralization, the model of which was the Papal court itself at Avignon. A considerable number of articles served as a basis for future medieval legislation concerning religious orders.

As the *Clementina* introduced a constitutional reform, so the *Benedictina* was basically a reform of financial administration. Those years were long past when, following the Rule's prescription, one cellarer was able to manage alone the material needs of a monastery. The once modest Cistercian farms became enormous feudal estates, while the evolution of European economics rendered their administration increasingly complicated. With the accumulation of material wealth there was increased the danger of possible natural disasters, wars or illegal demands and immoderate exactions of avaricious princes together with the impending problems of a basically changing economic system. Hence, despite the vast extent of their possessions, a large number of monasteries became victims of unfortunate circumstances and were deeply submerged in debt. As a remedy, the *Benedictina* restricted the unlimited power of abbots in finances, establishing a system of controls through rights of supervision granted to the communities or to the General Chapter and in the most important cases reserving the decision to the Holy See. The documents of legal transactions, if concerning the matter in question the consent of the community was required, were to be corroborated by the official seal of the convent. The Constitution created the office of the treasurer, whose duty it was to record the incomes and expenditures of the monastery, and made compulsory annual financial reports by all those in charge of fiscal administration.

Further paragraphs emphasized the importance of General Chapters and urged regular attendance as against widespread absenteeism. Abbots were reminded that despite a sharp decrease in vocations, no novice should be admitted without proper qualifications for the religious life. The Pope also insisted on simplicity in clothing and food, although in some cases a general dispensation was granted from abstinence for abbots and their company. A new arrangement providing for single cells instead of the common dormitory was condemned and strictly forbidden.

In the first draft of the document there was an even more revolutionary innovation; the Pope proposed that besides the abbots, each community should be represented at the annual Chapters by a delegate elected by a majority of votes. The move most likely was inspired by the Dominican constitution; among the abbots of the Order, however, it caused a universal alarm. In a lengthy memorial they protested against this and other curtailments of abbatial powers and as a result the idea of a conventual delegate was dropped from the final composition. The controlling office of the treasurer was another unpopular item in the administrative part of the reform and upon the request of the abbots it was soon modified by Clement VI, Benedict's immediate successor.

It is evident from the *Benedictina* that, notwithstanding some minor and sporadic abuses or signs of mismanagement, the Order as a whole still observed the high ideals of its founders, worthily enjoying the widest reputation and deserving the eloquent acknowledgment of the Pontiff in the introductory paragraph of his Constitution. Those significant lines also solemnly recognized the Order's active character by attributing to it the role of both Mary and Martha: "Gleaming like the morning star in the midst of a clouded sky, the Sacred Cistercian Order by its good works and edifying example shares in the combats of the Church Militant. By the sweetness of holy contemplation and the merit of a pure life, it strives with Mary to ascend the mountains of God, while by praiseworthy activities and pious ministration it seeks to imitate the busy cares of Martha. Full of zeal for the divine worship so as to secure the salvation of both its own members and outsiders, devoted to the study of Holy Scripture so as to learn therefrom the science of perfection, powerful and generous in the works of charity so as to fulfill the law of Christ, this Order has merited to propagate itself from one end of Europe to the other. It has mounted gradually to the summit of the virtues, and it abounds in the graces of the Holy Spirit, who delights to inflame humble hearts."

7. The Crisis of the Renaissance and Reformation

The Constitutions of Benedict XII, with their elaborate administrative and disciplinary measures, aimed to promote and secure the quiet development of the largest and most influential religious bodies for centuries to come. But those centuries, instead of strengthening and stabilizing the well established order of medieval civilization, through a series of natural catastrophes, disastrous wars, social and political revolutions, shook the old world to its very foundation, threatened the religious orders with total collapse and seriously endangered the Church itself.

Only six years after the death of the zealous Cistercian Pope, the worst epidemic of the Black Death broke out (1348-1350); it carried away more than one half of the total population of Europe. The towns and monasteries were attacked with special severity and many of them lost almost their entire population. The economic crisis caused by the disastrous scarcity of labor could have been overcome, but the Hundred Years' War (1338-1453) between England and France prolonged the misery in those countries for a century. During the hostilities, Cistercian monasteries benefited to some extent from their relative independence and from their English affiliation. While Cluniac priories were seized by the victorious English as members of a foreign organization, Cistercian houses were left untouched. Nevertheless, a large number of Cistercian abbeys were seriously and repeatedly damaged, many completely destroyed.

Their estates were exposed to devastation by enemy troops and every one suffered from exorbitant taxation. The danger was so permanent and widespread that the Holy See in 1364 granted general permission for religious communities to leave their houses and flee to fortified places. The continuous insecurity exposed the General Chapters to peril and made regular attendance impossible. Moreover, in 1360, the whole community of Cîteaux was forced to seek refuge at Dijon; even the General Chapters were held there in 1421 and 1423 because of security reasons. In 1438 the mother house of the Order was completely ransacked by hordes of unpaid soldiers and Abbot John Picard was held in their hands as hostage for six weeks.

According to the system developed during the thirteenth century, due to the technical and financial difficulties of traveling, the most distant houses of the Cistercian orbit were not legally required to be present at every Chapter. For example, the abbots of Syria were permitted to visit the Chapter in every seventh year only; those coming from Greece and Scandinavia in every fifth year; from Ireland, Scotland, Sicily and Portugal in every fourth year; those from Friesland, Hungary and the western countries of Spain in every third year; many others came only in every second year. Even with that reasonable arrangement, the General Chapter truly represented the whole Order with hundreds of abbots gathered year after year at Cîteaux. But from the second half of the fourteenth century on, attendance dropped steadily so that in the troublesome years of the coming era there were rarely gathered together more than 30 abbots; in 1560 only 13 abbots convened.

In some cases, the early manifestation of nationalism impaired the successful control of discipline. In Ireland, the visitation of foreign superiors became increasingly difficult, while the traditional Irish-English differences and continuous skirmishes greatly affected monastic life. During the fourteenth century novices of English origin were not admitted and postulants were required to take an oath that they were not of English blood.

Military operations of the Hundred Years' War afflicted only France, but in the meantime the Great Schism of the West (1378-1417) extended the confusion all over Christian Europe. As the world was divided between Urban VI, the Pope of Rome, and Clement VII, residing in Avignon, so was the Cistercian Order. Cîteaux, with the General Chapter and the abbeys under French political pressure, inclined toward Avignon; the others toward Rome. Since the Roman Pope forbade any relationship of the Cistercians with the schismatic Cîteaux, the monasteries outside of France held their abbatial conventions elsewhere. Moreover, encouraged by the Pope, they organized their own General Chapters, one in 1383 at Rome, another in 1393 at Vienna, where the abbot of Morimond was presiding. The effects of the schism upon authority and discipline within the Order were disastrous. Cîteaux's unfortunate position undermined not only the general respect toward the mother house, but stirred national animosity and the spirit of separatism. Meanwhile, both Popes showered new privileges and dispensations upon the Order, which greatly weakened the uniform discipline.

The Schism finally came to an end at the Council of Constance (1414-1418) with the election of Martin V, but for Cistercians the same Council opened another era of severe losses and sufferings. The Council condemned as heretic John Huss, a professor at the University of Prague, and he was burnt at the stake. But his followers, the Hussites, honored him as a martyr and broke out in open revolt. Their well organized bands terrorized Bohemia, Moravia, Austria and the eastern provinces of Germany for decades, destroying churches, and killing Catholics. Between 1420 and 1440, some 30 Cistercian monasteries fell victim of their savage attacks, and each of them had more than one victim among those who were unable to escape.

Attempted Reforms

Besides plagues, wars and schism in the middle of the fifteenth century, the Church found herself confronted with a much deeper and more crucial problem, that of the challenge of the youthful and vigorous spirit of a new civilization, known in European history as the Renaissance. The character of the movement in its complexity is one of the most discussed problems of modern history. Concerning its religious implications, it has to be admitted that the Renaissance reversed the way of thinking of the medieval man, completely changed his interest, taste and style, and revaluated the whole field of his medieval heritage. The Church, Papacy, and religious orders, as representatives of the old world, became targets of a sharp criticism. Yet the rising new world, as a whole, was not antireligious or even atheistic. New devotions and feasts, an excessive veneration of saints and their relics, pious foundations and a flourishing religious art prove that faith and Christianity still remained vital factors in the formation of the new man until the era of Enlightenment.

The Church and religious orders readily recognized the necessity of far reaching reforms. There was no other era in the history of the Church when more efforts were put forth for an internal renewal than the fifteenth and the beginning of the sixteenth centuries. The Councils of Constance (1414), of Basel (1431) of Ferrara-Florence (1438) and, finally, the Fifth Lateran Council (1512) all emphasized the universal need for a radical reform of the Church in head and members; yet all their impressive resolutions were just as fruitless as the simultaneous attempts of single religious orders. The most energetic steps toward the restoration of ancient discipline did not result in anything but dissolution in different congregations. These measures caused further splits among the already divided Mendicants and endangered the unity even in those orders where it had been thus far preserved. The influence of sporadically successful reforms, like that of the canons of Windesheim in Friesland (1387), or the activity of some new religious orders with a severe austerity program, remained restricted within the surroundings of their headquarters. Moreover, the once highly respected religious vocation as such was losing its prestige. Contemporary literature, for example the popular *Canterbury Tales,* frequently sketched the humorous or malignant figure of an idle monk or a vagrant friar; there were signs in increasing number of a general contempt or even hatred of them. Everywhere the number of religious vocations dropped sharply. The one-time celebrated community of Fontevrault, which during the thirteenth century numbered almost one thousand members, in 1460 counted altogether only 33 monks. The once flourishing institution of lay-brotherhood became almost extinct, and the missing labor had to be replaced by hired workmen.

The tragic gap between existing forms of religious vocation and contemporary public opinion can not be explained with satisfaction by simply referring to the fallen state of original zeal and discipline in the monasteries or the low moral standard of the orders. Serious abuses and immorality were not so widespread as some modern scholars, generalizing the outbursts of coeval moralists and visitors, have concluded. Moreover, the still considerable number of well disciplined houses and the exemplary life of reformed congregations certainly counterbalanced irregularities on the other side. The ultimate reason for the instinctive aversion toward customary forms of religious life was founded on the basic differences between the Medieval and Renaissance mind. The new way of living and thinking penetrated the whole society with its revolutionary ideas and greatly changed spiritual needs and desires. The traditional monastic life, even in its spotless purity of ancient discipline, lost its former appeal and could no longer satisfy the masses, although the ideal of a new and modern religious community was still far from fulfillment. However, when St.

Ignatius of Loyola established his new Society (1534), the magnificent success of the Jesuits amply proved both the possibility and dynamic energy of a Christian Humanism, and the unbroken vitality of the religious life, which was revived on a high scale through a well-timed beginning, appropriate program, superior organization and competent leadership.

Undoubtedly, the circumstances mentioned above did not leave untouched traditional Cistercian discipline and simplicity. Transgressions of poverty, of strict enclosure, of fasting and abstinence were quite common, especially in communities farthest from the center of the Order and scarcely within reach of visitors. Nevertheless, there are ample contemporary references testifying that Cistercian monasteries in general, together with the Carthusians, were still widely respected for their exemplary life and regular observance. This was especially true in the Low Countries, where a veritable religious renaissance united the Cistercian houses into a "Confraternity." The evil influences of a turbulent world affected them less than other orders, including the hitherto uncommonly popular Mendicants. The strict reformers of Windesheim, like Thomas à Kempis, readily acknowledged the high standards of Cistercian discipline (*Imitatio,* I, 25). "These (Cistercians) never lost altogether the spirit which had inspired their founders; even in the sixteenth century, this Order was more alive, than the great mass from which it had broken off"—writes the extremely critical modern G. G. Coulton.

The General Chapters, though with shaken authority and crumbled means of control, did everything to curb abuses and maintain discipline. At the very beginning of relaxation the alert Chapter acted immediately by issuing a collection of former disciplinary regulations under the title *Institutiones Capituli Generalis* in 1240, revised in 1256. A code of similar decisions was published in 1289 and reviewed in 1316, as the *Libellus Antiquarum Definitionum* which, following the legislation of Benedict XII, was further modified and became compulsory in 1350, as the *Libellus Novellarum Definitionum.* In 1390, the Chapter ordered a general visitation of all abbeys in the vicinity of Avignon, whence alarming news came about laxity in regular observance. In 1405, the Spanish houses underwent a similar procedure, while the visitation of Germany, Bohemia, Poland and Hungary was committed to the Abbot of Morimond, in 1409. The strict uniformity of liturgical practice was enforced by a special committee of abbots in 1419. In 1439, a new and complete collection of Statutes was ordered to eliminate the excuses of ignorance of the law. These measures did not prove successful and the Chapter of 1473 turned to the Pope, Sixtus IV, to enforce the most important points of a universal reform. The Pope, deeply involved in Italian politics, refused to take any decisive steps; but his successor, Innocent VIII (1484-1492), demanded of his own accord an immediate reform in a sharp letter addressed to the General Chapter in 1487. The King of France, Charles VIII, showed an eager interest in the matter by convoking an extraordinary convention of abbots in Paris, at the College of St. Bernard, in 1493. Unfortunately, the convention's decree of 15 articles was never enforced, largely because of the renewed and prolonged struggle between the Abbot of Cîteaux, John de Cirey (1476-1503) and the Abbot of Clairvaux, Peter de Virey. The General Chapter condemned Clairvaux's selfish endeavors, but Abbot Peter turned with his claims to the *Parlement* of Paris and the danger of a schism seemed closer than ever. The scandal of the rebellion soon became public and the Pope hastened to interfere. In his Bull of 1489, he ordered the unification of Cîteaux and Clairvaux under one head, to eliminate further rivalries. But this drastic measure, like most of the other remedies of the decline, never materialized, and was soon forgotten. Despite the disappointing results of the reform, John de Cirey stood in the high esteem of the Pope who invested him with the unique privilege of administering to his subjects the sub-diaconate and diaconate, although the Abbot was not an ordained Bishop.

The Dissolution

Luther's reformation (1517), with the subsequent schism of England and the apostasy of the Scandinavian countries, was a terrible blow to the Church and also to the Cistercian Order. Hundreds of monasteries were secularized within a few years and the remaining ones were constantly on the verge of destruction though religious wars, until the middle of the seventeenth century.

In England, King Henry VIII, after his well-known breach with the Papacy, in 1536, proclaimed the dissolution of the "lesser" monasteries (those having less than £200 annual revenue or 12 members) and the monks were transferred to the larger houses. By the year 1539, an Act was passed vesting all monastic property in the King, and all the remaining "greater" houses surrendered to the secular power. Of a total of 62 Cistercian houses in England 22 were dissolved by the act of 1536; the rest of them belonged to the "greater" houses of considerable wealth and personnel. For the majority of abbots, who "voluntarily" assigned their Order's property to the King, a lifelong pension was granted. The monasteries in general did not show much resistance against the confiscation, but from those seven houses involved in the uprising following the execution of the Act, the so-called Pilgrimage of Grace (1536), four were Cistercians (Sawley, Jervaulx, Whalley, Kirkstall). Those abbots who refused to yield were hanged in front of their own monasteries.

The first among Cistercian martyrs was a monk of Jervaulx, George Lazenby, who courageously interrupted in the church a sermon attacking the Pope's authority; he was executed in 1535. The others put to death in 1537, condemned for treason and conspiracy against the King, were: William Trafford,

Abbot of Sawley; Richard Hobbes, Abbot of Woburn, together with two of his monks, Laurence Bloxam (Blonham) and Richard Barnes; William Thurston, Abbot of Fountains; Adam Selbarre, Abbot of Jervaulx; John Paslew, Abbot of Whalley, with two monks of his community, John Eastgate and William Haydock. In the same years, martyrdom was the fate of the Abbot of Kirkstead, with three of his monks and a member of Louth Park.

The monasteries in Scotland shared the same fate some twenty years later; those in Ireland were also dissolved by Henry VIII, although their vigorous spirit of resistance delayed the Act's effect and some communities survived amidst terrible trials and sufferings until the eighteenth century. The Cistercian Menology lists 46 martyrs in Ireland, who suffered death between 1577 and 1606. The procedure was much the same in Denmark, Sweden and Norway, where the confiscated monastic property was used to finance the expansion policies of those countries. In Switzerland, according to a visitation made in 1579, 4 houses survived, 6 others fell victims of the Reformation. In Holland and Germany, the Order also suffered heavy losses, losing about two thirds of its establishments. In France, where the Reformation never gained considerable ground, many abbeys were endangered by riotous Huguenots. Senanque and Longpont were burned by them; some other monasteries organized an armed resistance, although the General Chapter in 1565 condemned the use of arms. In Hungary, Cistercian life was ended independently of the progress of the Reformation, when the country was invaded by the victorious Turks (1526).

As a result of the advance of Lutheranism in Northern Germany the monks were either expelled by force or voluntarily deserted their monasteries. In the case of Loccum (Hannover) however, while gradually all the monks accepted the new creed, they continued their community life, thus creating a unique blend of Lutheran monasticism. The daily schedule and liturgical life remained almost intact during the sixteenth century; moreover the Lutheran abbot delegated one of his Catholic fellow-abbots as his representative at the General Chapter of 1601. In 1658, the language of monastic liturgy was changed to German, but celibacy was not abandoned until the beginning of the eighteenth century. Abbot Gerard Molan (1677-1722) as a leading Lutheran clergyman of the highest reputation became a close associate of Leibnitz in the endeavor toward unification of Christian churches. Later the abbey was transformed into a Lutheran seminary, and as such, still has a distinguished role in the spiritual and intellectual life of German Lutheranism.

The outbreak of the Reformation and the subsequent Catholic revival, starting with the Council of Trent (1545-1563), gave new impulse for the resumption of reform activities within the Order. Although the General Chapter had only five regular sessions until the end of the century (1565, 1567, 1573, 1578, 1584), it was better attended and regained its former international character. The topics of the decisions included all problems of contemporary religious life, with a special emphasis on the elimination of secular influence in monastic life regarding food, clothing, entertainment and private property. Every Chapter stressed the importance of studies, urged the sending of enough clerics to Paris, regulated the admission and education of novices, and gave an opportunity for those persons who, during the troubled years of Protestant uprising had left their communities, to return to the Order.

Knowing from past experience that decisions are of no avail without enforcement, a plan of extensive visitations was carried out chiefly by the abbots of Cîteaux. When Jerome Souchier (1567-1571) was elected Abbot of Cîteaux, he retained the seat of his former abbey, Clairvaux. To that extraordinary power was added the cardinalate in 1568, and the Abbot used all his influence to restore his Order's faded glory and reputation. His worthy successor, Nicholas Boucherat I (1571-

1585), was almost constantly on the road and the detailed report of his visitation in Germany (1572-1574) gave a fair picture of the condition of the Order in that country after the disaster of the Reformation. He found 33 surviving houses in Germany (not including Austria) and Switzerland. The buildings were for the most part in good condition and the property well administered. The total number of monks was nearly 600 and there were 62 novices and 21 lay-brothers. The general state of discipline was satisfactory; in some houses as in Salem (Baden), and in Kaisersheim (Kaisheim, Bavaria), it was exemplary in every respect. Abbot Boucherat's indefatigable activity found an efficient supporter in the person of Cardinal John Morone, the protector of the Order.

Abbeys "In Commendam"

Despite the best efforts of an able and zealous administration, there existed, since the early fifteenth century a problem in monastic life which hampered every reformatory endeavor and eventually did more harm both materially and morally than wars, disasters and the Reformation combined. That was the system of abbeys *in commendam.* Disregarding forms of feudal interference in abbatial elections before the Cluniac reform, this new evil originated under the Popes of Avignon. Simultaneously with tendencies toward strictly centralized administration, the Holy See took a deeper interest in the affairs of religious orders, and, justified by the promotion of current reforms, placed Papal nominees, mostly cardinals, at the head of the richest and most influential abbeys. Finally, Gregory XI (1370-1378), referring to his supreme jurisdiction, claimed the exclusive right of nominating abbots to all monasteries of men. This theory, when put into practice, caused the accumulation of benefices; and since secular power was always aware of Papal interference in domestic politics, kings and princes also tried to revive their feudal rights of nomination. Henceforward, the system of free election, the greatest achievement of medieval monastic reforms, was replaced by nomination, where political considerations prevailed over the vital interest of religion and discipline.

The right of nomination again became a matter of bitter dispute between the King of France and the Pope. Since the Council of Basel was unable to find a satisfactory solution, King Charles VII took action into his own hands and, backed by the French clergy, proclaimed the Pragmatic Sanction of Bourges (1438), which nominally restored the canonical election but actually opened a wide door to the King's overwhelming influence. During the second half of the fifteenth century, the hopelessly complicated political problems paralyzed every effort to eliminate the evil; moreover, the Concordat of Bologna (1515), negotiated between Pope Leo X and Francis I, King of France, completely suppressed the elective method. The King presented his candidates and the Pope retained the right of institution. Thus the Concordat legalized and upheld until the French Revolution a system which undermined not only the very existence of monastic orders, but also made any reconstruction extremely difficult. The situation was at its worst in Italy and France, but with the single exception of England commendatory abbots ruled monasteries everywhere in Europe. The majority of abbots were chosen from the ranks of the hierarchy, but even the appointment of laymen was not a rare exception. As a rule, commendatory abbots did not live in their monasteries, but if a lay-abbot intruded into the community with his family and kinsfolk, further monastic life became utterly impossible. Since the abbot was not a monk and his interest rarely exceeded the collection of abbatial revenues, the actual administration of the monastery became the duty of the Conventual Prior. The distribution of revenues between abbot and convent was legally determined, but what the monks received was barely enough for food and clothing. The system did not spare even the oldest and most influential abbeys. In the Concordat of Bologna only Citeaux's freedom was assured; La

Ferté was already *in commendam* since 1488, Pontigny became so in 1543, along with the majority of Cistercian abbeys in France. As soon as the Cistercians realized the evil influence of the system, they vigorously protested against it. As early as 1415, Pope John XXIII issued a decree insuring that in the future no Cistercian houses would be given to anybody, however, he failed to act against those who actually were in the possession of abbeys. This policy was officially reaffirmed in 1454 by Nicholas V and in 1459 by Pius II, but to little or no avail. With the increasing number of abbeys *in commendam,* not only the regular life of the houses was endangered, but also the central government of the Order, since commendatory abbots were unable to fulfill abbatial duties regarding the regular visitations and participation at the General Chapters.

A shocking picture of the disastrous influence of the unfortunate system was presented in a report by Nicholas Boucherat, who, as Procurator General, personally visited the houses of the Order in the Papal States and in the Kingdom of Naples and Sicily in 1561. All the 35 monasteries were under commendatory abbots. He found the buildings everywhere dilapidated, many of them in ruins. Sixteen monasteries were completely deserted; in some others a few secular priests or members of other orders were living. The total Cistercian population of all those 35 houses consisted altogether of 86 monks, subsisting in misery, without any vestige of regular discipline or liturgical service. Another visitation in Lombardy and Tuscany in 1579 revealed similar conditions, where some 17 monasteries were hopelessly struggling with their commendatory abbots for a bare subsistence. The sharp contrast between conditions in Italy and the findings of a similar visitation in Germany sufficiently illustrates the fact that the Reformation in the center of its origin, was less detrimental to monastic life than the fatal maladministration of ecclesiastical property tolerated by the Church itself. Cîteaux and the General Chapter fought vigorously against the heaviest odds from the first recognition of the danger, with very little success. The only concrete result of their unceasing contention was the Ordinance of Blois in 1577, in which King Henry III of France exempted from the commendatory system La Ferté, Pontigny, Clairvaux and Morimond.

Pastoral Activity

In opposition to the heavy losses of these critical times there were some gains, among them an extensive pastoral activity and organization of parishes on the Order's own lands. Active ministry among the faithful certainly did not belong to the original program of the first founders of Cîteaux; yet the development of organized parishes was a necessary consequence of the Order's expansion. Uninhabited territories were not everywhere available, and the growing communities, frequently in grave material need, must have accepted as donations estates with villages and churches upon them. Some monasteries, for example Fountains or Kirkstall in England, went so far in the observance of the earliest Statutes, that they ejected the inhabitants, allowed the houses to fall into ruins and destroyed the parish-church, thus reducing the village to the status of a grange. But such a procedure aroused the just indignation of both the people and civil authorities; moreover, it was evidently against the universal interest of the Church. Another unavoidable occasion of acceptance of pastoral duties was the incorporation of monasteries already possessing churches with regular service for the people. In both cases the General Chapter relaxed its traditional rigorous attitude, and, from the middle of the thirteenth century, did not oppose the possibility of Cistercians taking care of the spiritual needs of the people living within the borders of monastic property. The number of incorporated parishes grew rapidly and at the end of the sixteenth century virtually all Cistercian houses had some monks involved in pastoral duties. Referring to this development, the Chapter of 1601 regulated in three paragraphs the legal state of the parishes and the general conduct of pastors. Meanwhile, permanent work of single monks in diocesan parishes was always regarded as an abuse against monastic discipline and strictly prohibited.

Academic Studies

As a proof that Humanism was not entirely incompatible with true monastic spirit, higher education was another field of remarkable advancement. Since the middle of the thirteenth century the General Chapter was always deeply concerned with the promotion of academic studies. Special attention was given to the College of St. Bernard at Paris, and those who obtained their degrees there enjoyed extensive privileges in their own communities. In this matter the Chapter's encouragement met a genuine and universal fervor for higher studies. During the first half of the seventeenth century new colleges were erected in Avignon and in Dôle near Besançon; the abbeys of Alna (Aulne) and Villers built study-houses in connection with the University of Louvain (Belgium). The German abbeys made even more conspicious progress in higher education. During the fifteenth and sixteenth centuries, almost every significant German university recorded Cistercian students. The most frequented among them was the University of Heidelberg, founded in 1386. The faculty of theology was organized by a Cistercian doctor, a graduate of Paris, Reginald of Alna. The adjoining Cistercian College of St. Jacob was founded in 1391, and according to the records of the University, from its beginning until 1522, the total number of Cistercian students had mounted to 600. When during the course of the fifteenth century Heidelberg became a stronghold of nominalism, the University was gradually abandoned by Cistercians adhering to the doctrine of St. Thomas Aquinas. The majority of students were transferred to Cologne, those from Southern Germany, to Freiburg. Cistercians were also sent to the University of Prague founded in 1348, but after that faculty became infiltrated by Hussites, the University of Leipzig (founded in 1409) received the largest number of Cistercians; its records show that some 400 identifiable Cistercians attended the University up to the middle of the sixteenth century. A Cistercian college, affiliated with the University of Leipzig, was opened in 1461. In Cologne, where the foundation of a Cistercian house of studies goes back to the thirteenth century, the University (founded in 1388) recorded that some 100 Cistercian students were in attendance up to 1559. Quite popular was the new University of Dillingen (founded in 1550), to which the abbeys of Baden, Württemberg and Switzerland sent large contingents; by 1695 they numbered altogether 173. At the beginning of the seventeenth century, two-thirds of the members of Salem, the largest abbey of Baden, were Dillingen graduates. Until the end of the eighteenth century some German Cistercian clerics were studying also at the famous *Collegium Germanicum Hungaricum* in Rome under Jesuit direction, altogether 42 in number.

In the General Chapter of 1584, there emerged a plan for a new *Studium Generale* at Rome, sponsored by Cardinal Louis d'Este, Protector of the Order; Pope Gregory XIII also showed a warm sympathy toward the proposition. He offered to the Order for that purpose the monastery of St. Susanna at Rome, and for further support of the institution the incomes of two Cistercian abbeys which were at that time under *commendam*. Since the French abbots, however, were afraid that by the new foundation the position of the College of Paris might be weakened they hesitated to assume the heavy financial burden of such an institution and the promising plan was given up and eventually forgotten.

8. The Rise of the Congregations

The spirit of the Renaissance, which replaced the medieval ideal of a universal Christian Monarchy with strong centralized states based on national unity, dissolved the once exemplary unity of the Cistercian Order. From the beginning of the fifteenth century Cîteaux's power proved to be inadequate in keeping under control the rising tide of separatism and must have given way to the development of more or less independent Congregations.

There was a certain parallelism between the later Cistercian evolution and the provincial system of the Mendicants, which was imposed even upon the Benedictines as a consequence of the reforms of Benedict XII (1336). The Mendicant provinces, however, were integral constituents of a highly centralized government, while the Cistercian Congregations were the results of a defective centralization, organized in defiance of the original constitution. Undoubtedly, its strongest motive was a general desire for reform which Cîteaux was unable to enforce in its full extent. The organizers of the new Congregations took the initiative into their own hands and, with the cooperation of similar-minded abbots, put into practice their own program, formulated under the influence of other religious orders, local customs and contemporary religious trends. In the sixteenth century such endeavors were decisively encouraged by the authority of the Council of Trent, prescribing, in reference to former decrees of Innocent III, the formation of congregations for those monasteries which were not under the jurisdiction of general chapters or diocesan bishops, but under the immediate authority of the Holy See.

The early separatist attempts were regarded as rebellions against the *Charter of Charity* and met with the vigorous opposition of the General Chapter; however, since the Holy See usually approved reformatory endeavors and the states striving for a national unity also warmly supported them, the General Chapter eventually was forced to appease.

The first case of desertion did not result from the above development; it must be attributed to the personal influence of Joachim of Fiore (d.1202), a popular prophet and well known precursor of St. Francis of Assisi. As an ardent admirer of the eastern hermits, he became a Cistercian in the middle of his rather agitated career. He was a strong and original personality, and instead of accomodating himself to the Cistercian way of living, he tried to impose his ideas upon several monasteries of Southern Italy. His program was condemned by the General Chapter; he himself was branded as a fugitive, and his followers were excluded from the Order. The basic points of Abbot Joachim's teaching on an approaching third era of the salvation, the age of Love and of the Holy Ghost with a new kind of monasticism, proved to be heretical, but personally he was always regarded as a holy man and his influence upon the late Franciscan movement was remarkable.

Independent Congregations

The earliest Congregation, as a reform measure, was started in Spain by Martin Vargas (d.1446), a former member of the Order of Hermits of St. Jerome. After having joined the Cistercians he built a reform-monastery at Mont Sion near Toledo. Apparently, he never became acquainted with the constitution of the Order, since his program was much closer to Mendicant ideals than to those of the Cistercians. In the monasteries reorganized by him stability was abolished; instead of abbots, he installed priors for triennial terms, while he called himself Supreme Reformer, an office he was to hold for five years. Although he acknowledged the right of visitation of the Abbot of Cîteaux in person, the new Congregation severed every other connection with the Order, having their own chapters at Mont Sion. They sent, however, every third year one representative to the General Chapter at Cîteaux. In 1425, Pope Martin V, whose confessor Abbot Martin had been, granted him permission to carry out his plans, and the General Chapter of Cîteaux, in order to maintain peace, also recognized his position and activity. However, Cîteaux, realizing that a final and irreparable break was imminent, excommunicated the "Reformer" and ordered him to be imprisoned in his own monastery (1445). Abbot Martin died shortly thereafter but his ideas survived in the Congregation of Castile, which never managed to reach a better understanding with Cîteaux than it did during the lifetime of its founder. In 1710, this Congregation controlled 42 monasteries.

The Congregation of Lombardy and Tuscany also arose under Papal auspices, against the protest of the Order. Their customs of electing abbots for three years and the abolition of stability was again the result of a strong Mendicant influence and, as such, far from any monastic tradition. In their own chapters, which at first were held annually and in every third year from 1578 until 1656, and only in every fifth year after that date, the communities were represented by the abbots (or as they called them, *prelates*) and also by an elected *discretus*. The *prelates* held their office for five years. They had almost no connection with Cîteaux, refusing even the representation of their Congregation at the General Chapters. Nevertheless, the congregation was approved by Pope Alexander VI, in 1497, and its authority was extended over 45 houses. Although Cîteaux succeeded in obtaining a reversal of the Papal Decree, Pope Julius II, in 1511, restored the Congregation, exempting it from the jurisdiction of Cîteaux and placing it under the leadership of the Abbot of Chiaravalle, near Milan.

Its distant geographical location promoted the development of the Congregation of Portugal, which united 17 Cistercian establishments in that country under the Abbey of Alcobaça. Since the approval of their organization by Pope Pius V, in 1567, they had very little connection with Cîteaux. Their constitution followed the pattern of the Congregation of Castile. Similar reasons gave existence to the Polish Congregation, which was formed in 1580 at the provincial chapter of Wagrowice, and consisted of 15 houses for men, 5 for women.

The original character of John de la Barrière (1544-1600) and his rather peculiar reformatory ideas created the Congregation of the Feuillants. De la Barrière, a former commendatory abbot of the monastery Les Feuillans in France (Haute-Garonne), took the Cistercian habit without a regular novitiate, and persistently ignoring both the traditions of the Order and the authority of the General Chapter, introduced into his monastery a life of extreme austerity. His followers wore no shoes, slept on a plank with a stone for a pillow, took their meals on the floor, drank from skulls, renounced wine, fish, eggs, butter, salt and all seasoning, and fasted during Lent restricting their diet to bread and water. Besides France, the reform found its way to Italy, and Pope Sixtus V, who approved their Congregation in 1586, invited them to Rome. When Clement VIII learned of the death of fourteen members of this house within a week, the Pontiff mitigated their rigid rule (1595). During the first decades of the seventeenth century the Feuillants of Italy detached themselves from those of France and set up the new Congregation of the Reformed Bernardines (1630), which eventually reestablished the connection with Cîteaux. However, every Feuillant returning to the Order was required to start another novitiate, indicating that the General Chapter did not even recognize them as Cistercians. The Feuillant movement found a sympathetic echo in Luxembourg, where Dom Bernard Montgaillard reformed Orval in 1605. During the second half of the century, however, de Rancé's influence became preponderant in Orval and the abbey succeeded in organizing a small group of monasteries under her own direction (Conques, Lurich, Düsselthal, Heisterbach and Beaupré). The exaggerations of overzealous radicals soon drove the group into the camp of the Jansenists.

At the request of King Philip III of Spain, the Cistercians in that country outside of the Castilian Congregation were united under the title of the Congregation of Aragon. Pope Paul V recognized the new Congregation in 1616, which remained under the jurisdiction of Cîteaux, though having very little real connection with it. The approval of their statutes by the General Chapter became a matter of discussion for the entire century, because in Spain the custom of temporary abbots was widespread and the Chapter's insistence upon the traditional life-time term was never fully respected. They elected their abbots for 4 years.

Those few monasteries which survived the disastrous commendatory system in the Papal States and in Naples and Sicily, were united under the auspices of Pope Gregory XV, in 1623, as the Congregation of Rome. For a time it was under the surveillance of the Procurator General, but the stability was abolished and its customs were quite foreign to those of Cîteaux. Ten years thereafter, those monasteries in Southern Italy left out of this union were organized by Pope Urban VIII, as the Calabrian-Lucanian Congregation which included also the monasteries once reformed by Joachim of Fiore. Their constitution was similar to that of the Congregation of Rome. However, these administrative measures were of little avail against the evils of the *commendam* and the true monastic life never revived there, despite the continuous efforts of the General Chapter.

The development of the Congregation of Upper Germany presented a more consoling picture. The movement started with the first "National Chapter" of German abbots in 1595, held in the Bavarian abbey of Fürstenfeld. Its chief motivation included the traditional antagonism between France and Germany as well as a sincere desire for necessary reforms, which hardly could be achieved otherwise, since the regular visitations of French abbots in Germany were regarded as unwanted foreign interference in domestic politics. Cîteaux, in protecting the unity of the Order, was as reluctant toward the proposition as it had been in similar cases elsewhere; but behind the lengthy negotiations the real problems were the attitude of the French court with its open Gallicanism and its determination to control the Church, and the Holy See, anxious to restrain the French political influence. Hence, it can be understood why the Popes promoted the organization of Congregations independently from French mother houses, as in the case of a German Congregation. With this powerful support, the able Abbot Thomas Wunn of Salem succeeded in effectuating the long debated plans, which were ratified by the General Chapter in 1623. The new Congregation numbered 26 monasteries for men and 36 convents in Southern Germany and Switzerland; and was divided into four provinces under the presidency of the Abbot of Salem (Baden).

Notwithstanding the differences between Cîteaux and the German abbeys, the latter were more faithful to the General Chapter and stood much higher in morals and monastic discipline than any other Congregation of the Order. They exhibited an amazing vitality during the Thirty Years' War, when Emperor Ferdinand II promulgated the Edict of Restitution (1629), which constrained the Protestants to restore to the Church all ecclesiastical goods, including more than five hundred abbeys, convents and churches, secularized since the peace of Augsburg. Naturally, the unexpected spoil challenged all ecclesiastic organizations to take possession of the derelicts, but the Cistercian abbeys of Kaisersheim, Salem, Lützel, Camp and Fürstenfeld not only claimed the former properties of the Order for selfish material interest, but in a matter of years resettled many of the deserted houses with great sacrifice of both finances and personnel. Unfortunately, as a result of the Treaty of Westphalia (1648), all these new acquisitions were lost to the Church forever.

Political motive in the formation of congregations was most conspicuous in the case of the short-lived Belgian Congregation established in 1782, upon the insistence of Emperor Joseph II's government. It contended that the "subordination" of those monasteries to "foreign superiors, subjects of the King of France," was an intolerable abuse. This group included, until the secularization, 53 well organized houses: 14 for men, 39 for women.

There were several other monastic organizations which, although they never belonged legally to the Order, followed its customs or accepted its spiritual leadership. Thus the Guillelmites, organized in Tuscany by William of Maleval (d.1157) wore Cistercian habit; their group survived until the end of the eighteenth century. The Congregation of Corpus Christi was formed in Umbria in the fourteenth century with the special purpose of the adoration of the Blessed Sacrament. In 1393 they accepted Cîteaux's jurisdiction and although their dependent state lasted only for about twenty years, they retained Cistercian customs for a long time.

Central Administration

The separation of the Congregations and the continued commendatory system influenced not only the discipline and customs of individual houses but also affected the central government of the Order. The new development greatly weakened and restricted the authority of the General Chapter and completely disrupted the regularity of visitations based upon the power of father-abbots, both cornerstones of the *Charter of Charity.* Unfortunately, the measures of the Chapter, applied in order to remedy and supplant the staggering traditional organization, lacked the clarity and thoughtful planning of St. Stephen's legislation; they were often rather vague and contradictory, and, most of all, never were enforced to their full extent.

The Chapters themselves did not truly represent the whole Order, since the abbots of the independent Congregations seldom attended, and the abbeys under *commendam* were mostly without representation, although the Conventual Priors were obliged to appear at the Chapters after 1546. Even for those who would have taken their part in the sessions willingly, the difficulties of regular attendance were so great that in 1605 the Chapter decided to convene only every fourth year; as a matter of fact, yearly Chapters had not been observed during the previous century. This rule was modified in 1666, by prescribing the Chapters for every three years. Nevertheless, neither plan was respected and during the whole of the seventeenth century the General Chapters held only 13 regular conventions; from 1699 to 1738 the Chapter never met at all.

As a result of the long chapterless years, there arose the influence and authority of the Abbot of Cîteaux. Since he represented the Order to the outside world and there was no other permanent organ of central administration, public opinion regarded him as a general superior, after the fashion of the newly organized religious Congregations. Concerning his person, in official documents, the title "Abbot General" became more and more common, and from the middle of the seventeenth century the usage was almost universally accepted. Meanwhile, both the General Chapter and the proto-abbots, suspiciously vigilant in regard to their constitutional rights, attempted to restrict Cîteaux's dominant position. Thus the same Chapter of 1605, which abolished the system of yearly Chapters, ordered an annual convention of the proto-abbots as a consultative body to the Abbot of Cîteaux in order to discuss current issues of major importance. There are very few records of such formal sessions until 1666, when the Constitution, *In Suprema,* of Pope Alexander VII revived the institution in a changed form as the Intermediate Chapter. The members of this assembly, in addition to the proto-abbots, were the Presidents of the Congregations, the Visitors, the Procurator Generals and the Provincial Procurators. The time of its convocation depended on the decision of the Abbot of Cîteaux, within the newly established triennial terms of the General Chapter. The same Apostolic Constitution tried also to restore the original role of the Chapter Fathers against the overwhelming power of the *Definitorium,* by securing their rights to vote in any matter proposed for final decision. However, like some other measures of the same Constitution, the Intermediate Chapters never gained any popularity or importance. Until the French Revolution it convened only ten or twelve times, debating mostly financial problems of the central administration.

More significant changes took place in the executive branch of the Cistercian Constitution when the spreading commendatory system and the rise of independent Congregations overthrew the traditional rule of controls and annual visitation exercised by the father-abbots toward their direct affiliations. As a substitution, beginning with the fifteenth century, visitors for certain monasteries were nominated occasionally by the General Chapter. If their authority was extended upon a larger territory with far reaching powers, they were frequently called Reformers. In 1433 a special Visitor was appointed for each province under the authority of a General Visitor. For such an important task usually the most influential abbots or even the Abbot of Cîteaux was appointed, but, with the commitment of the Chapter, simple monks also acted as visitors. At the same time, for other extraordinary duties, like arbitration or collection of contributions, the appointee of the Chapter was called a Commissary; this office became increasingly important.

The new system of administration took a more steady and specific shape when, during the sixteenth century, those abbeys not belonging to the newly established Congregations were organized into provinces or vicariates, under the direct authority of the General Chapter. When the Chapters failed to convene, this authority was exercised by the Abbot of Cîteaux. These Cistercian provinces, unlike those of the Mendicants, were administrative units without any autonomy or constitutional role, and territorially they corresponded to the political provinces of the countries concerned. The new scheme first developed in France, and, during the seventeenth century, spread throughout Continental Europe; in 1683, besides the Congregations, there were 39 Provinces. Control over the monasteries of a Province was the duty of the Provincial Vicar who, appointed by the General Chapter, was, as a rule, an abbot of the same Province. The regulations of this new and important office were laid down by the Chapter of 1605 and further developed by the subsequent General Chapters. The chief obligation of the Provincial Vicars was the annual visitation of all the monasteries under their care, reporting their findings to the Abbot of Cîteaux. These appointments lasted until the next Chapter, but since decades frequently elapsed without a regular Chapter, the Vicars were nominated or relieved by the Abbot of Cîteaux after consultation with the proto-abbots; distinguished abbots often held the office for a lifetime. When the Abbot of Cîteaux assumed the title of Abbot General, the Vicars became known as Vicars General. An official subordinated to the Vicar General was the Provincial Procurator, in charge of the defense or support of the abbeys in legal cases. This office originated during the struggles against the *commendam* in the fifteenth century. Their title was changed in 1565 to *Syndicus* or *Promotor;* the whole institution was suppressed in 1699. The rising influence of the French Court in religious matters was indicated by the appointment of a Procurator General to the King's Court at Paris in 1601, with a similar authorization for that of the other Procurator General to the Holy See. In spite of these substantial innovations, the original *Charter of Charity* never was formally amended or even revoked; where the original affiliation was still in existence the Chapters always encouraged the abbots to exercise their constitutional rights in cooperation with the Vicars General.

The same historical factors, which necessitated these administrative changes, affected also the reorganization of the education of novices and of young professed members of the Order. As a result of the evil circumstances analyzed above, a large number of abbeys decreased both in members and regular discipline, thus becoming unable or unfit to maintain properly their own novitiate. The detailed reform-scheme of the Chapter of 1601 demanded the establishment of common novitiates for certain groups of abbeys; and, since the same institution proved to be a practical means of supporting a uniform discipline in many other religious congregations, the plan found a warm support in Rome. Undoubtedly, such a resolution vitally affected the basic rights of single monasteries, and was vehemently opposed by all those abbeys where the traditional Cistercian life was still alive, especially in Germany. Nevertheless, the common novitiate, as an unavoidable necessity in France and Italy, became a provincial institution, but the right of single abbeys to maintain their own novitiate was always respected, as far as they were able to fulfill the minimum requirements for its proper management. The houses of common novitiate were usually connected with a subsequent course of theology, where the young professed students were trained further in monastic discipline. Because of the great importance of these educational centers concerning pending reforms and general spirit of the Order, the manner of their direction and supervision was a subject of heated debate during the struggle of observances throughout the seventeenth century.

The internal administrations of the autonomous Congregations show about the same pattern in a more concise form. The most efficient among them was the Statutes of the Congregation of Upper Germany, drafted in 1618. Its preamble emphasized fidelity to Cîteaux and to the General Chapter and the intention of the constituent abbeys to remain in the union. The

President of the Congregation was to be elected in the Congregational Chapter; he was an abbot and enjoyed all the rights of a Vicar General. His chief duty was the annual visitation of the monasteries of men and the visitation of convents in every fourth year. The President's own monastery was to be visited by an abbot and two monks appointed by the Congregational Chapter. The office of the President included a Commissary and a Secretary, both members of his own community, who in case of any impediment were delegated for visitations and always accompanied the President in his tours of visitation. In case of the President's death, his duties were to be taken over by the Commissary. The Congregational Chapter convened one year before and one year after the General Chapter, but could be convoked any time in case of emergency. Its place was Salem, where all abbots were due to present themselves. In the session preceding the General Chapter it was decided who would represent the Congregation at Cîteaux. At the abbatial elections either the President or the Commissary was to be present and the newly elected abbot had to be blessed by the President. The right to admit new abbeys to the Congregation belonged also to the Abbot President. The organization of a common novitiate at Salem together with a full course of philosophy and theology had been decided; but in the education and instruction an equal part was guaranteed for each abbey.

Here, as in the case of the new constitutional development in the central administration of the whole Order, the simplicity of the *Charter of Charity* was virtually replaced by a modern scheme with an obvious resemblance to the provincial organization of the new religious orders of the sixteenth and seventeenth century. Nevertheless, it is remarkable that the basic elements of the ancient customs continued to prevail, and that while the traditional constitutional system in its original form ceased to function a century ago, these new attempts to establish and preserve order and discipline were unmistakable signs of a firm will for survival.

9. The War of the Observances

The reformatory efforts of the previous two hundred years culminated in the middle of the seventeenth century, when the movement, after finishing its course in Spain, Italy and Germany, revolutionized the center of the Order, Cîteaux. Its unusual impetus cannot be attributed only to the vigor of a minority group among the numerous French abbeys; like every real reform of importance, it emerged as an organic element of a universal religious renewal, which reached its climax during the first half of the "Great Century." It was the highest tide of the Baroque, a return of an exuberant religious sentiment with a fresh inspiration not only for poets and artists, but also for the men full of zeal for the final victory of the Church, which never seemed to be closer than after the defeat of the Protestant armies during the first period of the Thirty Years' War.

Religious Renewal

The enthusiastic spirit of the Catholic revival gave origin to scores of new religious congregations and also regenerated the old religious orders. The most efficient reform was that of the Discalced Carmelites in Spain by St. Teresa of Avila and St. John of the Cross, which quickly passed into the other Catholic countries of Europe. The reformed French Benedictines formed the Congregation of Saint-Vanne (1604) and somewhat later the famous Congregation of Saint Maur (1621). The movement soon spread to the Canons Regular, Franciscans, Capuchins, Dominicans, and Augustinians. The new spirit also penetrated the secular clergy and inspired a new system of education for the priesthood with the organized assistance of the new French Oratory.

The spectacular success of this universal religious renewal was supported by a new spirituality which, in sharp contrast to the Humanism of the sixteenth century, turned its interest toward the supernatural, and in its asceticism imitated again the Fathers of the Desert and revived the golden age of medieval mysticism. Naturally, the ideals of the new piety were also far removed from the ruling style of Jesuit spirituality and the clash between old and new—as so many times in the past—became inevitable. At the same time, the innovations aroused bitter passions within the reformed orders and the divergent trends dissolved the communities into observant and non-observant members, resulting in a final schism between the opponent observances. The vehement debates were accompanied by a flood of polemical literature and the Holy See, with all its alertness, was hardly able to restrain the combatants from abusive exaggerations.

The discipline of the Church, following the Council of Trent, was strict enough to prevent the danger of a serious breach, yet the overheated atmosphere of boiling emotions produced the characteristic heresies of seventeenth century France, Jansenism and Quietism. Their dogmatic errors concerning the correlation of nature and grace concerned only a handful of theologians, but the practical consequences of their teaching, their morbid exaggerations and peculiar demands of individual piety profoundly infected the French religious mind.

Although Quietism, an unhealthy outgrowth of contemporary mysticism, was not lacking influential representatives, the Jansenistic movement found a much wider and louder echo. Cornelius Jansen, a professor of the University of Louvain, whose name trade-marked the heresy, died in 1638 and left the task of editing his work, entitled *Augustinus,* to his friends. The responsibility for the propagation of his thoughts was largely due to Abbé de St. Cyran, the spiritual director of the Cistercian convent of Port Royal near Paris, and Anthony Arnauld, whose sisters, Angelica and Agnes ruled the group of congenial sisters from within. The Cistercian Order as such, had nothing in common with the future role of Port Royal, since it denied entirely its Cistercian allegiance. Their appeal found an enthusiastic response among the highest intellectual and social classes of French society. A small circle of the most devoted friends, among them Pascal, lived in solitude near the Convent, after the fashion of the eastern hermits, while the movement was supported from the outside by a much larger number of sympathizers such as Racine, Boileau and Madame de Sévigné.

The root of Jansenistic piety is a moral pessimism: human nature is so deeply corrupted that all actions corresponding to its inclinations are sinful, consequently salvation will be granted only for a small number of the elect, who abandon their nature and follow grace; their lives must be given heroically to God, in the spirit of penance, retired from the world in the severe asceticism of the Desert Fathers; natural virtues and the love of learning are at best worthless, and the Church herself had been taking a wrong direction ever since the twelfth century by advocating Scholasticism and the Renaissance. In other words, Jansenism with its wholesale pessimism and ultra-supernaturalism, together with an antiquarianism unfriendly to development, is the clearest example of the counter-renaissance, characteristic of the whole century. Jansenism as a doctrine was condemned by Pope Innocent X in 1653, after a long war waged against it by the Jesuits, but the incurably self-conscious defenders of the sect did not give up fighting until, after the death of the first Jansenist generation, Port Royal itself was dissolved and razed to the ground.

The "Strict Observance"

The Cistercian reform in France, as an integral component of the general religious revival, took its first steps in the last years of the sixteenth century at the abbey of Charmoye followed by Châtillon, but the movement did not exceed local importance until Denis Largentier, the Abbot of Clairvaux, entered the picture. Through his personal example and his influence upon his affiliations the reform met with remarkable success. By 1618, eight monasteries had followed Clairvaux's lead, and their number continued to grow steadily in spite of increasing dissensions between the new observance and Cîteaux. In 1624, more than 40 abbeys belonged to the reform; by the year 1660, it was adopted by a total of 62 houses. During the lifetime of Abbot Largentier there was complete harmony between him and Nicholas Boucherat II, the Abbot of Cîteaux, who sincerely welcomed the reform and did not even oppose Clairvaux's efforts to organize the observant abbeys into one congregation. However, the General Chapter of 1623, mindful of previous schismatic attempts inaugurated by the same Clairvaux, sharply rejected the proposed congregation, without condemning the reformatory endeavors behind it. Apparently, the reform in this early stage progressed without too much pressure from either side. Moreover, not only full houses but also individuals were free to embrace or reject it until 1628, when the Chapter ordained that for the sake of internal peace the non-observant members of reformed communities should be transferred to non-observant houses and those who wanted to join an observant abbey were free to do so. Doubtless, in the atmosphere of a continued good will and understanding between Cîteaux and Clairvaux, both the necessary reform could have been achieved and the unity of the Order might have been preserved. Unfortunately, Abbot Largentier died in 1624 and Abbot Boucherat also passed away in the following year. Neither one of their successors followed either of them in the spirit of peaceful cooperation.

The abbatial elections in both places were held against the vigorous protest of a very active minority. In Cîteaux, Peter Nivelle took the seat of the Abbot General; in Clairvaux, Denis Largentier was succeeded by his nephew, Claude Largentier.

As soon as it became evident that the new Abbot of Clairvaux was by no means a wholehearted promoter of the reform, Stephen Maugier, Abbot of Charmoye, assumed the leadership of the Strict Observance; Maugier was determined to impose the reform without delay upon the whole Order at any cost, should the General Chapter refuse to yield to his demands. When the Chapter Fathers in 1628 declined to enforce drastic measures against a solid majority, the Strict Observance adopted a resolution which inflicted an unparalleled humiliation upon the whole Order by opening wide the door to outside interference and arousing the passions on both sides. This excluded any reasonable solution and prepared a fatal and irreparable breach between the two observances.

The intransigent members of the reform kept in touch for a longer time with Cardinal La Rochefoucauld, who had been Apostolic Visitor of all religious orders in France since 1622, and now they convinced him that the time had come for action. The partially informed Cardinal, without any formal visitation at Cîteaux, issued in 1634 a charter containing the following measures: Cîteaux and the four proto-abbeys were to be turned over immediately to the Strict Observance; the members of these communities were to be transferred to other houses. Those who accepted the new observance might stay where they were, but they also were deprived of any active or passive rights in voting for monastic officials. The abbots of these five houses were allowed to keep their titles, but the government was to be exercised by Assistants of the Strict Observance. The authority of the General Chapter was suspended and the supreme power was to be executed by a Vicar General and four Assistants until the election of a new Abbot General from the members of the reform. The Cardinal himself appointed the Vicar General in the person of Stephen Maugier. The houses of the Strict Observance alone and exclusively enjoyed the right of receiving novices; thus the other houses were condemned to extinction.

Since Cîteaux was deeply convinced that the Cardinal's procedure was perfectly illegal and that the applied measures exceeded by far his authorization, the Abbot General appealed simultaneously to the Pope and to the King in order to obtain the annulment of the decree. Pope Urban VIII promptly nullified the ordinances, but Cardinal Richelieu, the all-powerful minister of Louis XIII, welcomed the unexpected event as a long awaited opportunity to interfere in the affairs of that mighty and influential Order. These years signalized the climax of his bitter discord with Rome on the issues of Gallicanism, and he used every means to establish a state-controlled Church under his own direction. In order to strengthen his position against Rome and to secure his influence within France, Richelieu eagerly intervened in every religious reform, but it was plain enough that he wanted not merely to reform the monastic bodies, but also to unite them into a national system to be controlled from Paris instead of Rome. After reforming the Capuchins, Dominicans, and forcing even the Jesuits to submission, he assumed the title of Abbot of Prémontré and in 1629 appointed himself Abbot of Cluny with the purpose of welding the Benedictine Congregations into a French union.

After a consultation with the Abbot General and the protoabbots at Royaumont in March, 1635, Richelieu ordained the convocation of a National Chapter at Cîteaux in the fall of the same year. Characteristically enough, besides the presence of both observances, he also insisted upon inviting the reformed Benedictines. Obviously he believed that the gathering might become the first step toward some sort of fusion between Benedictines and Cistercians. Nevertheless, not only the Benedictines but also the Strict Observance boycotted the sessions and the Chapter was dissolved without results. The indignant Cardinal decided to take the initiative into his own hands. In 1636, he appointed Peter Nivelle as Bishop of Luçon, simultaneously declaring himself Abbot General of the whole Cistercian Order. The circumstances of the procedure are not known, but there is certainly no trace of any legal or even formal election, and the Holy See never acknowledged his position as Abbot of Cîteaux. The missing formalities, however, did not prevent Richelieu from acting as an absolute master of the Order. The measures which followed surprised no one, because the Cardinal had proceeded exactly in the same manner a few years before at Cluny. He placed 26 monks of the Strict Observance at Cîteaux in charge of the central administration and dispersed all those members of the community who were not willing to cooperate; of the original personnel of the abbey only ten remained. The next step toward thorough-going unification and control was the suppression of all novitiates of the Order in France, except one at Cîteaux, which was to serve as a common novitiate for the whole country. It is doubtful how far these drastic and wholly illegal measures were carried out, since Cardinal Richelieu died in 1642, leaving the Order in a state of complete turmoil.

After having received the first news of the Cardinal's death, the outcast members of Cîteaux attempted to take possession of their abbey, but the inflexible observants kept the doors closed, flatly denying them admission. Thereupon, the excluded group of some 40 monks retired to Dijon and there, in January of 1643, in the so-called "Little Cîteaux," unanimously elected the Prior of Froidmont, Claude Vaussin to the vacant see of Cîteaux. The King still insisted that a member of the Strict Observance should be elected and vetoed the action, but did not object to submission of the case to Rome. The Pope appointed a committee of three bishops to investigate the confused situation; the committee recognized the right of election of Vaussin's party but denied the legality of the January voting. Through a compromise, a new election took place at Cîteaux on May 10, 1645, where all the forty votes were cast again for Claude Vaussin. Nevertheless, fifteen members of the "abstinents" refused to accept the new abbot and for their part elected John Jouaud, Abbot of the reformed Prières. The ominous consequences of the double election, however, were this time eliminated by the quick approval of Abbot Vaussin's election by both Pope Innocent X, and King Louis XIV.

The new Abbot General clearly realized that his first duty was the pacification of the disturbed sentiments, but the thorny problem of the College of St. Bernard in Paris increased the tension. When, in 1647, Abbot Vaussin declared his determination to take possession of the College which had been held by the Strict Observance since 1635, enmities flared up again. In 1649 Vaussin contacted John Jouaud in order to work out a possible compromise and to restore peace between the observances; moreover, in case of a favorable reply he expressed his readiness to nominate Abbot Jouaud, the leader of the "abstinents," as General Visitor over the whole Order. Nevertheless, the subsequent abbatial convention of the Strict Observance flatly refused the idea of any compromise. As a further sign of his sincere desire to discuss and solve the most ardent problems, Abbot Vaussin convoked the General Chapter as soon as the political situation permitted. The Chapter met in 1651, the first time since 1635. After the decades of embittered debates, it is rather surprising to read in the first point of definitions that the whole Order as such accepted the strict observance in its full extent, except the perpetual abstinence. It was added, accordingly, that novices and clerics everywhere in the Order must be educated in the same spirit of reform in perfect uniformity. The statement unmistakably proved on the one hand the existence of a genuine reform spirit throughout the Order, and it illustrated on the other hand the fact that, with the single exception of abstinence from meat, which after all was by no means a cardinal point either of the Rule of St. Benedict or of the Cistercian constitution, there was no essential difference between the regular observance of the opponent parties. Yet, the Strict Observance could not be appeased by any compromise. They never forgot the time when, with Richelieu's help, they ruled the Order. They now took their various grievances to the supreme secular court, the *Parlement* of Paris. The prolonged litigations caused the cancellation of the Chapter already announced for 1661, and due to the fact that the possibility of an agreement seemed to be farther away than ever, the Holy See decided to intervene. Pope Alexander VII, with his Brief of 1662, ordered the representatives of both observances to Rome for the purpose of working out an acceptable formula for both parties in cooperation with a committee of cardinals appointed for the detailed investigation of every point of disagreement.

The Constitution of Alexander VII

The lengthy negotiations lasted from December, 1664, until April, 1666. The delegation of the Common Observance was headed by Abbot Vaussin himself, while as a representative of the Strict Observance there emerged now for the first time the name of Abbot de Rancé of La Trappe who, although he had just completed his novitiate, became the key figure of the future development. The results of the negotiations were summed up in the form of a Brief, the *In Suprema,* signed by Pope Alexander VII, on April 19, 1666. The purpose of this important document, as the Pope himself emphasized in the introductory chapter, was to strengthen the unity and reestablish peace and mutual understanding within the Order through a point by point explanation of St. Benedict's Rule in every question of common discipline. Thenceforth Cistercian life in both observances was regulated by this Constitution until the French Revolution. Concerning the legal status of the Strict Observance, the Pope assured them of equal rights for their abbots in the General and Intermediate Chapters and in the system of visitation; in the monasteries *in commendam,* only members of their own observance could be appointed as conventual priors. It was prohibited to transfer monks from one observance to the other without the consent of the major superiors, and the Pope strictly forbade the use of pressure in order to force monks to join the Strict Observance, if they were not educated in it. The houses of the Strict Observance were to keep the perpetual abstinence; in the other houses meat could be served thrice a week except during Advent, during Lent from Septuagesima Sunday on, and on the other days of abstinence established by the universal law. Concerning the education of novices everywhere, it was emphasized that they were obliged to follow the strict discipline with the exception of perpetual abstinence, which was the only difference between the Strict and Common Observances. Since the ultimate aim of the Brief was to maintain the unity of the Order, it could not agree to the organization of an independent Congregation for the Strict Observance, but it did accede to the division of their houses into distinct provinces under their own Provincial Visitors, which meant a considerable degree of autonomy.

For the solemn promulgation of this new document, the Pope ordered the convocation of a General Chapter in 1667, at which, besides the Abbot General and the proto-abbots, ten *definitors* were to represent the Common Observance and another ten the Strict Observance. This arrangement, considering the fact that the Strict Observance was still a strictly French institution and a minority even in France, was a generous gesture made in the hope that the "abstinents" would sincerely cooperate in the execution of the Papal order.

Unfortunately, contrary to optimistic expectations, the blind passions and personal enmities which had characterized the relationship between the two parties ever since 1634, caused a ruthless struggle for power and domination, which annihilated the foundations of a possible peaceful settlement. The General Chapter of 1667 turned out to be the stormiest ever held. Instead of preparing the way for the desired unification, it became a decisive step toward inescapable separation.

The reading of the Papal decree was scarcely terminated, when Abbé de Rancé stood up to protest, with the unanimous support of the abbots of the Strict Observance. He argued that the Brief was largely the result of intrigue, that its content was against the Rule and against the traditions of the Order, even against the will of the Pontiff. Other abstinents opposed the composition of the Chapter and its officials, especially the *Definitorium,* and in the turmoil of charges and countercharges any reasonable discussion became utterly impossible. The Strict Observance obstinately insisted to the very end not only upon privileges virtually identical with the erection of an independent Congregation, but also upon the right to reform further houses as soon as the majority of the members would be in favor of the move. Since the first point obviously was directed against the Brief and the second would have created a state of permanent revolution in the whole Order, the Common Observance also stiffened its position and the promising convention dissolved in bitter resentment.

Since Richelieu's interference in behalf of the reform, the Strict Observance did not enjoy the best reputation in Rome; but now its attitude toward the Papal Brief aroused the deep dissatisfaction of the Holy See. Pope Clement IX, the successor of Alexander VII, issued a new Brief, sharply rebuking the protesting abbots, the Abbot of La Trappe by name, and energetically upholding and confirming the *In Suprema*'s authority. De Rancé understood the lesson, retired to his monastery, and, with relentless energy, set about the reform of his own abbey, which was to become the cradle of a new spirituality and later of the Order of Trappists. However, his fellow-abbots readily took up the gauntlet, and the battle went on.

The General Chapter announced for 1670 was deferred because of the death of Abbot Vaussin. His immediate successor, Louis Loppin, died in the same year, and, as another sign of the sincere will for peace, John Petit was elected Abbot General; Petit was one of the ten monks who had remained at Cîteaux after the "abstinents" came into power during Richelieu's regime. Nevertheless, the General Chapter of 1672 failed to create any relief in the overheated atmosphere. Clement X, addressing the Chapter in his Brief stated that the equal number of *definitors* for both observances was meant only for the Chapter of 1667 and that to continue the practice would be unjust to the majority of the Common Observance. When the Chapter consequently resolved to reduce the representatives of the Strict Observance from ten to six, the storm broke out again. The abbots of the "abstinents" boycotted further sessions and this time they tried to weaken the authority of the Papal message by charging that it was not approved by the King.

The first sign of a break in the constant tension was shown during the Chapter of 1683. After having heard the complaints of the Strict Observance that their original discipline was dangerously declining almost everywhere, the Chapter Fathers readily acceded to the two major demands of the Strict Observance—so severely opposed two decades before—namely the right to have their own annual abbatial conventions and the power to incorporate full houses into the reform as soon as the majority of the members might request it. By that arrangement the long debated autonomy of the Strict Observance became legally established and, through a silent agreement of non-interference, the two observances coexisted within the same Order until the time of the French Revolution without any serious dissensions. At any rate, after the departure of the first fighting generation the maintaining of the peace became a much simpler task than before, because the General Chapters, the only occasions for a full scale combat, were very rarely convoked. On the eve of the Revolution there were even indications of a complete reconciliation. At the Intermediate Chapter of 1784, the Strict Observance proposed a new scheme of unification worked out in detail by the Abbot of Châtillon, and the serious negotiations were continued during the General Chapter of 1786. Apparently, the plan already had been kept in evidence for a long time and had found universal approval, but the bloody events of the following decade changed the picture so completely, that the problems of bare survival must have preceded other considerations.

La Trappe

Since the Strict Observance preserved its exclusive French character until the Revolution, the dissolution of all religious organizations in 1790 was even more disastrous for them than it was for the universal Order, which managed to survive in some other countries of the European continent. However, a last minute establishment in Switzerland by the abbey of La Trappe not only perpetuated the Strict Observance but eventually resulted in the formation of the well known Trappist Order.

Although toward the end of the seventeenth century the impulsive personality of Abbot de Rancé (1626-1700) and the life and discipline he introduced at La Trappe aroused the admiration of contemporary society, the influence of his peculiar monastic ideas was far from penetrating the whole reform. In the majority of the houses belonging to the Strict Observance, the traditional Cistercian life and spirituality remained in full vigor. Moreover, after the disappearance of the initial rivalries, in both observances the will to restore formal unity prevailed. But the fact was that only one house of the Strict Observance, a filiation of La Trappe, survived the disaster of the French Revolution and that explains why the extraordinary personality of its reformer, de Rancé, and his resurgent spirit dominated the movement of the reorganizing Strict Observance. In other words, the nineteenth century Trappists cannot be regarded simply as the direct descendants of the seventeenth century Strict Observance as such. La Trappe, with its rather eccentric piety and discipline constituted even among the "abstinents" a clearly distinctive minority faction, a reform within the reform, and, while ideological differences between the two observances before the Revolution were negligible, the surviving lineage of La Trappe accentuated de Rancé's spiritual heritage, thus creating a new crisis of divergent ideas concerning Cistercian monasticism during the nineteenth century.

With full respect given to de Rancé's personality and to the Order based upon his foundation, it is undeniable that the most conspicuous characteristics of his reform at La Trappe were novelties in the history of the Order, although deeply founded in his own internal development and in the spirituality of the seventeenth century France. The main reason for his numerous innovations—as was true of so many similar cases of reformations in the past—was the incompleteness of his Cistercian education and his extremely self-conscious and combative personality. After his conversion, he had felt no religious vocation and even years later he was still undecided whether to join the Carthusians, Grandmont or the Cistercians. In his final resolution to become a Cistercian, an internal inclination toward the traditional Cistercian spirituality and way of living as befitting his own personal needs had no place at all. He assumed the Cistercian habit with the definite purpose of reforming La Trappe, of which he happened to have been the commendatory abbot since his early youth. When he entered the novitiate as a man of forty, the outlines of his reformatory ideas were in his mind firmly established, and the year of his novitiate under Cistercian discipline at Perseigne was not sufficient to give him a solid Cistercian foundation.

According to de Rancé's views, monasticism was basically a form of penitential life; monasteries were like prisons; their inmates were to be considered as criminals, doomed to spend the rest of their lives in severe penances. The chief duty of the abbot was to create for his monks all types of humiliations and to encourage them to practice every self-chosen austerity even at the cost of ruining their health. The monks were never to be permitted to feel any satisfaction in their works or exercises; their proper activity was to lament their sins. The discipline of the house, menu and daily schedule were to be arranged accordingly. De Rancé and his followers multiplied the time spent in prayer, returned to hard manual labor, restored perpetual silence, and banned not only meat from their table, but also fish, eggs and butter. To a certain extent, the heroic spirit of the first Cistercians had resurged at La Trappe, but instead of the inspiration of the first crusaders, the main force behind their admirable efforts was the guilt-complex of a highly sophisticated society. The frame of their daily routine bore some resemblance to the first glorious days of Cîteaux; but for the wonderful clarity of St. Bernard's contemplative spirit they substituted the gloomy and pessimistic air of contemporary rigorism. Only de Rancé's close adherence to this ruling spirituality can explain the strange fact that, despite conspicuous deviations from the traditional interpretation of monastic vocation, he always insisted that the life at La Trappe was nothing but the restoration of the twelfth century Cistercian monasticism.

Nevertheless, if we accept the thesis that every century has the right and duty to adapt traditional ideas to its own needs and desires, de Rancé's procedure, in spite of his historical errors, found its perfect justification in the admirable success and tremendous impression that La Trappe made upon the contemporaneous civilization which not only appreciated their superhuman sacrifices, but included many who enthusiastically followed their example.

10. On the Verge of Extinction

If material progress, a feverish planning and building activity can be considered an adequate criterion of an internal revival, the eighteenth century certainly must have matched the glorious times of the Founding Fathers. To the new generation the old medieval structure of churches and monasteries appeared too narrow, dark and uncomfortable; hence, the larger and still prosperous abbeys changed their features completely. With little understanding of the noble simplicity of Cistercian Gothic, they tore down indiscriminately the monuments of the past and replaced them with new buildings full of the gleaming splendor of the late Baroque architecture, where space and light were the dominant elements. Even the smaller houses, which could not afford a full scale rebuilding program, tried at least to remodel the old interior, and scarcely any of the medieval foundations kept their original style intact. However, both time and material resources proved to be insufficient for carrying out the magnificent plans, and most of them faced incompletion and indebtedness before the approaching Revolution.

The abbeys east of the Rhine furnished a more convincing sign of unbroken vitality. The excellent spirit of the German Congregation has been discussed above. In Austria, Bohemia, Moravia and Lausitz, following the Hussite wars and the Reformation, the Order was in a state of desolation. However, a vigorous reorganization movement started with the visitation of the Abbot of Cîteaux, Edmund de la Croix, in 1581, and these communities rose steadily both materially and morally until the end of the eighteenth century. The era of relative peace produced many new attempts at restoring extinguished monasteries; moreover, there are records of a number of new foundations. Thus, German, Austrian and Bohemian abbeys successfully reestablished first Ossegg in Bohemia (1626), then four Hungarian monasteries after the liberation of Hungary from the Turks (1686). Among them was Zirc (founded in 1182), the center of the future Hungarian Congregation. Between 1670-1710 Polish monks founded three new houses in Lithuania which marked the farthest Cistercian expansion toward the East.

The Decline of the Order in France

Despite the deceptive or real prosperity of religious communities, the contrary powers, ready to overthrow the remnants of the old feudal world together with the foundations of traditional monasticism, gained ground with fearful rapidity. The intellectual revolution of the Enlightenment replaced faith with reason, religion with philosophy, and prepared to change the course of European civilization entirely. The first practical applications of the new theories of society, religion and economics had been attempted during the Old Regime, with the powerful assistance of the "enlightened" despots and the old ruling classes both deeply infected by the new ideas. Though skeptical themselves in matters of creed, the rulers realized the importance of religion for the successful governance of the masses, but strictly upheld the thesis of a state-controlled Church. The clergy was generally regarded as a branch of the civil administration, subject to the direction of the state, rather than under the jurisdiction of Rome.

In order to break the possible resistance, the champions of the Enlightenment first of all turned against the Jesuits, the order which always had been the symbol of Catholic allegiance to Rome. After a long and ruthless campaign, characterized by incredible calumnies and open violence, Pope Clement XIV, yielding to the increasing political pressure, declared the suppression of the Society of Jesus in 1773. This great victory was only a signal for a frontal attack against the other religious orders. In 1766, Louis XV instituted a Commission of Regulars, made up largely of laymen, which raised the age of religious profession, and prevented any further expansion of religious life by forbidding congregations to have more than one house in each city of a province; moreover, it provided for the dissolution of monasteries which did not possess a fixed number of professed members, and in fact suppressed eight orders and a total of 450 religious houses. Only the Cistercians and Carthusians were spared. The Black Monks suffered the heaviest losses, almost 30% of their establishments.

Concerning the Cistercian Order, the attempt of the French government to influence Cîteaux's legislative and administrative activity was exerted by special Royal Commissaries, who since 1738 had played an increasingly important role during the sessions of the General Chapters. At the beginning, they were only passive observers of the regular procedures. But they soon took over the initiative and acted as presidents of the convention. No matter of importance could be arranged without their permission. Unfortunately, just as a century before the debate of the observances furnished the opportunity and justification of secular interference, so now a renewed dispute between the proto-abbots and the Abbot General resulted in the same disastrous effect.

The strife between Cîteaux and its first four daughter-houses was almost as old as the Order itself, but the long chapterless years with their direct consequence, the rising power of the Abbot General, created a new prolonged crisis of unusual intensity. The General Chapter of 1765 was opened in the presence of 53 abbots, with a remarkable representation of German houses. The party of the proto-abbots tried to strengthen its well organized French group with the support of the Germans, but the majority of the foreigners lined up solidly on the side of the Abbot General. When the petty claims of the proto-abbots concerning titles, precedence and influence especially in the appointment of the members of the *Definitorium* failed to win a majority, the proto-abbots together with their followers walked out of the session and appealed to Paris. Although the Court decided against them, the government soon recognized the party of the proto-abbots as a natural ally in an endeavor to establish state control over the Order, and the Royal Commissaries, appointed to the General Chapter of 1768, were instructed to support the proto-abbots. One of the Commissaries, Jean Armand de Roquelaure, Bishop of Senlis, a true courtier, under the pretext of a general settlement, proposed an entirely new constitution with the obvious intent of imposing a royal protectorate upon the Order. A committee of five abbots was chosen to work out the statutes in detail, but the final draft was the composition of the Royal Commissaries. The Chapter of 1771 was convoked upon their insistence with the single purpose of enforcing the acceptance of the new constitution without discussion. This ruthless pressure resulted in an embittered resistance. Since the political implications of complete control over the Order by the French government were evident, the German abbots again joined with the Abbot General in protest, thus creating such an overwhelming majority against the proposal that the King agreed to a point by point debate. The disputes led nowhere, and the Commissaries abruptly dissolved the Chapter.

During the twelve years that elapsed until the next General Chapter in 1783, the position of the Church greatly deteriorated not only in France but also in the Habsburg Empire. Since the ecclesiastical policies of Emperor Joseph II prevented the majority of German abbots from attending the Chapter, the Royal Commissaries, this time four in number, succeeded in securing some important prerogatives for the proto-abbots. Moreover, the Commissaries sharply criticized the general condition of Cistercian houses in France; following the decree of the famed Commission of Regulars, they threatened the suppression of monasteries having less than 9 professed members. The disaster, however, was for the moment avoided, and the Chapter of 1786 proceeded without serious consequences; nevertheless, the new constitution of 1783 was never put into effect, because meanwhile the final catastrophe of the Revolution approached with inevitable necessity.

Meanwhile, the rule of Joseph II (1780-1790), a typical representative of "enlightened" despotism, weighed heavily upon religious orders. In 1781, he forbade any communication between religious institutions and their foreign superiors, the exemption was suspended, the admittance of novices, through complicated regulations became almost impossible. These measures were only a preparation for the suppression of all religious houses which were not directly serving the public interest by the maintenance of hospitals, schools or by extensive pastoral duties. The contemplative orders, declared "useless," were all dissolved and their property confiscated. Within four years after the decree of 1782, no less than 738 monasteries and convents had closed their doors forever. The Cistercians almost everywhere possessed a considerable number of parishes. Consequently, their houses could have been exempted, but in fact very few escaped the suppression; thus Zirc in Hungary, which was an affiliation of Heinrichau under Prussian domination and could not be abolished without diplomatic consequences. Since the educational system after the suppression of the Jesuits was in constant crisis throughout the Habsburg Empire, the Hungarian Cistercians, Benedictines and Premonstratensians made an attempt to secure their livelihood by assuming teaching duties in secondary schools. Thus Pásztó took over the abandoned Jesuit Gymnasium (high school) in Eger as early as 1776; Zirc and St. Gotthárd soon followed the example, operating additional high schools, thereby laying the foundation of the future vocation of the Hungarian Congregation, namely the education of youth especially in secondary schools. The first Cistercian community which embraced the teaching and education of youth as vocation was perhaps the abbey of Rauden in Silesia. In 1743, during the War of Austrian Succession, when the province was cut off from other centers of learning, the abbey opened a Latin school which soon developed into a full scale Gymnasium. The number of students, mostly boarders, grew rapidly and in 1788 the monastery housed 243 pupils. Teaching was free; for board a small fee was charged. The school enjoyed a country-wide reputation and survived the abbey's dissolution in 1810.

The French Revolution and Secularization

The year 1789 marks the beginning of the French Revolution, the turning point of modern history. Within a decade surviving feudal establishments gave way to a new free society; but the burning ruins of the old world buried also the material structure of ecclesiastical organizations upon which the public life of the Church had been built since the early Middle Ages. The Revolution launched its program with the abolition of all privileges of the nobility and clergy, including the ecclesiastical tithes, the vital financial foundation of every benefice and institution. Secularization of all ecclesiastical property soon followed and an inventory of goods was taken immediately. A law annulled religious vows and to the monks who consented to leave their monasteries a pension was promised. Estates and buildings were sold at auction, while valuables and works of art were taken into the treasury of the state. All that remained was to deprive the clergy of their liberty. The Revolution, in order to free the Church from the jurisdiction of the Pope and make her a servant of the state, demanded an oath of allegiance to the new constitution from every member of the clergy. For those who refused to yield to pressure there remained only two possibilities: to flee abroad or face the most violent persecution.

The outbreak of the Revolution found 228 Cistercian monasteries for men in France: 34 regular abbeys and 194 *in commendam,* a surprisingly large number if we consider the adversities of the previous six centuries. On the other hand, a total personnel of 1,914 monks in both observances clearly demonstrated the disastrous consequences of the commendatory system regarding membership and monastic discipline. There were still many communities with a considerable number of professed members living exemplary lives, but some 75 of them, mostly under commendatory abbots counted less than 5 monks, and in these regular life was all but impossible. The picture of the rapid decline is even more striking in comparison with the findings of the Commissions of Regulars in 1768. At that time, the total number of Cistercians in France was still 2,429, indicating a loss of 515 members (21%) within 22 years. In this respect the Strict Observance was no more prosperous, having been decreased in the same term from 578 to 350. Equal or heavier losses characterized the state of other religious orders throughout France. Nevertheless, here we must emphasize again that any generalization based merely on the lamentable state of the Order in France, does not apply to the Order as such. Since the end of the sixteenth century, the center of activity within the Order exhibited a tendency to shift eastward, as indicated by the decisive influence of the German abbots in the General Chapters during the eighteenth century. Not only did the Congregation of Upper Germany show a favorable picture but so also did less significant groups, such as the Vicariate of Bohemia. The latter's nine monasteries, according to the statistics of 1699, numbered 261 priests, 70 clerics, 25 novices and 18 lay-brothers; a total of 374 persons. The same Bohemian houses, in sharp contrast with the situation in France, increased their total personnel to 426 by the year 1780, each house having an average membership five times higher than contemporary French monasteries.

For the leaders of the Revolution, the state of single monasteries was no problem; they were all dissolved. On May 4, 1791, Cîteaux was sold at auction. The sacred remains of the Founding Fathers had been transferred to Dijon but in the turmoil of the following years they disappeared without trace. A considerable part of the archives and library are still available in the municipal library of Dijon. The last Abbot General, Francis Trouvé, who governed the Order since 1748, in prevision of the dissolution of Cîteaux, delegated his power as general superior to Robert Schlecht, Abbot of Salem; he then sought refuge among his relatives, dying in 1797. The same fate awaited all other Cistercian institutions and only technicalities caused some delay in the routine procedure. Meanwhile, the persecution of the priests who refused to take the oath of allegiance to the Civil Constitution of the Clergy broke out everywhere with increasing cruelty. According to the information of the Abbot of Wettingen (Switzerland), only about one third of the former Cistercians obeyed the law. For the majority, there was no other choice but to escape abroad or to face imprisonment, deportation or even death. Exact records are not available concerning their further trials; beyond doubt, large contingents found temporary homes in Cistercian houses in Belgium, Germany, Switzerland and in the Papal States, but many of them died as a result of the inhuman conditions in French prison camps or at the penal colony of French Guiana.

The refugees could not count on the lasting hospitality of their foreign brethren. The victorious French troops soon invaded the surrounding countries, propagating the same revolutionary doctrines by force of arms. Belgium, their first victim, was treated with special severity. Monasteries were visited, detailed inventories taken, abbeys arbitrarily taxed, and the religious incessantly molested. Finally the laws of 1796 decreed that all monastic goods be confiscated. Here again refusal to take the loyalty oath was the pretext for the persecution of priests. Moreover, a decree in 1798 sentenced the entire Belgian clergy to deportation. The decree was only partly carried out, but hundreds fell victim to the tyranny, among them 37 Cistercians. The wars of Napoleon extended the destruction to Italy; and, though the Church might have breathed more freely in France after the Concordat of 1801, a severe blow was still to follow. After the annexation of the left bank of the Rhine to France, in order to appease the German states, Napoleon proposed compensation through the secularization of Church property in Germany. The "enlightened" princes welcomed the opportunity to seize the long desired spoils and, consequently, the decree of 1803 was immediately executed. It completely destroyed the fabric of the Church of Germany, together with the flourishing Cistercian Congregation. Abbeys and churches were sold to the highest bidder, priceless objects of art bargained, entire libraries dispersed, while the homeless monks were promised a small and ill paid yearly allowance. With Napoleon's further advance, the secularization became effective in Prussia and Poland in 1810, although the actual seizure of the monasteries did not follow immediately; some of them survived until 1833.

French domination in Spain resulted in the same destruction of ecclesiastical goods; but, after Napoleon's fall, the revived national kingdom restored the old order and returned to the monks their confiscated property. Nevertheless, anti-clerical parties again gained the upper hand, and in 1835, all religious establishments were suppressed, with the exception of a few engaged in teaching or missionary activities. The Cistercians, divided into two congregations, that of Castile and Leon and the Congregation of Aragon, still possessed altogether 65 monasteries with a combined personnel of 1,205 monks; none of their houses survived the secularization. In Portugal similar events had abolished monastic life some years earlier. In Switzerland, where during the Revolution many Cistercian refugees had found a friendly reception, only three abbeys survived the general dissolution. These were former members of the Congregation of Upper Germany. In 1806, they formed the independent Swiss Congregation, but a rising anti-Catholic feeling sealed their fate. In 1831, a law prohibited the admission of novices and ten years later the abbey of Wettingen was suppressed followed by suppression of the others in 1848.

The fortunes of the three Lithuanian monasteries revealed a rather peculiar development. After the partition of Poland (1795), religious orders under the Russian regime became entirely isolated and, in 1803, Benedictines and Cistercians formed a united Congregation which the Camaldolesians and Carthusians later joined. The whole group consisted of eight monasteries headed by a president elected for a three year term. In 1832, following the crash of the Polish insurrection of 1830-1831, the Russian government abolished the orders in Lithuania; only the Cistercian house of Kimbarowka survived but the acceptance of novices was forbidden. This monastery, too, was suppressed in 1842; however, the monks were permitted to stay there until 1864, when, as a reprisal for a new Polish revolt, the Orthodox Church took over the property and the last Prior and his seven monks were deported to Siberia.

As a final and disastrous consequence of the French Revolution, no Cistercian establishment was able to continue its monastic life in peace except for some few houses within the borders of the Habsburg Monarchy. The general destruction and the growing anti-clerical attitude of the nineteenth century prevented the expelled monks from founding permanent institutions elsewhere on the Continent. The older generation of the homeless religious depended on the hospitality of their relatives, while the majority of the younger priests found employment in diocesan service.

The abandoned church buildings and monasteries, many of unique artistic value, shared everywhere the fate of their former inhabitants. First, the official state commission expropriated the valuables, and as soon as the monks departed, the neighboring population stripped the edifices of everything movable. During the stormy Napoleonic era, the buildings were occupied mostly by the military; but after the restoration of peace the bare constructions were abandoned since they had become inadequate for civilian use. The people of the surrounding villages helped the elements of nature in their destructive work, by utilizing the fine carved stones as building materials. When finally museums and art institutions discovered the value of the noble ruins, there was not much to save. Thus the magnificent monuments of Cistercian prayer and toil of seven centuries became almost completely annihilated, but the spirit could not be entirely extinguished.

11. The Reconstruction

After the downfall of Napoleon, the Congress of Vienna (1815) seemingly reestablished peace and the Old Regime; but, under the surface, the ideas of the Revolution continued to gain ground among the young generation of intellectuals. The following period of European politics was characterized by a sharp cleavage between the supporters of the traditional order, called "conservatives" or "reactionaries," and the "liberals" or "radicals," direct descendants of the eighteenth century "enlightenment" who now favored the achievements of the Revolution. The Church, which had suffered so much from the Revolution and under Napoleon, sided with the conservatives without being able to check the ever increasing power of the liberals who, of course, regarded the clergy as their first enemy. This chronic political instability became a constant danger for the Catholic Church. Repeated revolutions in France and sudden political changes elsewhere usually brought a more or less open persecution of the Church; this as a rule, meant restrictions on the activities of religious bodies, dissolution of their houses and the expulsion of their members. Until the end of the century the Church had lost not only her former predominant state and privileges but stood under the vehement fire of the combined forces of anti-clerical elements.

The other idol of the nineteenth century, extreme nationalism, was also an obstacle to the revival of religious orders of international organization. It presented a new incentive for continued state control over the Church even where the government was not directly hostile, inasmuch as every communication of religious organizations with their foreign superiors was regarded with suspicion. Such an official attitude not only rendered the central administration of the orders extremely difficult but also affected the spirit of solidarity within the orders and fostered the formation of peculiar national characteristics, which were hardly compatible with the aims of a universal direction.

The only element in the complexity of intellectual movements during the first half of the century in favor of religion in general and of the Catholic Church in particular was "romanticism." After the bloody tragedy of the Revolution, romanticism had appeared as a reversal of the unbound confidence in reason, emphasizing the importance of emotional life with more understanding of nature, tradition, history and also of religion. Its inspiration having been exerted predominantly on art and literature, it had little direct influence upon the distressed state of the Church, but it did undeniably encourage contemplative vocations frequently sponsoring the restoration of ancient monasteries, with considerable effect upon the rapid revival of the Trappist Congregation.

In addition to the generally hostile political trends, the Cistercian reconstruction was particularly handicapped by the fact that, after the suppression of Cîteaux and the death of the last Abbot General, nothing remained of the once elaborate system of central administration. The chaotic years that followed annihilated all the Cistercian Congregations; not a single Province remained intact. The dozen odd monasteries which managed to survive, isolated in the Austrian Empire, desperately struggling for their own subsistence, were unable to furnish the needed leadership for a planned work of reorganization. Hence, it is understandable that the first sign of revival appeared in Italy, where the Pope himself took the lead in this enormous task.

Pope Pius VII, after his return to Rome, immediately began the work of reconstruction in his own domain. Thus, in

1814, the Abbey of Casamari (province of Frosinone) was restored; it had suffered much following the seizure of Rome by the French troops. Not only were the abbey and the church ransacked, but six monks were killed while protecting the Blessed Sacrament. In 1833, the abbey regained the monastery of San Domenico (province Caserta) and, although Casamari was repeatedly plundered in 1861 and 1871, it was again recovered through the liberality of Pope Pius IX. In 1864 the Pope also donated to the abbey the ancient monastery of Valvisciolo (province Littoria), which was restored at his own expense. Casamari had been following the Strict Observance since 1717, but, under the direct jurisdiction of the Holy See, it remained independent until 1929, when the whole Congregation joined the Common Observance.

Pope Pius VII also reestablished in 1817 two other Cistercian houses at Rome. One of them, the monastery of Santa Croce with the adjoining ancient Basilica (Santa Croce in Gerusalemme) had been under the care of the Order since 1561; the other, the monastery of San Bernardo, had been formerly an establishment of the Feuillants. These two houses lay at the root of the future Congregation of St. Bernard in Italy (founded in 1821) which, during the course of the century, revived three former Cistercian houses and in 1876 founded the new monastery of San Antonio at Cortona.

After the secularization of Heinrichau in Prussia (1810), Zirc, its daughter-monastery, the only surviving Cistercian house in Hungary, became independent. Under the condition of taking over two abandoned Jesuit Gymnasiums, Zirc regained Pilis and Pásztó with the adjoining high school at Eger, which were formerly suppressed by Joseph II. Thus, in 1814, the Abbot of Zirc became the head of the two other united abbeys. When during the 1870's the liberals gained the upper hand in Vienna, a new wave of secularization seemed imminent. In order to escape the danger, the monastery of St. Gotthárd, an affiliation of the Austrian Heiligenkreuz, joined the Hungarian union in 1878 but, upon the insistence of the government, Zirc had to accept the obligation of conducting a fourth high school. Through its educational activity the popularity of the Order grew rapidly in Hungary and from the community of a handful of monks, Zirc developed into the largest Cistercian abbey by the end of the century.

The revolution of 1830 separated Belgium from Holland, and the new Belgian government, unlike the former regime, showed much good will toward the Catholic Church. The remnants of the homeless Cistercians who remained organized under the successors of their last legitimate abbot, succeeded in opening a monastery at Bornhem (province Anvers) in 1835 while the last living member of the Abbey of Val-Dieu, Dom Bernard Klinkenberg, repurchased the same monastery of which he became the first superior in 1844. After the restoration, the first Belgian novices were educated at Santa Croce in Rome, but the abbeys remained independent, following their own statutes approved by the Holy See.

The revival of the Common Observance in France was launched as a personal endeavor of a pious diocesan priest, Lucas Leo Barnouin, who in honor of the Immaculate Conception (defined as a dogma in 1854) restored monastic life at the ancient Cistercian abbey of Senanque, in the diocese of Avignon in 1855. Abbé Barnouin, receiving the name of Bernard, finished his novitiate at Rome, and the new foundation remained for a while affiliated to the Congregation of St. Bernard in Italy; but the flourishing community soon became independent after forming the Congregation of Senanque in 1867. Within a short time, the abbey revived three other abandoned Cistercian houses, among them the famous center of the pre-Benedictine French monasticism, Lérins (Provence), which later became the headquarters of the whole Congregation. This group is the only one in the Common Observance retaining a life of a purely contemplative character. Their discipline, however, was not as strict as that of the "Strict Observance"; it was called frequently *Observantia Media.*

The expelled monks of Wettingen (Switzerland) purchased the old Benedictine monastery of Mehrerau in Austria (Vorarlberg), where, since 1854, they have continued their exemplary monastic life. After the wrath of the *Kulturkampf* had diminished the prosperous community was able to reopen its first German house since the secularization, that of Marienstatt (Westerwald) in 1888. The Cistercians at Mehrerau also embraced teaching as their outside vocation and their well managed boarding school still enjoys an excellent country wide reputation.

The Restoration of Central Government

The only group of Cistercian establishments which survived the general secularization of the early nineteenth century was situated within the Habsburg Empire. It included 7 monasteries in Austria, 2 in Bohemia, 2 in Poland (under Austrian occupation) and one in Hungary. These houses which were scattered remnants of former Provinces with different customs, languages and local interests, remained independent of one another, and solely under the theoretical authority of the Holy See. Nevertheless, after the collapse of the wars of independence of 1848-1849 in Italy and Hungary, the Viennese government, being engaged in the forcible unification of the vast polyglot state, welcomed the plan of a united Austrian Cistercian Province. As its first step, an abbatial convention was held in 1852, where the idea of a common novitiate was sharply rejected, but a general study-house at Heiligenkreuz soon became a reality. A decisive approach was made toward the government-sponsored goal by the nomination in 1854 of the Archbishop of Prague, Cardinal Schwarzenberg, to the post of Apostolic Visitor of all religious orders of the Empire. Under his presidency, a provincial chapter was convoked at Prague in 1859 which proclaimed the formation of an Austrian Province under the leadership of an elected Vicar, and drafted compulsory uniformed statutes. In the following year, the new Province published its first official directory with rather impressive figures: it counted 516 professed members, among them 429 priests.

The union born under pressure was neither sincere nor of long duration; yet it constituted a powerful inspiration toward the restoration of a central administrative organ for the whole Order, something that had been completely lacking since the outbreak of the French Revolution. Although shortly after the restitution of the Cistercian houses in the Papal States, the Abbot of Santa Croce assumed the title of the President General of the Cistercian Order, he had no constitutional authority nor direct connection with any of the Cistercian houses north of the Alps. How far some well-meant but premature endeavors toward an international organization were from reality was clearly proven by the attempt of Joseph Fontana, Abbot of Santa Croce, in 1825. In a personal letter to the Abbot of Wettingen he proposed some sort of legal connection between the Italian and Swiss Congregations, but the offer was politely declined. The fear of the Swiss abbots concerning the unfriendly reaction of such a foreign relation upon their government was perfectly justified by the subsequent secularization of their abbeys. The idea, however, was kept alive and after the greater part of the existing communities had been already united in the Austrian Province, the time seemed ripe for the resumption of negotiations.

When Theobald Cesari, Abbot of San Bernardo in Rome, was appointed by the Holy See as Visitor of the Belgian Congregation, he called on the Cistercian abbeys in Austria and noticed everywhere the desire for a universal organization. Based on his information, the Congregation of Religious, in 1868, issued a decree subordinating the Austrian and Belgian houses to the jurisdiction of the President General in Rome. Invested with this power, Abbot Cesari announced a General

Chapter for the following year, 1869, to be assembled at Rome, the first such meeting since 1786. With few exceptions, all abbots attended personally or sent their representatives to the Chapter, which in fourteen sessions laid down the foundation of the modern Cistercian constitution. As its most significant innovation, the convention resolved that any abbot of the Common Observance could be elected as Abbot General with residence at Rome. As a basis for common discipline, the Statutes of Prague were accepted, modified by approved local customs. A house of studies was organized at Rome, accessible to the whole Order, and each abbey promised financial support for the institution as well as a disbursement for the offices of Abbot General and Procurator General. The resumption of the function of a central organization was certainly modest and the first meeting left much to be desired for the future, but at least the ice was broken and the door stood wide open for further development.

The next General Chapter convened at Vienna in 1880, electing Gregory Bartolini, a member of the Italian Congregation, as the successor of the deceased Abbot Cesari. During the following years intense preparations were made for the worthy celebration of the eight hundredth anniversary of St. Bernard's birth, in which the Austro-Hungarian Province excelled with fundamental contributions to Cistercian history. A critical edition of St. Bernard's works was begun under the title *Xenia Bernardina;* Leopold Janauschek, a monk of Zwettl, completed his monumental work, *Originum Cisterciensium Tomus I,* a critical list of 742 Cistercian monasteries of men, still indispensable for historians. The community of Mehrerau started the publication of a German language monthly, *Cistercienser Chronik* under the direction of Gregory Müller; the monthly survived both World Wars and soon became the richest treasury of the Cistercian past. In Hungary, after long years of research, Father Emeric Piszter completed the two giant volumes of his *Life and Works of St. Bernard,* matching Vacandard's widely known standard biography; unfortunately, its language (Hungarian) prevented a well deserved publicity. Remigius Békefi, later Abbot of Zirc, started at the same time the publication of the richly documented series on the history of Hungarian abbeys. A short-lived periodical, *L'Union Cistercienne,* was the contribution of the Congregation of Senanque, while the Trappists arranged a revised edition of the *Nomasticon Cisterciense,* a code of Cistercian legislation.

The General Chapter of 1891 at Vienna, was celebrated in solemn atmosphere of the jubilee, and some decisions of consequence were made. The Abbot General had died the year before, and now, since the Holy See acceded to the universal desire that the head of the Order might reside elsewhere than Rome, a German, Abbot Leopold Wackarz of Hohenfurth, was elected to the high office. The same Chapter approved the formation of a Swiss-German Congregation consisting of Mehrerau and its new foundation Marienstatt, in Germany. On the same occasion there was published the combined statistics of both observances including Cistercian convents. In 1891, the Order possessed 82 monasteries for men, 114 for women, with a total personnel of 11,008. Among the men the Trappists counted 52 houses with 2,929 monks, leaving far behind the Common Observance with 30 monasteries in 6 Congregations, having altogether 940 professed members. However, this was the last time the Cistercian Order, despite differences in regular observance, impressed the Christian world with figures based on its undivided unity. The following year witnessed the final stage of the age old feud between the Strict and Common Observances, considerably aggravated by a divergent development during the nineteenth century.

The Separation of the Two Observances

For the Strict Observance the dissolution in revolutionary France became even more severe in its tragic consequences than for the rest of the Order, because, being established largely in France, they lost everything at once. It was only due to the providential skill and energy of Dom Augustine de Lestrange that in 1791 a considerable number of the monks of La Trappe managed to find a new home at the deserted Carthusian monastery of La Val-Sainte, in Switzerland. When in 1811 Napoleon banished the Trappists from his whole Empire, Abbot Augustine kept his community together and, in seeking a place for a permanent establishment, traveled with his monks in a quite unusual manner throughout eastern and central Europe. Though the adventurous pilgrimage was not particularly successful, after Napoleon's fall in 1815 they were able to return to France and restore the ancient mother-house of La Trappe. From that time the growing community revived in rapid succession a number of former Cistercian houses in western Europe and in 1847 the Trappists again possessed 17 well disciplined monasteries.

However, life under Dom Augustine's rule, with its intense emphasis on the penitential character and increased austerities, was much harder than it had been under the original regulations of de Rancé, and growing opposition under the leadership of Eugène de Laprade soon broke up the unity of the reform. This faction formed an independent Congregation with Septfons (France) as its center, while in Belgium political necessity compelled the monks to group themselves in a separate Congregation around the abbey of Westmalle. Thus, in 1821, there were already three distinct Congregations and only La Trappe remained faithful to Dom Augustine; the others returned to the rule of de Rancé. Following the death of Abbot Lestrange (1827), the French monasteries in 1834 undertook a short-lived union; but in 1847 they split again. This time, however, even the group of La Trappe abandoned Dom Augustine's regulations in an attempt to return to the original discipline of Cîteaux, while the others still kept faith with de Rancé. Despite internal dissension, the Trappists continued their spectacular development and at the end of the century they surpassed both in number and reputation the old stock, the Common Observance.

In these circumstances, the Trappists felt increasingly embarrassed that, according to a decision of the Holy See in 1847, they were still subjected to the President General of the Common Observance, although his interference scarcely exceeded the confirmation of their abbatial elections. More distressing was the fact that the Strict Observance was not invited to the General Chapters of 1869 and 1880; moreover, they were positively excluded from eligibility for the office of Abbot General.

Nevertheless, behind these just grievances, there were much deeper causes of dissension. The Trappists, throughout the whole century, stressed ostentatiously the usages and spirituality inaugurated by de Rancé, which had evidently little in common with the original ideas of Cîteaux. On the other hand, the majority of the monasteries of the Common Observance tended toward the other extremity, surrendering monastic traditions to an increasing tide of outside activities. More than half of their houses were engaged in pastoral duties; seven of them in Austria-Hungary maintained secondary schools, others administered elementary schools or orphanages. Once these activities had saved the communities from imminent dissolution and during the course of time these institutions became so closely attached to the monasteries that neither the younger generation of monks nor the Bishops nor the people welcomed the idea of abandoning them. In some instances the Trappists themselves yielded to pressing necessities by conducting several educational institutions, yet they regarded the practice of the Common Observance as utterly incompatible with Cistercian ideals.

Finally, the ruling spirit of extreme nationalism at the end of the century alienated emotionally the two groups, due to the fact that the Common Observance was predominantly German, while the Strict Observance was French. After the defeat of France by the resurgent German Empire in 1871, the mutually hostile sentiment grew so intense that even religious bodies were unable to restrain its harmful influence. When the General Chapter of 1891 elected a German as Abbot General, the Trappists' patience came to an end. Enjoying the special benevolence and powerful support of Pope Leo XIII, they convoked an abbatial convention at Rome in 1892; the three Trappist Congregations were united into one entirely independent order under the official title of "Reformed Cistercians of Our Lady of La Trappe," without any further legal connection with the other group of the same monastic family, the Common Observance, or, officially, the "Sacred Order of Cistercians" (S.O.Cist.). On the occasion of the eight hundredth jubilee of the foundation of Cîteaux in 1898, the Trappists politely insinuated a fusion of the Common Observance into their Order, but in the circumstances neither group could give serious consideration to the matter. Meanwhile, as a result of their ardent endeavor to approach the original scheme of twelfth century Cîteaux, the Trappists gradually abandoned de Rancé's bequest and from 1902 they call themselves simply "Order of Cistercians of the Strict Observance" (O.C.S.O.); only their popular name, "Trappists," refers to their seventeenth century origin.

12. Cistercians in the Twentieth Century

The turn of the nineteenth century brought new trials and new successes for the Order. In France, to a certain extent, the story of Abbé Barnouin had been reiterated. A wealthy and devoted priest, Bernard Maréchal, formerly a member of the Congregation of the Blessed Sacrament, was searching for a community willing to sponsor his plan to found a contemplative monastery for the special purpose of perpetual adoration of the Blessed Sacrament. Finally, Fontfroide of the Congregation of Senanque adopted the idea; Dom Maréchal joined the Cistercians and in 1892 built a new monastery at his own expense at Pont Colbert near Versailles, himself being appointed the first abbot of the new establishment. However, the peaceful monastic life could not be continued for a long time. The persecution of religious orders broke out in France again and between 1900-1904, hundreds of monasteries and convents were dissolved, their members exiled; among these were Senanque, Fontfroide and also Pont Colbert. Some of the monks sought refuge in Italy, others in Spain, but the community of Pont Colbert succeeded in founding a new monastery in 1904 at Onsenoort (Marienkroon) in Holland. After World War I, the dispersed Cistercians were admitted to France again, resuming monastic life at Senanque and Pont Colbert, while the community of Fontfroide, unable to regain its old home, settled down in 1919 in the Pyrenees at an ancient abandoned Benedictine monastery, St. Michel de Cuxa. Onsenoort continued its life as an affiliation of Pont Colbert until, very recently, it joined the Belgian Congregation.

In 1898 Mehrerau revived the old Cistercian abbey of Sittich (Stična) in Slovenia (founded 1135; suppressed 1784) as its second daughter-house. For this flourishing community the end of World War I presented a crucial problem. Since the abbey fell within the borders of the new state of Yugoslavia, the Austrian monks of the community were forced out of the country. The exiled fathers found a temporary home (1921-1931) in Germany at Bronnbach (Baden), a former Cistercian abbey, now the property of the family of Prince Löwenstein; finally they purchased the abandoned Cistercian convent of Seligenporten (Oberpfalz) where the new monastic life was resumed in 1931. Stična revitalized in 1925 the Polish monastery of Mogila, at one time a famous *Studium Generale* of the Order, which, after a long period of *in commendam* under the administration of the University of Krakow, was greatly weakened in membership. Through the work of Slovenian monks it was now joined to the Congregation of Mehrerau.

Similar causes resulted in the further increase of the family of Mehrerau; its new member was the resurgent Himmerod (Eifel), one of the largest Cistercian abbeys of medieval Germany (founded 1134; suppressed 1802). The German members of the Trappist monastery of Mariastern in Bosnia (Yugoslavia) were also unable to continue their lives under the new regime and purchased the ruins of the ancient monastery of Himmerod in 1919. Since the Archbishop of Trier insisted that the members of the new establishment must actively cooperate in pastoral duties—a condition unacceptable to Trappists—the monks turned to the Common Observance for assistance. Marienstatt accepted the sponsorship of the new foundation and, within a short time, a magnificent new monastery arose from the ruins. Marienstatt became the mother-abbey of another revived Cistercian house at Hardenhausen (Westfalen) in 1927. When the Nazi regime confiscated their property in 1938, the monks found a temporary shelter in the city of Magdeburg until the end of the war. In 1933, the Congregation of Mehrerau was increased again through a new foundation at Untermais (Italy, province Bolzano), sponsored by the abbey of Stams, while Mehrerau itself revived in 1938 the ancient Swiss abbey of Hauterive, suppressed in 1848.

The military operations of World War I, with the exception of the Polish houses, left the establishments of the Order untouched; the subsequent peace treaties, however, led to the regrouping of the existing Congregations. The partition of Austria-Hungary loosened the bond among the members of the Austrian Congregation. Hohenfurth and Ossegg, now within the borders of the new Czechoslovakia, formed the Congregation of the Immaculate Heart of Mary in 1920; Zirc, with its dependent houses, constituted the long desired Hungarian Congregation in 1923; Mehrerau also gathered its own foundations into a separate Congregation; while the remaining Austrian houses were united into the Congregation of the Sacred Heart of Jesus. More important than these administrative changes was the fusion, in 1929, of the Congregation of Casamari with its three affiliated houses to the Common Observance. This group, although originally quite close to the discipline of the Trappists, refused to support the separatist move of 1892, and remained independent. Now, in union with the main body of the Order, the Congregation proved its real vigor by the foundation of eight new houses in Italy within twenty years, and by doubling its membership. The Congregation of St. Bernard in Italy also contributed to the general expansion by the revival of the first Spanish house since the secularization; the mighty medieval Poblet (province Tarragona) was restored in 1940. The ancient Cistercian monastery of Boquen (Bretagne, France) was revived by a group of former Trappists in 1936, and is now under the direct jurisdiction of the Abbot General of the Common Observance.

The General Chapter, convening in every fifth year, resumed its routine work of central administration, although greatly impaired by the fact that neither the assembly nor the Abbot General had a permanent residence, properly provided office or adequate staff. Thus, the Chapter of 1900 was held at Rome, those of 1905 and 1910 at the abbey of Stams in Austria; in 1920 it convened at Mehrerau. When, as the successor of Abbot Wackarz, Amadeus de Bie, Abbot of Bornhem, was elected supreme head of the Order in 1900, he decided to reside at Rome, temporarily as a guest at Santa Croce, later in a rented apartment. However, after his death in 1920, the new Abbot General, Cassian Haid, Abbot of Wettingen-Mehrerau, accepted the election only under the condition that he might stay at his beloved Mehrerau. His wish was respected, but since the Congregation of Religious stressed anew the necessity of establishing the headquarters of the Order at Rome, Cassian Haid resigned in 1927 and an extraordinary Chapter elected Francis Janssens, Abbot of Pont Colbert, with the obligation of procuring a permanent residence at Rome. In the same year the Order purchased a house at the Monte Gianicolo (Villa Stolberg), which served as the residence of the Abbot General until 1950, when a new building was finished at a more convenient location, worthily housing not only the highest officials of the central government, but serving also as a general study-house for the whole Cistercian Order.

Nevertheless, the final and satisfactory solution of mere technicalities did not eliminate another problem of vital importance: the successful function of the Order as an organic unit. The monasteries of the Order which survived the French Revolution and the secularization of the early nineteenth century never had a real connection with Cîteaux, not even during the previous period, when the authority of the General Chapter effectively controlled at least France and Germany. The abbeys of the Habsburg Empire and Italy, as remnants of once more or less independent Congregations, each with its immemorial customs and privileges, willingly reestablished the office of the Abbot General and the General Chapter, but the idea of a unified discipline, strict control, and direction exerted from outside was always vigorously opposed. The main subject of discussion at all Chapters from 1900 on was the precise definition of the power and authority of the Abbot General as well as of the General Chapter. A patient and understanding approach to the problem by all interested parties finally brought success. After several previous attempts and after years of experimentation, the General Chapter of 1933 composed a constitution of the supreme government of the Order; this was approved by the Congregation of Religious in the following year. The *Charter of Charity,* which served as its basis, was adapted to the new Canon Law and to the changed circumstances and in its present form is a skillful accordance of Cistercian traditions with modern requirements.

Missions Overseas

An excellent proof of the efficiency of the revitalized General Chapter on one hand and of the Order's spontaneous will toward cooperation on the other, was the beginning of active missionary work and through it a rapid expansion outside of the European continent. The Chapter of 1925 wholeheartedly supported the new program of extensive foreign missions sponsored by Pope Pius XI; it outlined carefully how a monastic community could do missionary work without sacrificing its basic characteristics. Cistercians, instead of putting single monks in isolated missionary stations, were to establish properly organized communities and through their living example and educational activity promote and deepen true Christian life and culture.

This difficult task found a zealous promoter in Abbot Aloysius Wiesinger of Schlierbach, whose monastery soon became the center of the movement. At the extraordinary Chapter of 1927, the Abbot reported the results of his previous investigations concerning North and South America, and the work was begun immediately. Himmerod, though itself struggling with the difficulties of an arduous beginning, sent out its pioneers to Itaporanga (São Paulo, Brazil). While the fathers were engaged in their pastoral duties, the brothers successfully adapted themselves to the local methods of ranching and in 1939 they laid the foundations of a new monastery. Today the flourishing foundation has attained the rank of an abbey, and besides extensive parish work, the monks operate a high school.

Through the united efforts of Wilhering and Schlierbach there sprang up in 1928 the Cistercian mission of Apolo (Caupolicán, Bolivia). The fathers were followed by Cistercian Sisters, whose work in gardening and teaching effectively supported the heroic toil of the small colony among the most neglected Indians. A donation of the large estate of Jequitibá (Bahia, Brazil) was the beginning of the foundation of a mission by Schlierbach in 1938. By 1945, they had finished a considerable part of their building program and besides their routine missionary activities they conduct a high school for boarders and day students with a special agricultural curriculum. In 1950 this monastery also was elevated to the rank of an abbey. Very recently three new foundations were started in Brazil; one, sponsored by the Congregation of St. Bernard in Italy, at San José de Rio Pardo (1943), another by Casamari, at Garimpo dos Cañoas (1950) and the third, by the homeless community of Hardehausen, near Itatinga (São Paulo) in 1951.

Beginning in 1930, by the commitment of Pope Pius XI, the Congregation of Casamari trained in its own seminary a large number of native African boys from Eritrea, then an Italian colony, for the monastic vocation. After finishing their studies, they were sent back to their country, where a new and flourishing Cistercian monastery came to life in 1940 (Belesa, Asmara, Ethiopia). In their liturgy they follow the Ethiopian rite, but remain affiliated to the Congregation of Casamari. Another African mission was begun in 1930 by Pont Colbert in the French colony of Madagascar, near Tananarive which, however, after some years was suppressed.

In Indochina (Viet-Nam), since 1918, several houses have been organized by local missionaries for contemplative vocations under diocesan authority and without formal adherence to any existing religious order. In 1933, they accepted the Cistercian Rule, My-Ca joining the Congregation of Senanque, Phuoc-Són (Annam) remaining independent under the direct jurisdiction of the Abbot General. The growing community of Phuoc-Són, with numerous native vocations especially for lay-brotherhood, founded in 1936 the new settlement of Châu-Són (Tonkin). The recent invasion of Indochina by Communist forces made the existence of these communities precarious. The former superior of Châu-Són, Msgr. Le-Huu-Tu, now titular bishop and Vicar Apostolic of Phât-Diem, is a well known champion of the movement of resistance against Communism and the organizer of his much publicized "private army."

America

Because of the much higher material and personal requirements involved, foundations in North America presented the most difficult problems; however, the Abbot General exhibited the warmest interest in the matter. Shortly after the Chapter of 1927, Fr. Thomas Roos of Schlierbach, Fr. Edmund Frey and Fr. Cornelius Knüsel of Mehrerau, landed in New York, October 6, 1927. Father Frey headed toward Richmond, Indiana, where he had already worked in 1924, while the two other fathers went to St. Louis, where Archbishop Glennon invited them to foster an agricultural school to be established at a large farm, "Selma Hall," which was at that time up for sale. Unfortunately, however, Msgr. Holweck, the soul of the whole enterprise, died, and as the negotiations proceeded, the price of the property was gradually raised to more than $200,000 and, as a result, this promising plan had to be abandoned. The discouraged fathers contacted various other dioceses and from Bishop Kelley of Oklahoma City they soon received a favorable reply concerning the organization of a diocesan minor seminary under Cistercian management. Again financial difficulties prevented the fathers from accepting the otherwise suitable offer.

Father Roos during his further investigations on May 11, 1928, had an audience with Archbishop Messmer of Milwaukee, who warmly welcomed the fathers into his diocese and promised his full cooperation and advice in the foundation of a monastery. After receiving the good news, Abbot General Janssens arrived in New York on June 3 in order to reach a final decision. There were two available properties in the vicinity of Milwaukee: a large building at Hales Corners, formerly belonging to the Dominican Sisters, and "Spring Bank," near Okauchee. Since the fathers were unanimously in favor of the latter proposal, the property, evaluated at $200,000, was actually purchased for $75,000.

The estate of "Spring Bank," surrounded by 55 acres on Lake Oconomowoc, was built by a wealthy Chicago businessman, Capt. Thomas L. Parker, between 1874-1880, and at that time it was regarded as the finest estate in Wisconsin. However, the property soon changed ownership and during the 1890's it was operated as "Hotel Spring Bank." Later the Catholic Hospital Association bought the place as a vacation home for its members; in the meantime the Marquette Retreat League occasionally rented some of the buildings for week-end retreats, and the spacious grounds were frequently occupied during summer by camping boys. When the Cistercian Order acquired "Spring Bank," there were six buildings on the grounds: three of stone and brick, three of wooden structure.

The solemn opening of the monastery was celebrated on August 20, 1928, on the feast of St. Bernard of Clairvaux, by a field Mass in the presence of some 120 Church dignitaries and priests from all over the country. The first postulant asked for admission even before this date, and was soon followed by others. In addition to the routine liturgical and domestic duties, retreats, missions and assistance at neighboring parishes kept the few fathers well occupied, providing the small community with the necessities of life; but it was also obvious that any future development would need further effective help both in material and personnel.

The Abbot General reported the start of "Spring Bank" at the abbatial convention at Mehrerau, February 7, 1929, when Schlierbach officially accepted the sponsorship of the new foundation under the leadership of Father Roos as Prior, and with other Austrian abbeys promising their full support. The promises were fulfilled, and Abbot Janssens again came to America, on June 14, 1929, accompanied by three fathers from different Austrian abbeys and four brothers from Schlierbach. One of the fathers, Hermann Hahn, in his civilian life an accomplished architect, immediately worked out a large scale plan for a new monastery, while the brothers demolished the three dilapidated wooden buildings. Providentially, a generous benefactor offered to defray the expenses of the greatly needed chapel, and construction was started on the first anniversary of the opening of the monastery. The joy over the great success was overshadowed by the grave illness and death of Father Knüsel, a severe loss for the small community.

The building of the simple but tasteful chapel was completed during the spring of the next year and solemnly blessed by Archbishop Messmer on Pentecost Monday, June 9, 1930. The internal decorations were continued during the summer; the mural in the apse and the stations are the works of the Milwaukee artist, August Christian. The picture above the Blessed Mother's altar, a donation of its last owner, Prof. Vladimir Shamberk of Chicago, is a fifteenth century copy of the famous miraculous image of the Blessed Virgin, venerated at the ancient Cistercian abbey of Königssaal, Bohemia. In 1934 the largest building, the so-called "Manor," was remodeled and operated as a vacation home for priests under the management of

Franciscan Sisters. In the same year, on the lake front of the monastery, a new, roomy dining hall was erected.

Meanwhile, the Abbot General, who never hesitated to intervene personally when the matter of the American foundations was at stake, repeatedly spent long months in this country and succeeded in the acquisition of three other properties: two in Canada and a large farm in Mississippi. The Canadian Val d'Espoir (Gaspé) was sponsored by Abbot Janssen's own abbey, Pont Colbert (1930), while the other, Rougemont (Quebec), became the filiation of Lérins (1932); the third foundation in Mississippi (Paulding, diocese of Natchez) could not be opened because of lack of personnel.

In spite of the apparently successful start, the life at "Spring Bank" became increasingly problematical. The crucial issue was still the small number of fathers, unable to fulfill their multiple duties at home and outside of the monastery. Indeed, there were too many new foundations in development at once and neither one of the European abbeys was in the position to fulfill the personnel needs of "Spring Bank" alone. Thus, in addition to the usual difficulties of language, different customs and ways of living, the life of the small community was greatly complicated by the fact that the group consisted of Austrian, German, Dutch and Polish members of different Congregations, which rendered smooth cooperation rather difficult. The lay-brothers, whose toil secured the material success of the foundation, were unable to obtain visas necessary for permanent residence and the prolongation of their six month terms as "visitors" became increasingly difficult. Furthermore, the greatest disappointment of the hard working fathers was that none of the American vocations persevered for quite obvious reasons; at "Spring Bank" the first foundation of the Order in this country, the postulants and novices scarcely knew what to expect; some could not endure the hardships of the pioneer work; others confused the Order with the Trappists, or just could not find their place within a foreign community.

In addition to the personnel problems, the years of the depression prevented the monastery from building on a basis financially sound enough for future development; moreover, the Abbot General, full of zeal and sincere good will, but without any experience in business, involved the monastery in a very disadvantageous loan that brought grave consequences for years to come. Unable to furnish further personnel and to carry the financial responsibility, the Abbot of Schlierbach resigned as father-abbot of the new monastery in 1934, and gradually recalled his subjects or transferred them to the abbey's new Brazilian foundation. The sponsorship of "Spring Bank" was taken over by Pont Colbert and the Austrian fathers were replaced with members of Pont Colbert's Dutch daughter-house, Marienkroon (Onsenoort); monks of the same community started the Cistercian life at Paulding, Miss., in 1935 (Our Lady of Gerowval). Following the custom of Pont Colbert, daily adoration of the Blessed Sacrament was introduced at "Spring Bank"; it was discontinued however in 1949. When, as a consequence of the further deterioration of the financial situation, Pont Colbert was forced to give up the Canadian Val d'Espoir in 1937, some of the Dutch fathers were transferred to "Spring Bank." In the following year Abbot Janssens resigned as Abbot General, largely on account of the collapse of his dearly cherished hopes regarding the success of his American foundations. The long years of World War II made any communication with the European mother-house impossible, and although the lack of personnel and local vocations still remained a difficult problem to solve, able leadership, sacrifice and hard work redeemed "Spring Bank" completely from its debts; moreover, through the purchase of an adjacent farm of 50 acres in 1947, the house developed into a self supporting unit.

In Europe very few houses survived World War II without considerable material damage; in France, Germany and Austria, where priests and religious were not exempt from combat service, even the loss in personnel was severe. Nevertheless, the ruins caused by aerial attacks, bombardments and looting hordes soon could be repaired, but the fatal effects of the Yalta agreement, which granted a free hand for the Russians behind the "Iron Curtain," turned out to be a tragic disaster for the whole Christian civilization under the Communist yoke. The one-sided battle against the religious orders started in Hungary, where they had the most influence through the control of the whole field of education. Right after the Russian invasion of the country, under the pretext of an agrarian reform, all ecclesiastical properties were confiscated in the belief that the institutions based upon the old system of large estates would automatically collapse. But through the generosity of the people, themselves in grave need, every Catholic school continued in operation as before, whereupon the government resolved to launch an open attack against them. In 1948, every educational institution operated by religious was confiscated by the state, among them the five Cistercian high schools. Moreover, since the further activity of former teachers, even the mere existence of them, was considered as dangerous, in 1950 the religious orders were simply dissolved, with a few exceptions, all monasteries and convents closed, the wearing of religious garments prohibited, and large numbers of their members were put in slave labor camps or prisons. Thus ended the formal community life of more than 200 Cistercians, the largest single group of the Order.

In the midst of the seemingly inconsequential tactics of the Communists, the Polish houses shortly after the war managed to regain three former Cistercian monasteries which were united in 1950 under the leadership of Szczyrzyc into a Polish Congregation. But it is very doubtful how long the present regime will tolerate their activities; as a matter of fact, the monastic properties were already confiscated in 1950, and the schools lost the right of publicity. The time table might be different in different countries, but not the end. If there is no hope for essential changes in the near future, Christian life in its whole extent will be reduced to an underground movement everywhere within the Communist orbit.

A number of Hungarian Cistercians who succeeded in escaping from their country found a permanent home at "Spring Bank," still in ardent need of fresh reinforcement; moreover, in 1947 the monastery became legally affiliated to Zirc as an independent Priory. Since then, the community has gained considerably in personnel, not only through immigration but through promising American vocations.

PART II

Cistercian Culture

13. Spirituality and Learning

The stimulus which animated the great spiritual renewal of the Gregorian Reform was a general desire to return to the very sources of Christianity in order to rejuvenate and purify the world in conformity with the exalted ideals of the primitive Church. Those who endeavored to free the hierarchy and secular clergy from the allurement of the world looked to the example of the Apostles; various lay-movements found new inspiration for their programs of religious and social reconstruction in the Gospel, while within monastic communities the appeal of the earliest traditions of the Desert Fathers grew stronger steadily.

The movement resulted in a growing interest in eastern Christianity and especially in the Holy Land, while, on the other hand, the actual connections with the Near East greatly invigorated the sway of the movement itself. The universal enthusiasm reached its climax in the First Crusade, filling Christian society as a whole with a heroic zeal for Christ and His cause, ready for any sacrifice.

The monastic reform of the eleventh century, permeated by the same spirit of heroism, found itself confronted with a peculiar problem, which consisted in the obvious antagonism between the challenging model of the Desert Fathers and the still predominant Rule of St. Benedict. Leading and influential authorities, such as St. Peter Damian, did not hesitate to solve the dilemma in favor of the eremitic life, boldly declaring that the Rule was written only for beginners, while the imitation of the Desert Fathers was meant to lead to perfection. A number of religious communities were reorganized according to the new ideals, the most significant among them being Camaldoli and Vallombrosa.

The direct influence of St. Peter Damian and his followers was not decisive north of the Alps. In France, however, a long series of more or less successful reforms revealed similar aspirations. Stephen Muret, Bernard of Tiron, Bruno of Cologne, Robert of Arbrissel, Vitalis of Mortain and many others were unanimous in their criticism of the contemporary state of monasticism and, under the inspiration of the heroic virtues of the Desert Fathers, sought its reorganization through a return to the more severe asceticism of pre-Benedictine models. Perfect detachment from the world, great poverty and strict penance were the common characteristics of their program, although in details it varied considerably.

The Early Cîteaux

In the atmosphere of feverish reform activities it was nothing unusual when St. Robert, a restless champion of monastic renewal, with the understanding support of a small group of former hermits founded the monastery of Molesme, as another experiment in the approach to the common ideal; their aim was not far removed from those of their predecessors and contemporaries laboring in the same endeavor. Their effort was rewarded by remarkable success. With the increase of personnel, however, there emerged once again the crucial problem: the proper interpretation of the Rule of St. Benedict. The heated debates utterly disturbed the peace of the young community; moreover, the Abbot and his faithful disciples were repeatedly forced to seek refuge and consolation in the solitude of neighboring hermitages. Meanwhile, as a result of the prolonged discussions, Robert's circle reached a significant conclusion: in order to reconstruct the basic ideals of monasticism, one must return to the very letter of the Rule, disregarding later interpretations or modifications of any kind. The theory put into practice, through the strictest literal interpretation of the almost six hundred year old document, led to the establishment of a life full of hardships, worthy of the heroic example of the Desert Fathers, although in its severity it was undeniably beyond St. Benedict's genuine intention. The reformers of Molesme were scarcely aware of such a possibility; moreover, their continuous reference to the Rule constituted a firm legal support for their case against any attack or opposition.

This uncompromising will to live according to the letter of the Rule, combined with an ardent desire for solitude, became the cornerstone of Cîteaux. In this skillful combination of the ascetic ideals of the uncommonly popular eremitism with the traditional form of Benedictine monasticism consists the real importance of the Cistercian reform. Cîteaux provided ample opportunity for those ready to follow the heroic virtues of the Desert Fathers and also saved in their entirety both the cenobitic character of monastic life and the absolute authority of St. Benedict and his Rule.

The consolidation of the "New Monastery" was the work of Robert's immediate successors, Alberic and Stephen. It is rather difficult to determine exactly what share each of them had in further specification of Cistercian spirituality. However, in the first pages of the *Exordium Parvum,* dealing with Alberic's regime, poverty, simplicity and detachment from all worldly affairs seem to be the most vigorously stressed virtues. The poverty and extreme simplicity in every field of their life was a natural consequence of the arduous circumstances; their complete segregation from society required their own hard manual labor, which other contemporary monasteries had provided by serfs. This humble and exhausting toil became another distinctive feature of the Order; later it came to be shared with a growing number of lay-brothers. Nevertheless, at the beginning, the heroic work of clearance and tillage only aggravated the monks' already heavy burdens to such a degree that anyone who intended to join the community was deterred by the "unusual and almost unheard-of austerity of their lives." (*Exord. Parv.*)

Despite all difficulties and disappointments, the intrepid warriors of Cîteaux did not surrender. On the contrary, St. Stephen, stressing further the idea of undisturbed solitude, protested against the visits of their noble benefactors, and extended the rule of simplicity over church vestments, vessels, furnishings and equipment. However strict and uncompromisingly ascetic Abbot Stephen was, amidst all the hardships of life, Cîteaux became under his regime a unique center of monastic learning. It is difficult to conceive how a small community in a remote monastery managed to accomplish such difficult tasks as a large scale liturgical reform, the collection of authentic hymns and Gregorian melodies, the revision of the Bible and the composition of a constitution of admirable wisdom and foresight. In carrying out these assignments, St. Stephen certainly relied upon the substantial contributions of his able companions. Concerning his predecessor, Alberic, the *Exordium Parvum* explicitly stated that he was a man of letters, well versed in divine and human sciences, and, when finally the flood of new candidates reached the monastery, the same document joyfully recorded that many of them were noble and learned clerics. Abbot Stephen himself made a significant exception in the application of his program of stern simplicity: he remained an ardent lover of beautiful books, and the manuscripts copied in the early days of Cîteaux belong to the most lavishly illuminated codices of the whole century.

St. Bernard

The merciless application of the principle of simplicity in those fields of monastic life which still remained untouched by it must be attributed to St. Bernard's growing influence. His famous essay on monastic art, the *Apologia ad Gulielmum*, became the commanding norm and the abdication of St. Stephen

Harding was followed by a series of legislative restrictions concerning not only the binding, decoration and illumination of manuscripts, but also intellectual activities, such as instruction within the monastery and authorship. In St. Bernard's rich literary bequest are numerous passages both in favor of and against science and learning, but his continuous fight against the extravagances of contemporary intellectualism created within the Order an air of distrust towards human learning, which prevailed until the middle of the thirteenth century. Significantly enough, even the great Saint could not escape a slight inconsistency. He who banished art from monastic precincts, was himself an unsurpassed master of medieval Latin prosaic art, the *Doctor Mellifluus,* author of a number of brilliant essays and the center of the most extensive correspondence of his era.

On the positive side, St. Bernard's influence upon spirituality within his Order as well as outside of it was enormous. His frequently quoted definition of Cistercian life, given in one of his letters, soon came to be regarded as the most authentic revelation of the quintessence of the Order: "Our life is a life of abjection, humility, voluntary poverty; of obedience, peace, joy in the Holy Spirit; our life is subjection to a superior, to an abbot, a rule, a discipline. Our life is the practice of silence, fasting, vigils, prayers, manual labor, and above all to follow the more excellent way which is charity, and to progress in all these things from day to day and persevere in them until the last day." (*Ep.* 142) With the motive of love in the center of his ascetic doctrine he became duly honored as the father of medieval mysticism. His inspired writings on the Sacred Humanity of Christ and the Blessed Virgin furnished an inexhaustible fountain for the school of Cistercian spirituality. In wide popularity all his other works were surpassed by different collections of his sermons, originally delivered for the community of Clairvaux, which were copied and circulated everywhere in the continent. St. Bernard's contribution to Christian theology and piety survived the Middle Ages, and, as all time classics of religious literature, were continuously reprinted and translated into every language of the civilized world.

The School of St. Bernard

First of all, the monks of his Order, his faithful disciples, worked for the further propagation and development of his teaching. His original approach to Christology and Mariology was further unfolded by Cistercians, thus giving a permanent character to the spirituality of the Order itself. The devotion of the Sacred Humanity of Christ must be regarded as particularly significant in prevision of the forthcoming devotion of the Sacred Heart of Jesus. Of course, Christ, both in His Divine and Human Nature, stood always in the center of Christian devotion; however, St. Bernard's emotional approach, his tender and compassionate love for the Child Jesus and the suffering Redeemer, was a great novelty, reechoed by thousands of his followers.

The mystery of the Sacred Infancy inspired the *Jesus at the Age of Twelve,* a gem of devotional literature by Aelred of Rievaulx, while meditation on the Passion led toward the contemplation of the wounded Heart of Jesus. In further explanation of the latter mystery William of St. Thierry, Guerric of Igny and Gilbert of Hoiland were closest to St. Bernard's genius. The Heart of Jesus remained a source of inspiration for Cistercian mystics throughout the Middle Ages. Apart from the famous convent of Helfta in Saxony, many others excelled in this devotion, especially in the Low Countries under the spiritual leadership of Villers, where Abbot Arnulph (d.1250) became its most influential promoter.

The cult of the Blessed Sacrament gained in popularity together with that of the Sacred Heart. The same Villers was the monastery where the solemn office of the newly introduced feast of Corpus Christi was first celebrated in 1252. As an interesting feature of this development within the Order, it is worth mentioning that at Kaisheim in 1393 a pious foundation was made for perpetual exposition of the Blessed Sacrament. The perpetual adoration, however, was not organized until the eighteenth century.

The veneration of the Blessed Virgin Mary took its rise at the very beginning of Christianity. However, while the early Fathers of the Church spoke primarily about her unique prerogatives and dignity as the instrument of the Redemption, St. Bernard and his Cistercian posterity changed the tone, approaching Mary as our Mother, with affectionate love of her children. To address her as "Our Lady"—in the age of chivalry—was made popular also by Cistercians. The first representation of the Blessed Virgin in the thirteenth century with the members of the Order under her mantle, became a pattern of similar symbolic pictures of "Our Lady of Mercy." As early as 1134 the General Chapter defined that all Cistercian monasteries should be erected in honor of the Blessed Virgin, although the first official allusion to Mary as special Patroness of the Order is to be found among the records of the Chapter of 1281. The Chapter of 1335 ordered that the Blessed Virgin's image be carved on the official seal of every monastery.

The development of Mary's role in Cistercian liturgy kept pace with an ever rising devotion to the Blessed Mother. In 1152, her commemoration in the daily office was introduced; in 1185, the Little Office of the Blessed Virgin became a community prayer; since 1194, a daily conventual mass has been said in her honor; in 1220, there appeared her Saturday votive mass in Cistercian Missals although the votive office was not intoduced until 1645. The origin of the *Salve Regina* reaches back to pre-Cistercian times; nevertheless, St. Bernard and Pope Eugene III did the most for its popularization, and since 1218 it has been sung in every Cistercian community as the closing devotion of the day. The *Sub Tuum,* following the Prime, was inserted into the office for the first time in 1533.

Among other Orders, the Franciscan spirituality was primarily enriched by St. Bernard's doctrine, especially through

St. Bonaventure's congenial adaptation. The so-called *Devotio Moderna* of the fifteenth century, particularly among the group of Augustinians at Windesheim, which included the author of the *Imitation of Christ,* was based largely on St. Bernard's spirituality. Naturally, St. Bernard's influence and popularity lessened somewhat in the changed world of the Renaissance and Reformation, although his works still inspired the spirituality of Cardinal Bérulle and his famous "French School" in the seventeenth century. Profane art and literature also paid its tribute of honor and respect to the Saint's irresistible personality throughout the centuries, beginning with such geniuses as Dante, who chose St. Bernard for his guide through his heavenly wandering.

Among Bernard's followers in his own Order, William of St. Thierry (d.1148), a Benedictine abbot, later Cistercian, contributed most to the foundation of mystical theology, in intimate friendship with the great Abbot of Clairvaux. A role similar to that of St. Bernard was played in England by Aelred, Abbot of Rievaulx (d.1164), a man of serene and modest spirit with an extraordinarily lovable personality. His sermons and essays, especially the *Mirror of Charity* and his *Spiritual Friendship,* enjoyed a lasting popularity. His life was written by one of his monks, Walter Daniel (d.1170), himself a prolific author of sermons of lesser originality. Another abbot of English origin, Isaac of Stella (d.1169), at once scholastic and Cistercian, agreed fundamentally with St. Bernard's teaching, but saw no opposition between mysticism and scholasticism. This remarkable synthesis was represented by his sermons and two essays, *The Soul* and *The Office of the Mass.* A collection of inspired sermons on the Blessed Virgin made the name of Adam of Perseigne (d.1221) well known in monastic literature; in one of his letters he outlined the proper method of education of novices, basing it upon six conditions: fervent faith, fear of God, love of wisdom, religious conversation with the master, the master's solicitude toward the novices, and finally, friendly and frequent discussion of spiritual and disciplinary matters. In England,

Abbot Stephen of Salley (d.1252) in his meditations presented the Blessed Virgin chiefly as Co-Redeemer and Mediatrix while at the same time in the Low Countries the Cistercian Gerard of Liège contributed essentially to the development of mystical theology. Among those who continued St. Bernard's unfinished commentary on the *Canticle of Canticles* the most successful was Gilbert of Hoiland (d.1172) and a French monk known as "Thomas the Cistercian."

Following in St. Bernard's footsteps, authors of noteworthy sermons were his secretaries, Godfrey of Clairvaux and Nicolas of Clairvaux; Ernaud of Bonneval, one of the Saint's biographers; Guerric of Igny (d.1151), suave and full of unction; the highly emotional Godfrey of Melrose; Baldwin of Ford, later Archbishop of Canterbury and preacher of the Third Crusade; Garnier of Rochefort, later Bishop of Langres; and Hélinand of Froidmont, once an erudite troubadour, compiler of a world-history and, after his conversion, author of a series of melancholic poems on Death.

In the initial period of Cistercian history, except for St. Bernard, few members of the Order contributed essentially to the development of theology. In this respect, the name of Peter Cantor, onetime professor in Paris, later Cistercian at Longpont, can be mentioned. One of the most learned men of the twelfth century, the *Doctor Universalis,* Alan of Lille (d.1203) retired to Citeaux only to die. Joachim of Fiore (d.1202) the famous Calabrian prophet, joined the Order, but only nominally, since his peculiar spirituality scarcely had any direct relation to Cistercian past or future.

Hagiography

The early Cistercians, like all of their contemporaries, displayed a lively interest in hagiography. Some of the *Vitae,* such as the *Life of St. Bernard,* successively continued by various authors, have considerable historical value; in others, legendary elements prevail, their primary purpose being the moral edification of the reader. In the collection of miraculous stories, Clairvaux established very soon a long lasting tradition. The first of its known contributors was John (d.1179), the Prior of the abbey, followed by Herbert of Clairvaux, whose *Liber Miraculorum* was composed around 1170. Goswin of Clairvaux (d.1203) finished his composition before the turn of the century, while the largest and most significant collection was the *Exordium Magnum* of Conrad, monk at Clairvaux, later Abbot of Eberbach. Besides the usual edifying character, the book exhibits a conspicuous apologetic tendency, defending the Order, especially the legality of its foundation, against the charges and criticism of the Black Monks. Concerning the miraculous contents, its main source was Herbert's previous collection.

One of the most significant books of legends which enjoyed the widest popularity throughout the Middle Ages, was the *Dialogus Miraculorum* by Caesarius of Heisterbach (d.1240), prior and master of novices of that famous monastery of the Rhineland. The *Dialogus* was most probably written between 1220-1235. The composition took the form of a dialogue between the master and novice; the stories always illustrated the beauty and usefulness of a certain virtue. Many of them may lack historical value, but the book is full of vivid details of the early thirteenth century folklore and monastic life. Caesarius is also the author of a large series of *Homilies,* based upon a symbolical interpretation of the Bible.

Similar books of legends circulated in large number all around the monastic world. One of the most voluminous was a collective work of Austrian Benedictines and Cistercians, which at the end of the twelfth century contained 580 miraculous biographies. The genre of legends retained its popularity until the end of the Middle Ages. Moreover, the fourteenth century brought about an aftermath of Cistercian mysticism not only within convents of nuns but in monasteries as well, especially in Germany. Heilsbronn, under Abbot Conrad of Brundelsheim (1317-1321); Kaisheim, in the time of Abbot Ulrich

Nubling (1340-1360), a personal friend of Tauler; Waldsassen, under the leadership of John Ellenbogen (1313-1325); and Königssaal, successively under Abbots Peter and Gallus, were widely renowned centers of monastic piety. All of the above mentioned abbots were also authors of mystical and devotional literature. In 1439 and 1447 the General Chapter itself encouraged the abbots to promote in their own houses the collection of stories of pious monks and nuns.

The life of St. Bridget of Sweden (1302-1373), the famous mystic and prophetess, bears witness to the unbroken vigor of Cistercian spirituality in the North. After her husband became a monk in Alvastra she lived for years in the neighborhood of the monastery under the spiritual guidance of the Fathers. Her piety was Cistercian in character with the passion of Christ and the glories of the Blessed Virgin as its center. The Rule of the Order of St. Saviour, founded by her, reflects Cistercian influence. Parts of her revelations were translated by the Cistercian Peter Olafsson.

Historiography

The first topic of profane studies which engaged a large number of Cistercian abbeys from the very beginning was history. The most outstanding among the historians of the Order and certainly the greatest in his century was Otto of Freising (d.1158), half brother of Emperor Conrad III and uncle of Frederick Barbarossa. Having finished his education in Paris under Abelard and Gilbert de la Porrée, he soon joined the Order, became Abbot of Morimond, later Bishop of Freising, and participated in the Emperor's company in the ill-fated Second Crusade. His *Chronicon* and *Gesta Friderici Imperatoris* conceived in the ideology of St. Augustin, attest to his extraordinarily clear vision and unparalleled originality.

In some instances Cistercian monasteries were founded with the express intention of fostering learning, primarily historiography. Thus Soroë in Denmark was established (1162) with the purpose "that therein men of prominent erudition would be boarded who would compile the annals of the Kingdom and record annually for posterity events worthy of memory."

Cistercian annalists secured for themselves a distinguished place in British historiography. Melrose, Waverley, Coggeshall, Margam, Stanley, Hayles, Dore, Stratfleur, Furness, Fountains and Meaux are those abbeys worth mentioning in this regard. The *Monumenta Germaniae Historica* published the chronicles of forty-eight Cistercian abbeys of great interest in German history; most of them were composed during the twelfth and thirteenth centuries. Among the chroniclers known by name, the following are the most outstanding ones: Ralph of Coggeshall, author of the *Chronicon Anglicanum;* Günther of Pairis, poet and historian of the Fourth Crusade, author of the work known as *Historia Constantinopolitana;* Alberic of Troisfontaines, the compiler of a history of his own times in the second quarter of the thirteenth century; Peter of Zittau, Abbot of Königssaal, whose *Chronicon Aulae Regiae* covered Bohemian history between 1305-1337; John, Abbot of Viktring (d.1347) whose *Liber Certarum Historiarum* is a first ranking source for German and Bohemian history, especially for the period of 1217-1341. Vincent Kadlubek (1160-1223), Bishop of Krakow, the father of Polish historiography, spent only his last years in retirement in the Cistercian abbey of Andrejow.

It is certainly conspicuous that in spite of the much emphasized simplicity of the early Cistercian life a surprisingly large number of excellent scholars exalted the fame of the Order through their literary activity. In order to solve the apparent contradiction, one must recall the extraordinary attraction of Cistercian ideals among contemporary men of learning as well as the fact that all the above mentioned authors received their education prior to their admission to the Order. Meanwhile, neither their scholarly activities nor the occasional diplomatic missions of abbots, preaching of zealous missionaries or crusaders, changed basically the spirituality outlined and exemplified by St. Bernard. All outside engagements of the Order which characterized its role as of the vanguard of the Church, however large their number, were restricted only to individuals or to isolated outposts in the peripheries of the Christian orbit, while the vast majority of the abbeys lived undisturbedly according to their traditional daily schedule.

Scholasticism

An overgrowth in monastic personnel, where a considerable number of candidates were attracted into the Order by reasons other than true contemplative vocation, may have caused a certain tension and some difficulties in discipline already in the lifetime of the second Cistercian generation; nevertheless, the first significant change of intellectual and spiritual outlook in the Order emerged as a result of the increasingly strong influence of Scholasticism, as represented in the activities of the Mendicant Orders. The ever growing authority of the University of Paris, the spectacular rise of the Friars and official emphasis on the intellectual education of the clergy left deep marks in Cistercian mentality. The establishment of the *Bernardinum* at Paris by Stephen Lexington represented not only the daring innovation of an able and ambitious abbot; it can also be regarded rightfully as the symbol of a new spirituality: St. Bernard's ideal of a somewhat rustic simplicity giving way to the new model of the "learned monk," physical labor being replaced by studies.

The obvious deviation from a century-old tradition caused a vehement though gradually subsiding reaction within and a puzzled amazement without. Among the popular explanations of Cistercian eagerness in scholastic studies, Matthew Paris, a contemporary English monastic historian, presented the most common one: "The Cistercian monks, in order to avoid the contempt of the Friars, both the Preachers and Minors as well as of literate seculars, . . . established houses in Paris and elsewhere where schools flourished, started to study . . . so that they would not seem inferior to others." Such an explanation may sound too simple and inadequate, yet it clearly attests the presence of a trend of extraordinary intensity.

The General Chapter, extremely alert in any other case of relaxed discipline, soon discarded its initial cautiousness and became the most strenuous promoter of scholastic studies. Significantly, the reform inaugurated by the famous *Fulgens Sicut Stella* (1335) of Pope Benedict XII, while stressing a return to the primitive discipline in many touchy points, strongly advocated the expansion of the already wide educational program. The spontaneous love of learning reached its climax undoubtedly in the Renaissance, when the Fathers assembled in the Chapter of 1488 did not hesitate to declare that "all glory and advancement of the Order depends mostly upon the multiplication of erudite members within the Order."

The development of Cistercian Colleges, parallel with the establishment of home courses of philosophy and theology in each monastery, supposed necessarily a respectable group of able teachers and scholars: however, scientific evaluation of their work is still largely wanting, and even the question of the existence of a specific Cistercian school of philosophy or theology is open for discussion.

The first known regent of the College of St. Bernard in Paris was John Waarde (d.1293), a member of Les Dunes, who was promoted to the degree of Master of Theology in 1275. In his time, the College already had been incorporated into the University of Paris. His successor was Francis Keysere (d.1294), author of a number of theological works. The first Cistercian member of the faculty to adopt in his lectures the doctrine named after St. Thomas Aquinas was Humbert of Prully (d.1298), known therefore as "The Father of Scholasticism in the Cistercian Order." Thomism, however, scarcely could have permeated the official Cistercian curriculum, because a certain monk, Bartholomy by name, was condemned as early as 1316, charged with nominalism. Richard of Lincoln, leaning toward the same doctrine, was silenced by Benedict XII for his "phantastic" opinions, although he was later cleared by Clement VI. The best known and probably the most brilliant defender of Ockam's doctrine was John Mirecourt, professor in Paris in the 1340's. A number of his basic theses were condemned in 1347. Orthodox theologians in Paris, members of the first scholastic generation, were Guy of L'Aumone, John of Limoges, Rainier of Clairmarais, John He, John Sindewint (d.1319), Jean Dun and Jacob Thérines (d.1321), defender of monastic exemption at the Council of Vienne; toward the end of the fourteenth century John of Neuville and Jacob of Eltville, participants in a debate on the problem of the Immaculate Conception; William Curti, later cardinal and protector of the Order; John Boissière, Abbot of Cîteaux and later a cardinal; and Peter Ceffonds, whose works perished.

Elsewhere, John of Cercamp was known as the organizer of the College at Montpellier, while William of Poblet acted in a similar capacity at Toulouse; both had been appointed to this duty by the General Chapter of 1335. In England, William Remington and Henry Crump, professors in Oxford around 1390, fought the heresy of Wycliffe. At the University of Prague and later in the Council of Constance, Matthew Steynhus acted in a similar role in the opposition against the heretic John Huss. In Austria, Nicholas Vischel of Heiligenkreuz (1250-1330), an expert in Jewish literature, was the author of several essays concerning theological problems of the Jewish faith. Outstanding theologian of his times was Conrad of Ebrach (d.1399), Abbot of Morimond, successively professor in Paris and Prague and finally the organizer of the faculty of theology at the University of Vienna in 1384. In his theological dissertations he criticized with keen accuracy the exaggerations of contemporary Thomists, remaining independent himself in the age old feud between the leading schools. The most accomplished Cistercian theologian and jurist of the Middle Ages was beyond doubt Jacob Fournier, Abbot of Fontfroide, better known as Pope

Benedict XII (1334-1342), whose substantial treatises on the much discussed subject of beatific vision earned him a well deserved fame and reputation.

Although the promotion of studies was a source of deep concern to the General Chapter throughout the late Middle Ages, courses in Canon and Roman law were strictly prohibited until the middle of the fifteenth century. The real cause of this strange restriction was never fully revealed and has puzzled historians ever since. As a matter of fact, Canon Law as a subject was still a novelty in the Universities; its study involved a number of debated current political issues and was constantly abused by restless troublemakers. Consequently, the general distrust toward law among the members of the Chapter was not entirely unfounded.

Libraries

In line with the eagerness for learning the number of well-stocked monastic libraries increased although, until the invention of printing, the process was extremely slow and was fostered almost exclusively by the monks themselves, who copied borrowed books in the *scriptorium*. For storing the ready manuscripts the *armarium*, a small chamber next to the sacristy was used, indicating that a large proportion of the available books were of liturgical nature. In the first two centuries there were no organized studies within the abbeys. Nevertheless, considerable time was spent each day in spiritual reading; consequently, depending on the number of monks, a relatively large stock of books was necessary to provide for the routine circulation. The library of Clairvaux, at the end of the twelfth century, included at least 340 codices, all of them copied in the same monastery, attesting to the fact that St. Bernard was by no means an enemy of books and that the *lectio divina* was for him just as important as manual labor. The body of this and similar other collections was always made up by the Bible and its classical commentaries by the Fathers of the Church.

As a result of scholastic studies the libraries soon became enlarged with theological and philosophical textbooks as well as with a collection of popular Latin classics. During the course of the fifteenth century, the General Chapter repeatedly encouraged the abbots to organize and maintain properly large libraries, for such collections were to be regarded as the real "treasury of monks" (1454). In 1495, the Chapter authorized the Abbot of Fountaines to solicit each English house for at least 8-10 books, "good and decent ones, worthy to keep in library," for the use of the College at Oxford.

By the end of the fifteenth century, many of the wealthier abbeys added to the traditional monastic plant a roomy library furnished with an impressive number of manuscripts. Thus, in 1480, Cîteaux owned 1,200 codices, while the building of the new library was finished at the end of the century under Abbot John Cirey. A fragment of the once rich collection is still available in the Municipal Library of Dijon. In 1472, Clairvaux stored more than 1,700 codices, now partly preserved at Troyes. Himmerod's library in 1453 counted over 2,000 volumes and the building of a new library was completed at the beginning of the sixteenth century. At about the same time the library of Lehnin with 1,000 codices was considered the largest in Brandenburg. The scriptorium of Heilsbronn was regarded as one of the finest in Germany: over 600 of these carefully copied parchment volumes are now in the possession of the University of Erlangen. During the 15th century the abbey of Altzelle rose to be a leading center of humanistic learning in Saxony, storing a large number of Latin classics in its growing library. In addition to the usual set of liturgical books the abbey possessed, in 1514, 960 volumes. After the suppression of Altzelle in 1540, the collection enriched the library of the University of Leipzig. In Portugal, Alcobaça played a unique role in the cultural advancement of the country. During the thirteenth century the abbey established a college at Lisbon and actively participated in the organization of the famous University of Coimbra. The abbey's library was rated as one of the largest in the country. Although its rich collection was repeatedly pillaged in 1810 and in 1833, the catalogue of the National Library of Lisbon still contains 456 manuscripts of Alcobaça, most of them copied during the thirteenth century. Even smaller houses were proud of their respectable libraries: the Austrian Zwettl owned in 1451 almost 500 books; the English Meaux in 1396 had 350 volumes. In order to appreciate the above figures we must remember that the richest secular libraries of the same era scarcely equaled an average monastic library. Thus the famous collection of Charles V of France in 1373 amounted only to 910 codices; that of the Medici family in Florence, almost a century later, numbered only about 800 volumes.

Shortly after its invention, the Order also made use of printing. The first Cistercian printing shop was established in Zinna, Germany, as early as 1492, and was followed in France by La Charité in 1496. In the subsequent centuries a number of the richest abbeys regularly operated their own printing shops. The large output of printed material soon necessitated strong measures in order to prevent the circulation of books and pamphlets advocating the Protestant heresy. Regarding nuns, who were considered incapable of recognizing the theological tendency of their spiritual readings, the Chapter in 1531 prohibited the possession of books written in other languages than Latin, and even those required the special approval of legitimate authority.

Renaissance

The study of Cistercian spirituality since the fifteenth century is far more complicated than it is of the previous period. Parallel with the weakening control of the General Chapter, the impact of alien influences became stronger and the more or less independent or isolated groups of monasteries soon exhibited a wide variety of discipline, liturgy and customs. The fateful commendatory system caused a tragic decline of the once rich abbeys of exemplary discipline throughout Italy and France; overzealous reformers separated whole countries from the vital unity of the Order, imposing new rules upon their followers in defiance of the traditional monastic institutions. After the disaster of the Reformation, the control of Cîteaux was practically restricted to France and the remaining abbeys of the Germanies. Thus the concept of "Cistercian Spirituality" as an active and formative power in the life of each Cistercian house became merely equivocal and its real meaning escapes any wider generalization. Since the few available essays dealing with the independent groups and Congregations scarcely would support definite conclusions in regard to the Order as a whole, the following remarks concern primarily those abbeys which remained under the jurisdiction of Cîteaux.

The destructive influence of the Renaissance and Humanism upon monastic life is usually exaggerated. It is certainly true that the number of vocations decreased and the overall emphasis on humanistic studies reacted upon the general spiritual outlook; however, the same era gave birth to the *Devotio Moderna,* witnessed an afterglow of mysticism, and a considerable number of Cistercian foundations, such as the members of the "confraternity" of the Low Countries, exhibited a genuine zeal for monastic perfection. The Reformation and the subsequent religious wars in many cases annihilated the material foundations of community life and the regular discipline, especially east of the Rhine. The vigor of the revitalized Church, however, following the Council of Trent, resulted in a large scale religious reform represented by a number of new orders, while the old ones successfully reorganized their ranks; in this movement the Cistercian Order, under the rule of Cîteaux, fully participated.

Regular life was soon restored in the Congregation of Upper Germany in accordance with medieval traditions. Austria and Bohemia followed suit, and the Papal reform decree of 1666 only stabilized the order already firmly reestablished. Despite contrary presumptions, it is rather surprising how little the monastic schedule had been changed during the crisis of the previous century. Originally, the time for the night office varied according to the seasons; however, the Chapter of 1429 fixed its hour universally for 2 A.M. on week days and 1 A.M. for Sundays and Holydays. In 1601, the schedule was changed so that the day began at 3 A.M. and 2 A.M. respectively. The same arrangement was renewed by the decree of Alexander VII in 1666, and was preserved intact until the French Revolution. As the only modification, the Chapter agreed in 1765 that in the houses with only six monks or less, the office could begin at 4 A.M. Contrary to the numerous attempts at reform before the Reformation, this time the legal prescriptions were obeyed with remarkable accuracy in every abbey having sufficient membership. The other items of the daily schedule also remained largely uniform and unchanged: Prime at 6 A.M., followed by the first Conventual Mass; at 8:30, Terce and Conventual High Mass, concluded by the Sext; at 12 noon the None; at 2:30 P.M. Vespers; at 7 P.M., Compline, after which the community retired in the strictest silence. A considerable part of the Divine Office was always chanted, in greater festivities in its entirety. The time and number of meals varied according to the seasons, while the intervals between liturgical services were used for private religious exercises, for reading or studies. The first mention of recreation emerged among the records of the Chapter of 1601 in the form of short walks or occasional excursions; as a short period for conversation after each meal, it was introduced somewhat later.

The seventeenth century brought about several innovations in spiritual exercises, which, however, after the Council of Trent, became standard requirements in any religious community. Thus formal meditation, already widely practiced, was legally prescribed in 1666 for twice a day, after the Matins and the Compline; meditation after the Compline was sometimes specified as an examination of conscience. As a novelty, an annual retreat for ten days was introduced by the decree of 1666; these retreats were arranged usually before Easter.

Behind the scheme of the well-regulated monastic discipline, the vital power was a reborn Cistercian spirituality, which, while preserving its traditional characteristics, was considerably influenced by prevailing contemporary trends. In France, the Cistercian renewal coincided with a general revival of vigorous asceticism. These tendencies were primarily reflected in the reform of the Strict Observance, but the same zeal permeated the Order as a whole. The most enthusiastic champion of a predominantly penitential life was de Rancé, Abbot of La Trappe, where the example of the Desert Fathers once again became a powerful source of inspiration. The continued trend toward rigorism attained its climax in the movement of Jansenism. Most of the Cistercian communities, however, were left free from the Jansenist exaggerations. Disregarding the well-known role of the convent of Port Royal, only Orval and Alna, both in Belgium, were involved in the famous controversy on the side of the Jansenists. The rather peculiar discipline of Orval, introduced by Bernard de Montgaillard, the "Little Feuillant," found a lively echo in some other monasteries too, established or reformed by Orval.

Baroque

At the same time, in Germany, Austria and Bohemia, the impact of the Jesuit spirituality was overwhelming. During the seventeenth and eighteenth centuries hundreds of the best Cistercian clerics were sent almost exclusively to universities under Jesuit direction and, in many cases, a sincere friendship developed between Cistercian abbeys and the nearby Jesuit college. The continued connections resulted not only in the adaptation of Jesuit doctrines in theology but also in a similarity of moral and ascetic training given to the young Cistercian generations. The fact that at Fürstenfeld, during the eighteenth century, the lengthy textbook of ascetics used for the instruction of novices followed closely the Jesuit pattern was most likely not an isolated phenomenon. The students not sent to Universities were educated for the priesthood in their own abbeys. In these home courses of theology, however, only Cistercians were employed as teachers, because, as the provincial chapter of Bohemia stated in 1652, "it is well known that there are sufficient in number among us who could fruitfully conduct such classes."

Studies and literary activity retained their momentous role in the era of the Baroque; moreover, the General Chapter created an honorary doctor's degree, conferred to distinguished members of the Order, which was actually granted for the first time in 1613. Bertrand Tissier, prior of Bonne-Fontaine, and Charles de Vish (d.1666), prior of Les Dunes, filled volumes with the bibliography of Cistercian authors. However, the evaluation of the Cistercian contribution to the development of contemporary science has never been made so far. In Spain, theology and history stood in the center of interest. In Italy, the Feuillants were active in various fields of Church history and liturgy. In France, a number of erudite debaters participated in disputes concerning problems of theology and spirituality, while a respectable number of German scholars justified the reputation of their large and flourishing abbeys as veritable centers of Christian learning and piety.

The libraries of the wealthier abbeys grew to be enormous collections of valuable manuscripts and printed materials. The library of Les Dunes, in 1798, counted 42,000 volumes, while at the same time the catalogue of Salem listed 90,000 items. Such collections naturally included works on a wide variety of subjects; moreover the Constitution issued by the Chapter of 1783 encouraged the librarians to provide material for physics, mathematics, natural sciences, and especially books on horticulture and forestry.

In spite of a prevalently spotless discipline throughout the Germanies, there is no doubt that the culture of the Baroque found its way into the monastic precincts. This culture preserved always its courtly character and imprinted the marks of a refined elegancy, both physically and morally, upon monastic buildings and gardens as well as upon their inhabitants. Not only the churches, the abbots' residences, libraries and dining halls were built or remodeled in Baroque splendor, but, as far as circumstances allowed, abbots and monks emulated also the manners and hobbies of contemporary aristocracy.

One of the most conspicuous manifestations of this spontaneous tendency was the passionate love of music. There were only a few original composers of wide reputation among the Cistercians, such as the Feuillant Lucretio Quintiani of Cremona, and Johannes Nucius (d.1620), Abbot of Himmelwitz, an accomplished follower of his Dutch contemporaries, especially of Orlando di Lasso; nevertheless, choir and chamber music became the monks' most popular past-time activity. The choir and on some occasions even the orchestra were regularly employed in the church, but the ambitious monk-musicians found ample opportunity to display their talents in frequent monastic festivities. On such occasions—just as at any other aristocratic gathering—the chamber orchestra entertained the convent and the invited guests at the dining table. In some otherwise well disciplined monasteries such customs were established without contradiction; elsewhere, however, they were branded as intolerable abuses. The problem was discussed at the provincial chapter of Bohemia in 1737, where the convened abbots condemned and prohibited the table-music in any form or on any occasion. A spokesman of the anti-musical opposition, the stern master of novices of Salem, Mathias Bisenberger, wrote in 1737 a scholarly study, entitled *De Musica Monachorum,* a document of extraordinary interest concerning the subject. In describing the universal enthusiasm for music, he certainly exaggerated; nevertheless, one bitter remark is worth quoting: "At the reception of candidates for the novitiate, he is questioned first and above all about nothing else but music. There is no allusion or inquiry regarding his education, moral qualities or studies; only, or at least principally, one question is asked: whether he knows music."

In imitation of their aristocratic neighbors each abbey took pride in fine pieces of art, paintings, sculptures, collections of historical or scientific interest of any kind. In some instances, they established well-equipped physical laboratories or even astronomic observatories. A Benedictine visitor, three years before its secularization, described Raitenhaslach as a true home of arts and sciences. An art-gallery included 150 fine paintings of famous masters; they had a richly equipped laboratory for physical experimentation, various botanical and zoological collections, and an excellent library, especially well developed in the natural sciences. Meanwhile, the guest was greatly impressed by the exemplary discipline of the abbey with a personnel of 43 monks.

At first sight, this strange blend of Cistercian monastic traditions and Baroque mentality may seem grotesque or even contradictory. However, just as the Baroque taste had no objection to the remodeling of Gothic churches in the new style, the rearrangement of the whole monastic environment also was accepted with the same natural ease and understanding. How simplicity and magnificence, poverty and wealth, discipline and relaxation could be combined in incomparable harmony, was ably described by Bartholomy Sedlak, secretary of the Abbot of Heinrichau, when, in 1768, on the way back from the General Chapter, he stopped at Salem, the great center of the German Congregation. Father Bartholomy, himself a member of a rich and flourishing community, had every reason to approach the abbey with prejudice and jealousy. Yet his report truly reflects his admiration of everything he saw and experienced. The Abbot of Salem, a highly educated and munificent patron of the arts and sciences, holding a prominent position in the government of the state, was honored with the title of "Excellency." Upon their arrival they were led to the dining hall, where they marveled at both the splendid service and the virtuous vocal and instrumental music played for their entertainment. Touring the magnificent building, they admired the treasury of the sacristy, especially a huge monstrance valued at 60,000 florins, the 14 bells of the tower, and the unique collection of the library, whose librarian was well-versed in seven languages. They admired the precise perfection of Gregorian chant and services, the pageantry of a solemn high mass with military parade; but they were impressed even more by the edifying recollection and discipline of the monks. "There," Father Bartholomy wrote, "while I observed such an exact regular discipline, I got the impression with consolation in my heart, that I was seeing Clairvaux at the time of our Father St. Bernard. There are seventy monks in the cloister, yet, though we passed through the corridors several times, we did not meet a single monk. This did not happen by chance, because they are engrossed in their studies and the habit of solitude is ingrained in their very nature. Although the monastery is wealthy, regarding the monks we noticed a great poverty. The material of their habit is cheap, they do not wear linen but only woolen under-garments. In monastic discipline they follow to the letter the reform constitution of Alexander."

The influence of the Enlightenment within the Cistercian monasteries was short-lived as well as superficial and affected only individuals. In this regard the famous Bavarian Kaisheim furnished a characteristic example. There, during the 1770's the young generation of clerics was greatly impressed by their outstanding professor, Ulrich Mayr, a graduate of the University of Ingolstadt and an enthusiastic disciple of "enlightened" philosophy. "I am glad to be a monk," he wrote to a friend, "because I believe that his profession is to serve the ideals of Christian philosophy. He is a man living in silent solitude, far from domestic duties, surrounded by learned friends, and yet always a virtuous philanthropist; oh, how much could he contribute to the general blissfulness!" He welcomed the abolition of the Society of Jesus as well as Emperor Joseph's measures against contemplative communities, while he did his best in order to conform his monastery to "enlightened" standards. However, the opposition of the majority grew steadily and in 1785 he left Kaisheim for a country parish in utter dismay. The conservative reaction against the Enlightenment was equally strong among Cistercians throughout Bavaria; in enlightened circles at Würzburg they were known as "the white Jesuits."

The French Revolution and the subsequent wave of Secularization brought to an abrupt end hundreds of Cistercian establishments while the surviving few faced their own crucial problems in perfect isolation. Each of them tried to consolidate its shaken existence in its own way and the reestablishment of a central administration two generations later found the Order divided on basic matters of vocation, customs and spirituality. The work of reorganization was slow, sometimes discouragingly difficult, but not entirely fruitless.

14. Liturgy

The divergence between Cistercian reform and Cluniac customs nowhere became so conspicuous as in the matter of the liturgy and Cîteaux's sharp criticism was nowhere more justified than in that field of contemporary monastic life.

As a consequence of the reform of St. Benedict of Aniane, who abandoned the manual labor and exalted the *Opus Dei* as the only worthy occupation for monks, the proportion of the monastic *horarium* spent at choir increased steadily until, by the middle of the eleventh century, it consumed almost entirely the daily schedule of the monasteries under Cluny's rule. As a preparation before the main parts of the canonical office, the monks said the *Trina Oratio* which consisted of three groups of psalms: for the living, for the deceased, and for special intention. The altars of the church were visited in procession while litanies and various other prayers were recited; the office itself was increased with various selections of additional psalms, such as the 15 Gradual Psalms, the Seven Penitential Psalms, and the first and last 30 psalms of the Psalter. Besides the canonical office, other offices filled out the time between the hours. The most popular among them was the Office of the Dead; others included the offices in honor of the Holy Cross, the Holy Trinity, the Holy Ghost, the Incarnation, the Holy Angels and later the Office of the Blessed Virgin. To the customary conventual Mass another official Mass, the *Missa Matutinalis* was added and the long processions, with stations and litanies, preceding the solemn high Mass became almost a daily routine.

With all these accretions the recitation of the Prime took almost as much time as the whole canonical office. The night office before greater feasts was begun on the preceding evening, since it was impossible to complete it otherwise until daybreak. While, according to the original arrangement of the Rule of St. Benedict, the monks were supposed to recite the 150 psalms of the whole Psalter during a week's term, now, in the Cluniac liturgy, the community said daily about 210 psalms. Some monasteries went so far as to pledge themselves to the *Laus Perennis* so that the monks and choir boys were divided into three shifts, to permit the various liturgical duties to be carried on incessantly.

Naturally, such exaggerations resulted in a general *taedium prolixitatis,*—weariness caused by immoderately protracted services. A growing dissatisfaction was spreading even within the Cluniac Congregation, while outsiders freely expressed their skepticism concerning the value of such devotional practices. The Cistercian author of the *Exordium Magnum* used unusually harsh wording when explaining the necessity of the return to the purity of the Rule in matters of liturgy, "cutting away entirely and rejecting all appendices of psalms, orations and litanies which were added (to the Office) arbitrarily by less considerate fathers."

Cistercian Simplicity

Although the founding fathers of Cîteaux took over their first liturgical books from Molesme, they were very anxious indeed to return to the original scheme of the Rule concerning the celebration of the Divine Office; all the more, because the only basis of their survival, the hard manual labor in the fields, never would fit into the Cluniac *horarium.* Except for a short Office of the Dead, they simply omitted all accretions added to the canonical office during the past two centuries and in the recitation of the remaining canonical hours followed precisely the directions of the Rule which distributed the 150 psalms equally among the days of a week. There are indications that even the Office of the Dead did not belong originally to Cîteaux's liturgy; perhaps it was added only around the middle of the twelfth century.

This radical reform immediately aroused the indignant protests of the contemporary monastic world, well-characterized by a letter of Abelard written to St. Bernard between 1132-36. In the list of the "scandalous" innovations, the first was the omission of the everywhere accepted hymns, replaced by "unknown and unusual" ones, which were chanted invariably all year around, disregarding the special demands of feasts and liturgical seasons. We know from other sources that those "unheard" hymns were adopted from the ancient Ambrosian liturgy of Milan, due to the reference of the Rule to them. Further items of Abelard's charges were the omission of various orations and commemorations of Saints, including the Blessed Virgin; the drastic reduction of processions (only those of Candlemas and Palm Sunday being retained), the omission of the recitation of the Apostles' Creed before the canonical hours, while only the Creed of St. Athanasius was said, and even that only on Sundays. However, in the eyes of contemporary critics, the most repulsive feature of Cistercian liturgical reform was the celebration of Lent, in which Cîteaux, wholly ignoring the traditions, continued the recitation of the Office without any change until Easter. Thus they did not cease to sing the *Alleluja* after Septuagesima, they ended the psalms even during Holy Week with the Gloria and continued to chant the same hymns as usual.

A copy of the earliest Cistercian Breviary from the times of St. Stephen Harding, recovered in Berlin during the Second World War, not only verifies the above list of distinctive characteristics but also contains the first authentic Cistercian calendar, another important proof of Cîteaux's conspicuous antiquarian tendencies. Although there were numerous commemorations of Saints, the number of feasts with a proper office was surprisingly low, totaling 57. Just as in the Rule, there is no trace of any ranking among them; all were celebrated according to the fashion of Sundays, with twelve lessons. The largest group of feasts was represented by the office of the Apostles; there were only four feasts of the Blessed Virgin (Purification, Annunciation, Assumption, Nativity) and the list of the remaining 26 Saints bears a definite Roman character with a slight Gallic sway.

During the course of the twelfth century feasts were ranked according to the manner in which they were observed. Thus, some of the feasts (originally about 20) were celebrated with two official Masses, which were later called "Feasts of Two Masses" (*Festum Duarum Missarum*). On the greatest festivities the abbot delivered a sermon in the chapter hall, consequently these became distinguished as "Feasts of Sermon" (*Festum Sermonis*), while the remaining simple feasts were known as "Feasts of Twelve Lections" (*Festum Duodecim Lectionum*). The time and liturgical basis of the further division of the first two groups into "Major" and "Minor" is uncertain; the establishment of the "Feast of Three Lessons" (*Festum Trium Lectionum*) followed much later.

The fact that the first Cistercians drastically reduced the length of the Divine Office and that even the remaining services were made to conform to the general pattern of an austere simplicity does not mean that the founding fathers of Cîteaux overlooked or belittled the importance of the liturgy in monastic life. On the contrary, the painstaking efforts of St. Stephen Harding and his collaborators to restore the liturgy to its original purity notwithstanding the certainly foreseen conservative criticism, gave ample evidence of their deep appreciation of its internal value. Their zeal for the perfection of liturgy went even further. In pursuance of faultless liturgical texts Stephen Harding, still as Prior of Cîteaux, undertook the critical correction of the whole Bible. His endeavor was not entirely unprecedented but the surprisingly advanced method applied in restoring the original text of the Vulgate was unequaled in his century. It consisted not only in the careful conjecture of a large number of rather discrepant Latin manuscripts, but, concerning the Old Testament, St. Stephen consulted renowned Jewish experts of the Bible in comparing the most difficult passages with the Hebrew original. After having been elected abbot in 1109, he published the wonderfully illuminated four volumes of his Bible "composed with much labor" as an official pattern for further copies and strictly prohibited any alterations in its text.

Gregorian Chant

The learned Abbot's attention was extended also to the musical qualities of the adopted liturgical books. Since it was generally believed that the liturgy of Metz still preserved the original melodies of the times of St. Gregory the Great, monks were sent there and they returned with a carefully copied Antiphonary. This and all other revised liturgical books of Cîteaux were declared by the *Charter of Charity* as official exemplars and the newly founded monasteries were obliged to copy and to preserve them intact so that perfect uniformity could be maintained in every detail of liturgy and customs.

However, St. Stephen's liturgical reform was not to live for a long time in its full integrity. No sooner had the great abbot passed away when the second Cistercian generation, under the leadership of St. Bernard, hastily reviewed the whole bequest of the founding fathers, applying inexorably the principles of simplicity and perfect detachment from the world in those fields of monastic life which had escaped their predecessors' attention. Thus, dissatisfied with the Antiphonary of Metz, the Chapter of 1134 appointed a committee under the presidency of St. Bernard himself in order to expurgate the liturgical chant used in the Order from all its alleged defects and superfluities. The Abbot of Clairvaux, having been engaged in other and more important affairs of the universal Church, the bulk of the revision was carried out by Abbot Guy, previously a monk of Longpont. Not discerning the evidence of authentic manuscripts, their procedure consisted in the application of recently developed and purely theoretical principles to St. Stephen's Antiphonary, such as the modal unity of melodies, the prohibition of exceeding the *ambitus* of a tenth, perfect separation of authentic and plagal tones, the possible elimination of the B flat and the omission of repetitions of text as well as melody by simplification and shortening exuberant phrases, especially in the *Allelujas.*

To the great disappointment of these fervent young theoreticians, their overzealous reformatory activity was considerably restricted, due to the vigorous protest of the still influential members of the older generation; consequently the new and revised Antiphonary, completed around 1148 and presented to the General Chapter for formal approval, was but a compromise which still preserved the characteristic features of the earliest Cistercian Gregorian chant. Most of the points of the above mentioned reformatory program represented a common tendency among contemporary Gregorian scholars; but the last item featuring a conspicuous predilection for brevity and simplicity in the melodies, was certainly a Cistercian speciality, advocated by St. Bernard himself.

The Cistercian Gregorian chant remained unchanged in this reformed state until the middle of the seventeenth century although—legally or illegally—the new-fashioned polyphony soon found its way into the Cistercian churches. As early as 1217, the General Chapter ordered an investigation against Tintern and Dore "in which abbeys, as it was rumored, the monks sing in the manner of seculars, in tripartite or quardripartite voices." Protests and renewed prohibitions proved to be vain efforts. The movement continued to spread and finally, in 1486, the Chapter acceded to the use of the organ. During the seventeenth century even the use of instrumental music was quite popular, at least in the larger abbeys for greater solemnities.

The Renaissance and Baroque which fostered the new style in Church music, reinterpreted the traditional liturgical chant itself according to the taste of the triumphant polyphony, with little understanding for the real nature of Gregorian plainsong. The fruit of the movement was the so-called "Medicean" edition of liturgical books published in Rome in 1614-15, with its mutilated melodies representing a drastic breach in the continuity of Gregorian traditions. The same style found its way unavoidably into the Cistercian liturgy, and the new Missal and Breviary published subsequent to the liturgical reform advocated by Claude Vaussin, Abbot of Cîteaux (1645-1670), exhibited the same alterations and mutilations of melodies as its model, the "Medicean." It was more than 200 years before the Gregorian, restored to its original beauty, largely through the efforts of the Benedictines of Solesmes, regained its worthy place in the liturgical life of the Church. The recent movement toward a general liturgical renewal inspired the Order to undertake the restoration of the Cistercian Gregorian to its twelfth century character. This work, based upon the achievements of the Benedictine researches, was carried out by the members of the Strict Observance and its result, the new and revised Gradual, was published in 1899, followed by the Antiphonary in 1903. The Common Observance also adopted the new editions and since that time both observances have used identical liturgical books.

The Mass

Since the Rule contained no hints concerning the celebration of the Mass, Benedictines everywhere followed the rite of the diocese in which they were established. The Cistercians, too, made use of the general custom and the early Cistercian Mass rite corresponded to that of the province of Lyons, modified by the usages of Molesme, which, on the other hand, were based upon the Ritual of Cluny. The liturgy of Lyons was a variation of the so-called Gallico-Roman rite, developed following the reforms of Charlemagne, when the ancient Gallic liturgy became conformed to the Roman rite although retaining a number of distinctive Gallic elements. The rather liberal procedure in the formation of a new liturgy was not a Cistercian privilege; similar principles were followed by the Carthusians and Premonstratensians, and later by the Dominicans and Carmelites. As a matter of fact, strict uniformity in rite, previous to the Council of Trent, was never enforced and in France almost every diocese practiced a variation of the generally ruling Gallico-Roman rite.

The contribution of Cîteaux to the liturgical development of the twelfth century was largely a negative one, namely the consistent application of the principles of poverty and simplicity in sharp opposition to the Cluniac exuberance. With the exception of a wooden crucifix, any superfluous decoration of the sanctuary or of the altar was strictly prohibited, the use of precious metals in making the sacred vessels and other necessary equipment was eliminated, the vestments were made only of linen or wool without any variety in color or quality. The number of official Masses was reduced to one which was sung after the Terce. On greater feasts, later clarified as "Feasts of Two Masses," a low Mass was added following the Prime. On week days the conventual high Mass was celebrated with only one server, possibly a deacon. A daily Mass for the deceased members of the Order and also for their relatives and benefactors belonged to the earliest Cistercian customs, but otherwise the daily celebration of private Masses was neither commended nor prohibited. Frequent private Masses during the Middle Ages were far from being universal; however, in Cistercian houses, an appropriate time between the canonical hours was always reserved for that purpose.

The medieval Cistercian Mass, corresponding to the Gallico-Roman rite, in comparison with the present Roman liturgy, exhibited a number of interesting peculiarities. Thus, at the foot of the altar, instead of the psalm *Judica,* the *Pater Noster* was recited; the *Gloria* and *Creed* were intoned at the Epistle side; the celebrant was not supposed to recite the text of those parts sung by the choir; in the Offertory rite the fact that the server was a deacon involved significant differences; at the *Lavabo,* all servers washed their hands; the *Secret* was recited at the Gospel side but the *Preface* was sung at the center; the Elevation after the Consecration was not prescribed until 1232; the singing of the *O Salutaris* following the Elevation was introduced in 1574; after the *Pater Noster* the Mass was interrupted by a series of prayers, called *Suffrages for Peace;* the large host was broken into three equal parts and one of them was reserved for the assistants; the Communion was distributed under both species, until 1437, and the second ablution of the chalice was taken by the servers; during the ceremonies, for both the celebrant and assistants, instead of genuflection, a deep bow was prescribed. Many of the feasts had more than one proper text in the Missal; on the other hand, for the days without a proper Mass, a variety of Votive Masses were at the choice of the celebrant for each day of the week.

Vanishing Traditions

The stern simplicity of the early Cistercian liturgy was another feature of the Order, which, during the course of the following centuries, gave way to the gradual development of a more elaborate rite and ultimately lost almost entirely its original characteristics. This development was effectively forwarded by powerful historical factors, e.g., the growing reputation and influence of the Order, the accumulation of Papal favors and privileges, the pontifical character of the abbatial office, the change in monastic occupation, especially the discontinuation of agricultural labor, and, most of all, the ever increasing influence of the Roman liturgy. The General Chapter was just as conservative in ritual changes as in any other field of the changing monastic customs; its resistance slowed down somewhat the precipitate onward movement but it could not halt the development altogether.

The most conspicuous phenomenon of the above mentioned tendency was the gradual increase of the number of feasts and their elevation in rank in the Cistercian calendar. By the seventeenth century, the number of "Feasts of Sermon" was doubled; the number of the "Feasts of Two Masses" increased from 20 to 32 during the period 1173-1259 and rose to 41 by 1300. The latter date coincided with the climax of Scholasticism when the original daily schedule of Cîteaux had already undergone a number of changes, replacing manual labor by studies. Without these precedents the increase of liturgical services never could be arranged because previously the monks' intensive work in the fields made both regular studies and prolonged services impossible. Thus the gradual departure of the Order from its initial simplicity in liturgy can be regarded as an indirect result of Scholasticism. Meanwhile the General Chapter played a delaying role against the popular trend which became most conspicuous in the belated introduction of the feasts of Cistercian Saints. The feast of St. Bernard was celebrated for the first time in 1174, the year of his canonization, and that of St. Robert in 1222, but St. Stephen Harding's feast was not introduced until 1623, while the feast of St. Alberic was established even later, in 1738.

Some of those accretions to the daily Office which were formerly so sharply criticized also found their way back into the Cistercian *horarium*. Thus the Office of the Blessed Virgin was prescribed for those traveling or staying in the granges in 1157; in 1185 it became compulsory in the infirmary, and at the choir preceding the canonical hours, although most likely it was said in many places much earlier. Another example of the general tendency toward liturgical amplifications was the return of the procession held before the conventual Mass. During the lifetime of St. Bernard such a procession was introduced on the feast of the Ascension; in 1223, it was introduced on the feast day of the Assumption. In 1441 there were already processions on every "Feast of Sermon" and at the same time processions were begun in France on Sundays, a procedure which soon became imitated everywhere. Eventually, during the seventeenth century, processions were seldom missing from the daily schedule of liturgical duties.

The rules of simplicity in vestments, vessels and other equipment became increasingly lax. In 1226, silk vestments were allowed if received as donations and in 1256, the permission was further extended. Some years later the use of cope for abbots and dalmatic and tunic for deacons and sub-deacons was permitted, formerly all forbidden liturgical garments. During the fifteenth century, the splendor-loving spirit of the Renaissance thoroughly permeated the monasteries while the classical simplicity of the early twelfth century Cîteaux sank into oblivion.

Facing the danger of the vanishing traditions, the maintenance of liturgical uniformity throughout the Order became one of the most difficult tasks of the General Chapter. The problem was kept well in evidence during the fourteenth and fifteenth centuries but the very fact that the same regulations had been many times repeated also proved their inefficiency. However, the technical difficulties of uniformity were largely solved by the extensive use of the newly discovered process of printing. The General Chapter soon realized the importance of the revolutionary technics and, by the Chapter's commitment, as early as 1484, the first printed Cistercian Breviary was published in Basel under the care of Nicholas Salicetus, Abbot of Baumgarten (Alsace), followed by the first printing of the Cistercian Missal in 1487 in Strasbourg, with the cooperation of the same Abbot Nicholas. Further printings of the most important liturgical books at various places (Paris, Lyons, Venice, etc.) appeared in rapid succession, so that at this time the question of authenticity and proper authorization caused considerable confusion; eventually in 1504 the General Chapter prohibited the printing and publishing of any liturgical books without the Chapter's special approval.

The Influence of Roman Liturgy

The program of the universal renewal of the Church inaugurated by the Council of Trent (1545-1563) included also a large scale liturgical reform, completed under Pope Pius V (1566-1572). The new Roman Breviary (1568) and the Missal (1570) were published with the explicit purpose of promoting complete uniformity of the liturgy throughout the world; moreover, the use of the same books was imposed upon all religious orders having a proper liturgy of less than 200 years. The different rites of the older religious bodies were approved; however, the Pope extended to them the general invitation to abandon their ancient liturgy in favor of the Roman. Although in this manner the integrity of the ancient Cistercian liturgy seemed to be secured, the moral pressure and the natural appeal of the masterly revised and purified Roman liturgy rendered complete preservation of the particular rite of the Order highly problematic. As a matter of fact, with some few exceptions, all other exempt orders readily adopted the reform and even those which, referring to their legal rights, refused to abandon their traditional rites, adjusted their own liturgical texts according to the principles of the Roman reform.

The movement within the Order in behalf of the Roman rite was especially strong among the independent Congregations. The general attitude toward the problem was characteristically expressed by no lesser authority than St. Francis de Sales, who in 1622 presiding at the General Chapter of the Feuillants, openly urged the embracing of the reformed Roman Breviary, charging that in the old Cistercian texts the "offensive, childish and obscure" parts were incompatible with the dignity of the Church. Indeed, it was no surprise when after years of deliberation, the General Chapter convened at Cîteaux in 1618, voted in behalf of the Roman Missal and at the same time decided on the revision of the Breviary. Because of well-founded practical reasons the resolution concerning the Mass met little opposition since the change was largely restricted to the Ordinary of the Missal and the Cistercian calendar was maintained together with many features of the ancient liturgy. Thus the well known Sequences of the Roman Missal (*Victimae Paschali, Veni Sancte, Lauda Sion, Dies Irae*) were further omitted from the Cistercian; on vigils and ember days there are fewer Prophecies in the Cistercian Mass and the liturgy of the Holy Week also shows many different characteristics with an emphasis on simplicity. The Congregations of Castile and Portugal having been separated from Cîteaux long before the liturgical reform, maintained the original Cistercian Mass rite until their dissolution in the 1830's; however, the surviving Spanish Cistercian convents preserved some peculiar elements of the ancient liturgy up to the present.

Due to the internal disturbances caused by the rise of the Strict Observance, the revision of the Breviary could not be accomplished until the regime of Claude Vaussin. Unlike the case of the Missal, there were no solid reasons to abandon the ancient rite of the Divine Office; on the contrary, Abbot Vaussin's reform was but a sincere endeavor to approach the original arrangement of St. Benedict's Rule. Since the greatly increased number of feasts (when the psalms of the Nocturns were taken invariably from the "Common of Saints") made impossible the recitation of the full Psalter during a week's term—the basic requirement of the Rule—the reform created a new type of feast, that of the "Feasts of Three Lessons" (*Festum Trium Lectionum*). On these occasions only the lections of the Nocturns were proper, the psalms were said according to the unbroken weekly order, an arrangement already adopted by the reformed Breviary of Pope Pius V. Now, a number of feasts, formerly of higher rank, were reduced to "Three Lessons" while a group of new feasts was established in the same rank without, however, disturbing the order of the ferial psalms. A considerable number of feasts and commemorations were simply suppressed, whereas three new votive offices of "Three Lections" were introduced: one for every free Saturday in honor of the Blessed Virgin; the office of St. Bernard on Tuesday, and another for Thursday in honor of the Blessed Sacrament. The biblical texts of the whole Breviary were amended according to the new edition of the Vulgate by Pope Sixtus V, and, satisfying the popular demand, the office of the last three days of the Holy Week was taken over in its entirety from the Roman Breviary.

The new revised Cistercian Breviary was published in 1656, under the authority of Abbot General Vaussin, amidst the vigorous protest of those in favor of the Roman Breviary. The malcontents found a powerful ally in the person of John Bona, then the General of the Feuillants, later Cardinal, who already had imposed upon his congregation the use of the Roman Breviary, which had been adopted even sooner by the Congregations of Lombardy and Tuscany and of Castile. The highly respected and influential Bona succeeded in obtaining a decree from the Congregation of Rites, which in 1661 abrogated Vaussin's reform and prescribed for the whole Order the use of the so-called *Breviarium Romano-Monasticum,* published by Pope Paul V, for the Benedictines. Nevertheless, the decree was never put into practice, because the pressure exerted by the Order was heavy enough for the reversal of the Congregation's decision. Eventually, Vaussin's Breviary became implicitly approved in 1666 by the famous *In Suprema* of Alexander VII, which secured the unopposed use of the Cistercian Breviary for the next two centuries.

A further contribution to the final formation of the Cistercian liturgy was the first printed publication of the Cistercian

Ritual in 1668, a collection of detailed regulations and various usages concerning the monastic life outside of the Mass and Divine Office. In comparison with the Roman Ritual, slight differences in the administration of Sacraments found their explanation in the fact that all these functions were performed within a monastic community. A revised edition of the same Ritual during the regime of John Petit, in 1689, was accepted as the standard guide for all liturgical functions throughout the Order, save the Feuillants and the Congregation of Castile. Abbot General Edmund Perrot, in his effort to conform some important items of Cistercian ceremonies to the Roman Ritual, issued in 1721 under his jurisdiction a newly revised edition of the Ritual, which was in general use until 1892, when the abbey of Lérins reprinted the 1689 text, adding in foot-notes the variations of the 1721 edition, leaving the decision to the free choice of each community.

The question of the rightful use of the Cistercian Breviary appeared once again rather unexpectedly during the 1860's. At that time the community of Bornhem (Belgium), in favor of the Romano-Monasticum, renewed Cardinal Bona's charges against the Cistercian Breviary, emphasizing the fact that Vaussin's reform was never formally approved by Rome, and that the Cistercian Breviary never kept pace with the liturgical development of the Church, ignoring popular and universally celebrated feasts, and failed in securing a proper place for the commemoration of recently canonized Saints. The dispute was referred to the Congregation of Rites, which, under the vigorous influence of the Trappists, upheld the legality of Vaussin's reform and in 1869 formally approved the Cistercian Breviary in its traditional form. However, in satisfying just demands, the same decree arranged the introduction of 40 new feasts universally celebrated in the Church; 9 among them in the rank of "Two Masses," 2 as "Twelve Lessons," and the rest of them as feasts of "Three Lessons," or as simple commemorations. This revision was solemnly sanctioned by Pope Pius IX in 1871, whose Brief has been reprinted ever since on the first page of every Cistercian Breviary.

In spite of the separation of the two observances, the liturgical books for both Orders remained identical, printed and published since 1854 under the exemplary care of the Trappists of Westmalle, in Belgium.

15. Art

The eleventh century Western World by its impressive development clearly manifested the arrival of a new civilization. Its roots may be traced to classical Antiquity or Oriental sources, but the thought behind the borrowed patterns was definitely unique and proper. The skill in self-expression soon achieved such spontaneous ease and perfection that the art of the era outgrew the period of childish imitations and developed the first great medieval style, the Romanesque.

Cluny, with its extensive network of affiliated houses, where a magnificently elaborated liturgy occupied the center of monastic life, naturally became the most zealous promoter of the new type of church architecture, for the purpose of creating worthy surroundings for the all important and almost continuous services. Another powerful factor in the development of the new style was the increasing popularity of pilgrimages. The monasteries having possession of relics of widely venerated saints, attracted, year after year, thousands of devout pilgrims; consequently the original churches, built to serve the needs of a small community, must have been remodeled or replaced by spacious structures to accommodate the crowds on festival occasions. Since the amount of donations and pious foundations grew in proportion to the number of visitors, no little effort was exerted for lavish decorations of shrines and churches with the obvious intention of attracting and delighting the pilgrims. A certain competitive spirit swept over the French monasteries and from the middle of the eleventh century the modest reliquaries were changed for splendid shrines made of precious

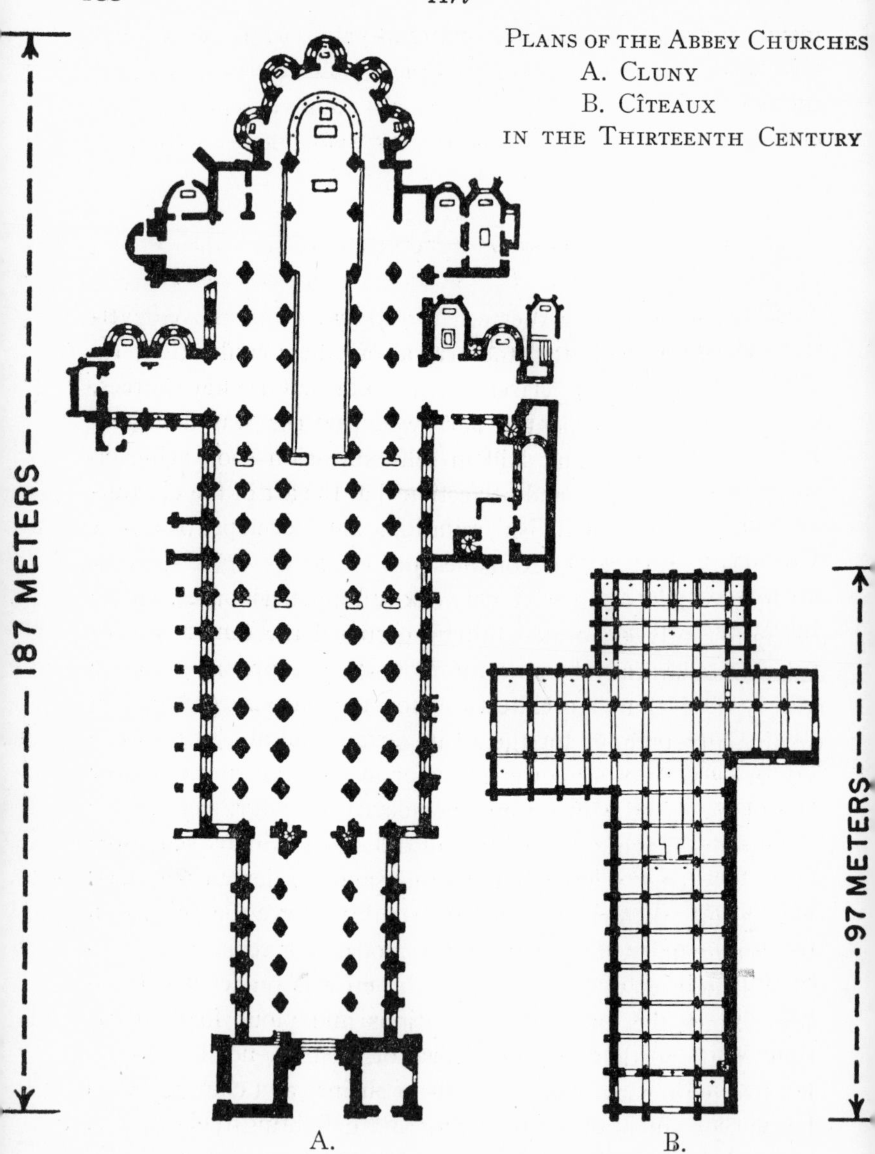
PLANS OF THE ABBEY CHURCHES
A. CLUNY
B. CÎTEAUX
IN THE THIRTEENTH CENTURY
187 METERS
97 METERS
A.
B.

PLAN 1

metals and stones of fabulous material value, while every available space in the huge church edifice, walls, portals, columns, capitals, even the floor, became richly adorned with the most elaborate carved or painted figures and symbolic decoration.

Cîteaux

The admirable memorials of the exuberant decorative spirit of French Romanesque art, such as the monastic churches of Vézelay, Moissac, Charlieu or Saint-Gilles, may still excite the unbounded esteem of modern scholars, yet they found little appreciation among the early Cistercians. The uncompromising spirit of poverty, simplicity and seclusion, which dared to reject the liturgical pomposity of Cluniac traditions, detested also the manifestation of the same inspiration in gold, silver and stone. Indeed, nothing was farther from the mind of the founders of Cîteaux, in love with eremitical solitude and silence, than the crowds of pilgrims; moreover, they instinctively despised the lucrative tendencies behind the ostentatious display of eye-catching splendor and beauty. Even if there had been at Cîteaux any temptation to imitate their wealthy Benedictine neighbors, the extreme poverty and hardships of the first two decades certainly must have taught them to be satisfied with a primitive setting with the bare necessities of life. (Cf. Plan 1.)

Of the earliest buildings of Cîteaux nothing remained; however, there is no doubt that both church and monastery were built in the same spirit of stern simplicity, which, according to the testimony of the *Exordium Parvum,* regulated the quality of liturgical vestments, furnishings and equipment. Nevertheless, during the regime of St. Stephen Harding, these regulations were only practical consequences of the Cistercian ideal of poverty and, where material value was not involved, as in the Gregorian chant or in the selection of liturgical hymns, the great Abbot's genius exhibited a deep understanding of good taste and beauty. Just how far removed from the mentality of St. Alberic and St. Stephen was the contempt of art was strikingly demonstrated in the pages of the first Cistercian manuscripts, which were exceptionally rich in fine and elaborate initials and miniatures. In this respect, the four volumes of St. Stephen's Bible (Fig. 1), completed in 1109, constitute the richest treasury of contemporary French miniatures. Next to the Bible stood in artistic value a copy of the *Moralia in Job,* finished in the same *scriptorium* in 1111. The skillfully drawn caricature-like figures illustrate the work of monks in different circumstances, such as hewing a tree-trunk, harvesting, gathering grapes and weaving cloth in addition to groups of jongleurs and riding knights in various postures. Other manuscripts completed at Cîteaux up to about 1125 are similarly decorated; around 1125, the young Bernard's rising influence greatly modified the early Cistercian attitude toward learning, literature and art, inexorably applying the principles of poverty and unworldly simplicity to the smallest details of monastic life.

St. Bernard's Principles

The change was inaugurated by one of St. Bernard's earliest treatises, the *Apologia ad Gulielmum,* a brilliant though not unprejudiced debate against Cluny, written between 1123 and 1125. The argument of the essay surpassed by far the importance of a family quarrel, and still belongs to the most quoted and most frequently misinterpreted documents of medieval aesthetics. After rebuking the Clunics because of their intemperance in food and clothing, Bernard sharply criticised the luxury of their buildings, "the vast height of the churches, their immoderate length, their superfluous breadth, the costly polishings, the curious carvings and paintings which attract the worshipper's gaze and hinder his attention"; however, he carefully restricted his criticism to the monastic churches while admitting the significance of art elsewhere for the common people, in order "to excite the devotion of carnal folk. . . . by bodily adornments." Nevertheless, for monks, whose devotion must be fomented through pure contemplation, every external impulse, in St. Bernard's mind, was necessarily more distracting than inspiring.

This evaluation of art was certainly far from the modern theory of "art for art's sake" but it was taught unanimously throughout the entire Middle Ages; moreover, the Church has always insisted that true religious art, instead of entertaining, must promote primarily the people's devotion. What St. Bernard urged was nothing but the consistent application to contemporary monasticism of commonly accepted principles. Furthermore, his rigid conclusion was not entirely unprecedented. St. Augustine, who in many other respects decidedly influenced young Bernard's mental development, had previously treated the problem of church music (*Confessions, Book X*) in a similar fashion. The only excuse St. Augustine found for the liturgical chant was that "by the delight of the ears the weaker minds may rise to the feeling of devotion."

Concerning the widely accepted opinion that St. Bernard was simply blind to the world with its beauty and despised art, the closing paragraph of his *Apology* may convince anybody to the contrary. After an ingenious though sarcastic description of the Cluniac decorative ensemble, he concludes: "In fine, on all sides there appears so rich and so amazing a variety of forms that it is more delightful to read the marbles than the manuscripts, and to spend the whole day in admiring these things, piece by piece, rather than in meditating on the Law Divine." He who wrote these lines certainly felt the charm of art but at the same time had the courage to repudiate it for the sake of divine contemplation.

Under St. Bernard's increasing influence, the principles of his *Apology* became the norms of Cistercian artistic activity and, after St. Stephen's death, the General Chapter freely adopted them in the form of prohibitions at the first sign of any transgression of the rule of a rigid puritanism. Thus the legislation of 1134, after reaffirming the requirements of the *Exordium Parvum* concerning simplicity of liturgical vestments and equipment, prohibited illuminated initials and the use of colors in copying manuscripts, banned the fine bindings of codices decorated with gold or silver, forbade stained glass windows, figurative carvings and murals, both in church and monastery. Sculptured portals were not allowed and the Chapter of 1157 prohibited even the coloring of the simple portals or church doors. The same Chapter condemned the towers built of stone; only a modest wooden bell tower was allowed and this could accommodate no more than two bells of small size. In 1218, decorative pavements were forbidden and the Chapter of 1240 ordered the removal of all pictures attached to the altars. These and a number of other prohibitions of a similar nature ultimately restricted the activity of Cistercian masons so greatly that their constructions during the twelfth and thirteenth centuries exhibited everywhere the same pattern of ascetic simplicity, the main characteristic of Cistercian art. Thus the Cistercians, although directly having no ambition to develop a peculiar style of their own, through the strict application of their spiritual ideals in art and especially in architecture created a style characteristically Cistercian, while other religious orders never achieved the formation of a school of art equal to it in conspicuous and uniform features.

The Monastic Plant

The earliest monastic buildings had all been of wood; however, as soon as funds permitted, they were gradually rebuilt in stone. The first accommodations of wooden structure were erected by the founders or by the monks themselves, but the permanent buildings were the work of skilled masons with the assistance of lay-brothers. The builders of Cîteaux and its first daughter-houses simply copied the plainest possible forms of the current Burgundian style, which, although still basically Romanesque, displayed some elements of the early Gothic, such as the pointed arches; consequently, the style which was

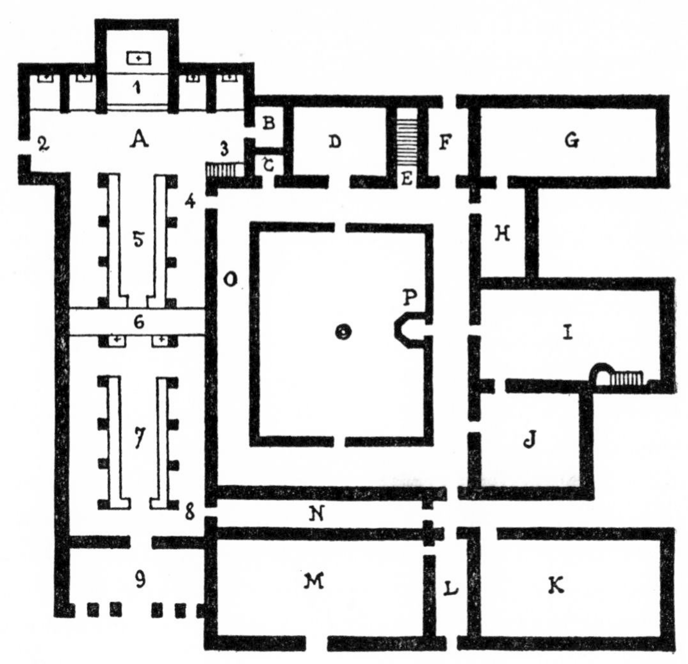

PLAN OF A CISTERCIAN ABBEY

A. Church
  1. Presbytery
  2. Door to the Cemetery
  3. Stairway to the Dorter
  4. Door of the Monks
  5. Choir of the Monks
  6. Rood-Screen
  7. Choir of the Lay Brothers
  8. Door of the Lay Brothers
  9. Vestibule
B. Sacristy
C. *Armarium* (Library)
D. Chapter-House
E. Stairway to the Dorter of Monks
F. Parlor
G. Community Room (*Sriptorium*)
H. Warming-House
I. Refectory
J. Kitchen
K. Refectory of the Lay Brothers
L. Passage
M. Storage Room
N. Corridor of the Lay Brothers
O. Cloister Gallery
P. Washing Fountain

PLAN 2

adopted and propagated by the Cistercians was called by many art historians the "transitional" style.

For the church, the traditional cruciform Benedictine plan was retained and only the rectangular apse represented a Cistercian characteristic (Cf. Plan 2). There were a nave and two aisles, regularly of east-west direction, introduced by a porch and crossed by the transept which was flanked with chapels of square or rectangular plan formed by party walls and used for private Masses. The choir of the monks began in the transept and extended toward the nave. Further west there were some stalls for the sick and disabled, while the rest of the nave was occupied by lay-brothers. Since Cistercian churches were unaccessible to the public, there was no space reserved for them. In the sanctuary there was only the high altar with other necessary equipment for solemn high Masses. Instead of the usual chevet with radiating chapels encircling the sanctuary—a familiar arrangement in both Romanesque and Gothic churches—in most of the Cistercian churches the rectangular apse was surrounded by angular chapels. The walls inside and outside were left bare; even the application of the highly decorative flying buttresses was rare. Only the traditional rose windows broke the monotony of the flat end walls of the façade, apse or transept, though they were usually small and of the simplest design. Since figured sculpture was not admitted, the only explicitly decorative element of the interior was found in the columns which ended in a formal capital with a wide plain leaf at each corner.

Although Cistercian churches, in a deliberate protest against Cluniac splendor, were lacking almost completely in ornamental elements, the effect of their purely architectural features became all the more impressive. The fine lines of the wide pointed arches, the quiet harmony of the cross vaults with powerfully emphasized ribs, the elegancy of piers and the beauty of proportion in every detail of the noble structure were distinctive characteristics of the early Cistercian architecture. These features in such purity are not found even in the most lavishly decorated Cluniac churches.

The usual site of the cloister was between the south wall of the church and the transept, the latter prolonged by a sacristy, chapter hall and scriptorium. Turning west along the cloister, there was a smaller warming room, the spacious dining hall set with its narrow end to the gallery of the cloister, and the kitchen. The remaining section of the cloister, closing the square toward the southern wall of the church, included the dining room for lay-brothers and different storerooms. On the second floor above the chapter hall the monks' dormitory was located, connected directly with the church by means of a stairway. The dormitory of the lay-brothers was above the storage room and their own dining room. Across the door from the refectory, the pavilion of the washing-fountain was usually located, a wide flat basin with many tubular openings (Fig. 2). The infirmary, the novitiate and the guest-house together with the workshops, mill and other buildings for gardening and farming were built somewhat apart from the monastery. In the early Cistercian monasteries, there was no library in the proper sense of the word, because of the scarcity of books; those few volumes absolutely necessary for liturgical services and spiritual reading were stored in a small chamber adjoining the sacristy, called *armarium.*

The largest and most beautiful rooms in the Cistercian monasteries were always the chapter-house (Fig. 3) and the dining hall. Although the rigid rules of simplicity were strictly applied in their interiors too, the skillful grouping of columns in one or two rows, the magnificent rib vaults of various design gave them a dignity no ornamentation could supply. The inside wall of the refectory held the balustraded pulpit in a recess with contiguous steps used by the reader during meals (Fig. 4).

Another decorative feature of Cistercian monasteries was the cloister itself. Though much simpler than the same part of Benedictine houses, the gallery, arranged in a quadrangular scheme with its open arcades, always presented a challenge to architects (Fig. 5). The cloister was really the artery of monastic life, connecting the vital parts of the building with one another. It was the place where the monks performed their domestic tasks, spiritual reading or meditation, where they spent their free time and where sometimes conversation was allowed; in a word, it was the monastic living room, filled with air, light and sunshine. The arches of the continuous arcades usually were supported by double columns, applied alternately with massive piers. The capitals were only modestly carved; with the spreading spirit of the Gothic, however, the original design was frequently changed to a more elaborate ornamentation.

The basic elements of Cistercian architecture, sober simplicity combined with good taste and excellent workmanship, were characteristic even of such humble buildings as forges, mills, tanneries and especially granges, where the fine vaulting was just as common as in the monasteries.

The earliest Cistercian establishments in France rarely survived the vicissitudes of centuries; they are with some few exceptions all in ruins or have vanished completely. Among the best preserved monuments, the church of Pontigny (Yonne) the second daughter-house of Cîteaux, can be regarded as the purest sample of twelfth century Cistercian architecture, while the almost intact building of Fontenay (Côte-d'Or) (Fig. 6) now a public monument, may serve as a model of the original Cistercian monastery. Likewise, Senanque (Vaucluse) (Fig. 7) now an abbey of the Common Observance, and Aiguebelle (Drôme), actually populated by the Trappists, have preserved essentially their twelfth century features.

Gothic

Despite the stubborn resistance of the General Chapter, the Cistercian severity of St. Bernard's times was greatly mitigated during the Gothic period. However, as a proof that the decorative instinct of monks could not be suppressed entirely even during the Saint's lifetime, a peculiar technic of stained glass windows is worth mentioning. This technic developed from the middle of the twelfth century in French monasteries and involved using, instead of colors, grayish tones for geometric, later figurative decorations (Grisailles).

As early as the beginning of the thirteenth century the new constructions showed conspicuous deviations from the initial simplicity. The church of Chaalis (Oise), consecrated in 1227, was built with a fine interior, imitating the cathedral of Châlons-sur-Marne. Royaumont (Seine-et-Oise) (Fig. 4) founded through the munificence of King St. Louis, in 1228, and built by his architect, Pierre de Montreuil, was as splendid as any contemporary secular church. This was the church where the King erected magnificent tombs for his ancestors, while a great number of similar monuments of prominent bishops or laymen adorned other Cistercian churches. Meanwhile the popular cult of relics found an increasingly important role in Cistercian churches, too, and the reliquaries and shrines were always richly decorated. At Obazine (Corrèze), the tomb of the founder, St. Etienne, exhibited a skillfully carved series of Cistercian abbots, monks, brothers and nuns in high relief, kneeling or standing before the Madonna, and on the opposite side, similar figures in the same grouping, rising from their tombs.

During the fourteenth century the rigid rules became further relaxed and the Renaissance ignored them almost completely. Not only did the new foundations follow the style of the latest Gothic period with its delicate ornamentations, but the old establishments also were remodeled according to the new demands, a magnificent library usually being added as another sign of the changing times. Such expensive improvements, however, scarcely could be afforded by the growing number of monasteries under the domination of commendatory abbots, where the communities must have been content with the preservation of their ancient plant.

The early monuments of Cistercian architecture outside of France bore similar characteristics to those in the motherland, though they soon adopted and continued to develop national artistic traditions. However, the real significance of the Order in this respect lies in the fact that they were almost everywhere in Europe the pioneers of the highly advanced French architecture, promoting especially the development of Gothic.

Nowhere on the continent did the Cistercians leave such a monumental record in the history of medieval architecture as in England. The first foundations skillfully combined the transitional style with the aboriginal late Norman elements, while during the twelfth century the monks mostly abandoned the well known sternly ascetic features and produced the finest masterpieces of the early English architecture.

The part of the country richest in comparatively well preserved Cistercian buildings is Yorkshire. Bayland, Jervaulx, Kirkstall, Roche and Sawley are all, even in their ruined state, noble witnesses of the toil, skill and taste of the White Monks; but the largest and most significant monuments are undoubtedly Fountains and Rievaulx, both founded in 1132. The exterior of the church of Fountains (Fig. 8) is the most impressive example of the transitional style in true Cistercian spirit of dignified severity. However, the most prominent feature was a superb bell tower, which in its magnificent proportions was certainly contrary to the rule of simplicity. Large parts of the monastery are also plainly discernible. The nave of the church of Rievaulx (Fig. 9) demonstrates the usual plain transitional forms; nevertheless the choir and transept, built about 1230, give the abbey an incomparable elegancy. The capitals are exquisitely molded, the triforium and clerestory singularly graceful, though all these decorative elements were built evidently in defiance of the early traditions. On the other hand, another remarkable ruin, that of Tintern in Wales, built some three decades later, still represents the purest Cistercian Gothic in the spirit of the so-called "geometrical" style, bare of any superfluous decoration. However, even here, the enormous windows on the east and west walls of the church with their elaborate design, hardly would have been approved by St. Bernard.

The final stage of the gradual departure from the principles established by the great Abbot of Clairvaux was set forth in Scotland by the rebuilt Melrose (Fig. 10), founded in 1136 by Rievaulx and completely destroyed by the revengeful English army following the defeat at Bannockburn in 1314. The reconstruction was soon begun through the generous donation of Robert the Bruce and continued until the sixteenth century. The abbey, rebuilt in the "decorated" and "perpendicular" style—the latest development of English Gothic—retained only the foundations of the old plan; in every other respect it was transformed into one of the most splendid memorials of monastic architecture in Great Britain. Though the church lacks the majestic proportions of Rievaulx or Fountains, the masons applied everything they knew in decorating pier sections, arch moldings, clerestory windows, tracery and vault shafts. Even now, after the vicissitudes of four centuries, it is still a matchless display of the finest decorative sculpture.

The dissolution of religious orders by Henry VIII also brought the death sentence for countless monastic buildings of inestimable artistic value. None of the Cistercian churches or monasteries survived the era of destruction without considerable damage; most of them were demolished entirely, although since the public has discovered the romantic beauty of the still remaining ruins, they are being well preserved under the care of private owners or by the Office of Works.

The first Irish Cistercian house, Mellifont, founded in 1142, was the fruit of the intimate friendship between St. Bernard and St. Malachy, Archbishop of Armagh. By the end of the century the number of monasteries grew to 25, all native foundations. With the fusion of the Congregation of Savigny and some late English foundations, the total number of Irish abbeys mounted to 36. A particularly strong early nationalistic trend soon rendered Clairvaux's control over its affiliations in that country rather questionable; however, the surviving monuments of Irish Cistercian architecture, some 16 more or less well preserved ruins of churches, exhibit a strong French influence. They cannot be compared in size or artistic beauty to the great English abbeys, but the flat surface decorations, related in design to the earliest Christian art, gives them a conspicuous local Irish character. During the fifteenth century a number of abbeys were partially rebuilt under English influence, with more decoration, elaborate vaulting, and with the addition of a central tower. The existing churches in the best condition are Mellifont, Boyle, Jerpoint, Corcomroe and Monister.

Nowhere was the influence of Cistercian architecture more decisive than in Spain, where the rather backward local Romanesque was enriched by Gothic elements, especially by the new vaulting system, produced for the first time through the efforts of French Cistercian architects. The earliest foundations of Clairvaux simply implanted without much change their Burgundian patterns; but those Spanish houses, founded by Fontfroide and Grandselve, soon developed a Catalan variation of the Gothic of Lanquedoc. The impact of Cistercian innovations was so overwhelming that almost all contemporary secular cathedrals were heavily influenced by them. Moreover, the majestic though ponderous architecture of the Order remained characteristic of Spain throughout the whole period of Gothic, without any effective attempt being made to develop the initial elements into the more advanced forms of the same style accomplished elsewhere in Europe. Walls remained as massive as ever, windows never grew larger and the use of flying buttresses was unfamiliar. The Cistercian monasteries themselves frequently had the appearance of a fortress, and, as a matter of fact, during the stormy centuries of the Moor invasion, that feature was perfectly justified.

The most magnificent monument of Cistercian architecture in Spain is the Royal Monastery of Poblet (Fig. 11) in Catalonia, the "Escurial of Aragon," the burial place of its most liberal protectors, the Kings of Aragon. The whole extensive plant is surrounded by fortified walls and bastions while the buildings themselves, under continuous construction and remodeling until the end of the eighteenth century, may serve as an illustration for the history of architecture from the early transitional style to the Baroque. Although the Order was suppressed in the country in 1835, the monastery is still in excellent condition, so that the recently resumed monastic life could have started anew without much difficulty. About half of the Spanish Cistercian foundations survived in fair condition, among them the very first one, Moreruela (1131) in Castile, Veruela in Aragon, the famous convent of Las Huelgas in Burgos, and a close rival of Poblet, Santas Creus in Catalonia; thus Spain became probably the richest country in well-preserved Cistercian monuments of architecture.

In Portugal, among the numerous establishments of the Order, the leading role was held undoubtedly in every respect by the mighty Alcobaça, some sixty miles north of Lisbon. Construction was begun in 1158, but was not completed until 1223. Its church was the largest in the country (365 feet long) and of unique artistic value. Its ground plan is an exact replica of Clairvaux; however, due to the fact that the side aisles are vaulted practically at the same level as the nave, it represents a rarity among Cistercian churches. The internal decorations were greatly enriched with the tombs of Portuguese royalty (Fig. 12). During the course of centuries Alcobaça was also incessantly remodeled, until the dissolution of 1834 when the monastery was converted into barracks.

In Italy, too, the Gothic was introduced by the Cistercians, although it was always regarded as the style of foreigners; indeed, the first Cistercian churches all faithfully copied the patterns of the early Burgundian school of architecture with heavy, plain structure, thick walls and small windows. Among the few early Cistercian monuments Fossanuova is the best preserved, erected toward 1190 in the likeness of Pontigny with interesting cloister galleries. Casamari, constructed between 1203-1221, shows similar features. Further examples of the Cistercian Gothic are Arabona in the Abruzzi, Castagnola near Ancona, San Galgano near Siena, San Martino al Cimino near Viterbo, and Colomba (Fig. 13) in the diocese of Piacenza. Although Cistercian austerity influenced Franciscan architecture remarkably, the style never became popular; its development stalled and the later monastic buildings of the Order were much more Italian in their features than Cistercian. An interesting example of how an originally simple Cistercian church was successively transformed according to the taste of the Italian Renaissance is Chiaravalle near Milan, founded in 1135. The monastery was destroyed but the church exhibits a Renaissance façade, an impressive octagonal bell tower while the interior decoration in the same style includes the famous stalls, each seat with a magnificent relief representing a scene of the life of St. Bernard, installed in 1645. The majority of Cistercian abbeys in the country fell as sacrifices to the commendatory system during the fifteenth century and most became so poor that they could contribute scarcely anything to the further development of Cistercian art. The present possessions of the Italian congregations, in large proportion, are not original Cistercian foundations.

In Germany, the earliest monuments of Cistercian architecture, such as Eberbach, Thennenbach and Bronnbach, made little impression upon the well advanced aboriginal Romanesque, however, during the flourishing period of Cistercian building activity in that country from 1200 to 1250, the churches of the Order represented the first real Gothic in its entire purity.

The first stage of this development toward a pure Gothic (1210-1220) was reached by Arnsberg (Hessen), Otterberg (Pfalz), Walkenried (Harz), Riddagshausen (Braunschweig) and by the famous church and monastery of Maulbronn (Württemberg) (Fig. 3) which was preserved almost in its original form, as well as by Ebrach in a close relationship to Casamari and Fossanuova, all following the pattern of Pontigny. The ruins of Heisterbach (consecrated in 1227) indicate another step forward, while the fulfillment of Gothic arrived with Marienstatt (Westerwald), begun in 1243, and Altenberg (Fig. 14) near Cologne, the foundations of which were laid in 1255. Their style marked the end of the steady Burgundian traditions in favor of the more advanced Gothic of the Ile de France, and also a departure from the spirit of rigid Cistercian asceticism. Their chevet with a system of radiating chapels and ambulatory, huge, stained glass windows and slender flying buttresses were novelties both in the Order and in Germany; nevertheless, towers were still missing and the cool and reserved simplicity of their interior (Fig. 15) still proved the active force of the original ideals.

The accomplishments of Cistercian Gothic were certainly surpassed by the great German cathedrals of the following centuries; however, the Order's greatest pride in the eastern part of the country, the creation of a Gothic brick structure where stone was scarcely available, remained without rival. The ruins of Lehnin (Brandenburg) and Kolbatz (Pommern) are fair examples of the unusual technics, but the largely intact church of Chorin (Brandenburg) (Fig. 16) with its delicate beauty survived as one of the most outstanding monuments of Cistercian architecture.

The establishments of the Order were the pioneers of Gothic also in Austria, taking even more liberties in the application of purely decorative elements. The first sample of real Gothic arrived in the country with Neuberg in Styria (1327). Similar features appeared in Heiligenkreuz (Figs. 2, 17, 28) and Lilienfeld (Fig. 18) but neither one of them could match the artistic riches and influence of Zwettl (Fig. 19) a treasury of art of almost every style from the twelfth century onwards.

In Belgium, the ruins of the once celebrated Orval belong to the most precious monuments of architecture in the country; however, the original church, consecrated in 1124, had no concern with the Order, since the monastery actually was not taken over by the Cistercians before 1132. Later the abbey was continually enlarged until its destruction in 1637, a consequence of the Thirty Years' War. During the following century the wealthy abbey was magnificently rebuilt in Baroque, but was destroyed again by the French revolutionary troops. The abbey was recently revived by the Trappists.

In Switzerland, the best preserved Cistercian building still exhibiting the original features of the early Gothic is that of Kappel, now a Zwinglian parish church. The church of Hauterive (Fig. 20) bears similar characteristics, though the present monastery is a Baroque structure. Wettingen also underwent a remodeling in similar style, while the monastery of St. Urban is generally regarded as one of the largest and most impressive memorials of Baroque architecture in the country (Fig. 21).

The majority of the Hungarian abbeys were founded directly from France and represented the advanced form of transitional style. The only building which has survived in perfect condition is the church of Apátfalva, a faithful copy of the plain Burgundian patterns, though its interesting polychrome portal shows Italian and its vaulting system German influence. Among the numerous Cistercian ruins only Kerc preserves its distinguishable transitional forms. Kerc, being situated in Transylvania, may be considered the farthest witness of Cistercian culture in south-eastern Europe. In Poland, a number of Cistercian churches conserved their medieval features in fair condition. The largest among them is Mogila, near Krakow. In its plan it is a classical example of Cistercian simplicity; whereas the church of Oliva, near Danzig, shows the well advanced forms of Gothic with an interestingly varied vaulting system. After the dissolution, this church served as the cathedral of the diocese of Danzig.

In Denmark, the remnants of the once rich Soroë are worth mentioning. The church is a simple Romanesque brick structure; even the monastery survived as a college until 1813, when it was destroyed by fire. In Norway, the Gothic was introduced by English Cistercians; unfortunately however, practically nothing remained of their establishments. The oldest monasteries in Sweden were French foundations. Alvastra, the largest and richest among them, was established by Clairvaux in 1143, and its plan shows some similarity to Fontenay. A part of the original transept of Nydala, another daughter-house of Clairvaux, built in the simplest Burgundian transitional style, is used now as a parish church. In Gutvalla, an affiliation of Nydala, only the nave remained, but the church of Varnhem, Alvastra's foundation, faithfully maintained its thirteenth century form and thus became one of the most significant monuments of Swedish transitional architecture. Its plain, massive square pillars supporting the circular arches of the nave exhibit unmistakably the Burgundian influence, and its circular chevet that of the thirteenth century Clairvaux.

Since the Chapter of 1157 prohibited Cistercian lay-brothers and artisans from assisting in the construction of secular buildings, the direct influence of the Order through its own trained architects was only sporadic. However, in those countries where Cistercians represented the only advanced style, their indirect influence, as models and sources of constant artistic inspiration, was considerable for centuries. Even in France, Cistercian influence prevailed until the era of the great cathedrals, especially among the newly founded or reformed religious orders. The Premonstratensians, the order of Grandmont and the Augustinian Canons copied exactly the austere Cistercian pattern in both their legislation and building activities. Through the Knights of the Temple, organized under St. Bernard's auspices, the Cistercian artistic program invaded even the Holy Land. Moreover, when, parallel with the further development of the Gothic, the Cistercians themselves were about to abandon their original simplicity, the Mendicants, lacking any ambition to create a style of their own, imitated the plainest available model of the Cistercians and continued to build their churches in similar fashion until the Renaissance.

The economic crisis of the fourteenth and fifteenth centuries necessarily slowed down the building activity of the Order and the catastrophe of the Reformation, with the subsequent religious wars, prevented the surviving abbeys from adding anything really momentous to their original plant in the new style of the Renaissance. In Italy and in Spain there are some beautiful Renaissance additions to churches and other monastic buildings, such as new façades, portals, altars and other pieces of internal decoration; however, the general poverty of these houses under commendatory abbots rendered large scale construction utterly impossible.

Baroque

From the middle of the seventeenth century until the end of the eighteenth, a period of relative peace and prosperity, the spirit of the victorious Baroque swept over the Continent. Within the Order there began an era of feverish building activity, especially in central Europe. In its prolific productivity it became almost equal to the glorious medieval beginnings. Unfortunately, however, the Baroque, with its diametrically different taste, had no understanding and respect for the monuments of the past and destroyed or substantially remodeled Romanesque or Gothic buildings in order to accommodate them to the changed requirements of the new style. The fate of the thirteenth century church of Zirc may serve as a characteristic example. Following the liberation of Hungary from the Turks, the rich Silesian abbey of Heinrichau revived the deserted Zirc in the first years of the eighteenth century. The once outstanding example of the early Gothic architecture, though damaged, survived in fair condition, so that the first settlers held their services therein. Yet, instead of the obviously easy task of repairing the building, they demolished it entirely and from the same stones erected the new Baroque structure, which, despite its splendor, was certainly far behind the artistic value of the original (Fig. 22)

In France, the fact that the great majority of the houses were under commendatory abbots made in most cases any large scale building activity impossible. Nevertheless, a magnificent plan was drawn up for a new monastery at Cîteaux. The work was begun in 1760, but only a small section was completed before the Revolution. At the same time, a similar endeavor completely refashioned the ancient Clairvaux, together with many other smaller houses throughout France.

The wealthy German abbeys proved to be more successful in carrying out their extensive building program, which resulted in monuments of unique importance in the history of Baroque architecture. In Himmerod, the old church was demolished and between 1735 and 1751 a splendid new Baroque church was erected while the monastery was remodeled even sooner (Fig. 23). Following the conflagration of 1697, Salem was rebuilt in the same brilliant fashion by the architect Franz Beer (Fig. 24). In a strange antithesis to the plain simplicity of the ancient Ebrach, a new monastery was constructed in 1716 by one of the leading geniuses of German Baroque, Balthasar Neumann; in its gorgeous beauty it was unrivaled even among the richest Cistercian Baroque monuments (Fig. 25). The same architect finished in 1728 the church of Schönthal in the diocese of Würzburg and somewhat later, the church of Vierzehnheiligen, a favorite shrine of German pilgrims in the valley of the Main, built under the auspices of the abbey of Langheim (Fig. 26). Fürstenfeld, near Munich, the mighty Waldsassen, Heinrichau and Grüssau (Fig. 27) in Silesia, Königssaal and Sedlitz in Bohemia, Oliva near Danzig, among many other Cistercian abbeys of lesser importance, are all leading representatives of Baroque art.

In Austria, all Cistercian establishments were more or less

substantially remodeled or completely rebuilt during the seventeenth and eighteenth centuries, representing the whole architectural development from the early stages of Baroque to the late Classicism (Figs. 28, 29). In this respect the richest treasury of art is the abbey of Zwettl; its tower and high altar (Fig. 19) are especially admirable masterpieces. Heiligenkreuz preserved many of its medieval characteristics, but the monks were engaged always in new decorative projects requiring the services of famous contemporary artists, like John Giuliani of Venice, the sculptor of the beautiful stalls completed in 1707 (Fig. 30). During the same period, the young Raphael Donner, one of the greatest personalities of Austrian Baroque, spent the years of his apprenticeship in the monastery's workshop. In Hungary, St. Gotthard, a real gem of noble design and virtuous craftmanship, represents the best Cistercian Baroque. Zirc (Fig. 31) rebuilt by Heinrichau, is a large though relatively simple structure with remarkable interior decoration.

It is needless to stress that the spirit of Baroque art, so eagerly adopted by the Order, entirely eliminated the tradition of stern simplicity characteristic of the early Cistercians, and only the financial status of each abbey set a limit to the sumptuous building and decorating activity. Halls, stairways (Fig. 25), dining rooms, and especially the library (Fig. 32) and the suite of the abbot were not far behind royal palaces in rich, glittering ornamentation; they were designed by the same architects who were employed by the highest aristocracy. However, in interior decoration and furnishing, Cistercian lay-brothers rendered an important service; in some instances, such as in Himmerod and in Heinrichau, their humble workshops, under expert leadership, developed into real schools of art.

16. Economy

Western Europe, from the ninth century onwards, developed into a purely rural society, where the condition of individuals and classes was determined by their relation to the land. After the establishment of the new social and political order, the increase of population began a rapid upward movement, while the traditional ways of cultivation made very little progress. Consequently, the middle of the eleventh century exhibited clear signs of a relative overpopulation, followed by an economic crisis and social disturbances. It became obvious that the feudal manorial organization could no longer support the growing masses, even though the gradually developing cities and expanding commerce played increasingly important roles in western economy.

From a purely materialistic point of view, the early Cistercian establishments, regarding the critical state of contemporary economy, scarcely could expect a prosperous beginning. Indeed, the Cistercians did not want too much from the world; they turned their back to the staggering system of feudal administration of monastic property and, in their love of simplicity, poverty and solitude, were content with lands no one else cared for: wild and uncultivated woods, heaths and marshes. As a matter of fact, there was hardly any other choice for them, since all arable lands were already occupied at the time of their appearance. At the beginning they had no far reaching economic plans; they procured the bare necessities of life through the work of their own hands. Undoubtedly, the original Cistercian program was a scheme of purely spiritual renewal and its development to a large scale revolutionary improvement of agrarian economy was only a consequence of the enormous popularity and expansion of the Order during the twelfth century, particularly in connection with the establishment of the Cistercian lay-brotherhood.

Agrarian Economy

The first Cistercian communities buried in the forests or in a marshy valley, such as Cîteaux or Clairvaux, literally starved for years until an increasing membership secured the necessary manpower for the most difficult task of clearance. After the bulk of the toil was accomplished, the fertility of the virgin soil richly rewarded the monks; however, there is no evidence of the use of any revolutionary new equipment or technics. The key to their marvelous success was the organized labor of hundreds of brothers known as *conversi* within the framework of a highly centralized economic administration.

The manorial system divided the large feudal estates into isolated and virtually independent units, where the peasantry, handicapped by servility of status and tenure was left alone to its own primitive devices without any large scale planning or unifying organization, for the lord's interest usually was strictly limited to the collection of revenues. To the contrary, the Cistercians, having the advantage of preparing the land themselves, established their farms all around the abbey in an unbroken unit, and, when their property grew larger, distant lands were exploited from sub-stations, known as granges. Everything they possessed was cultivated by lay-brothers with the assistance of choir monks or, if necessary, by hired labor. No matter how large the surrounding estate developed, there was always only one individual responsible for the whole management, the cellarer. This marvelous simplicity in administration, intelligent planning, strict discipline and the large number of *conversi* enabled the Cistercians to accomplish tasks far beyond the capacity of an ordinary manorial estate, bound by an overcomplicated and inefficient system of mutual rights and duties, where immemorial customs prevailed over economic reasons.

The greatest achievement of the early Cistercian settlers was the reclaiming of wasteland and woodland for cultivation by forest-clearing, drainage or irrigation. "Give these monks," wrote Gerald of Wales in 1188, "a naked moor or a wild wood; then let a few years pass away and you will find not only beautiful churches but dwellings of men built around them." Nevertheless, they never stripped the forests indiscriminately; a considerable part of them was always carefully maintained, where their animals found good pasture even during the hottest summer months; the sites of most of the ancient Cistercian abbeys are still surrounded by standing timber. The abbey of Waldsassen (Germany) practiced planned forest conservation from the twelfth century on, and, from the middle of the fourteenth century, its forestry can be followed documentarily, when, year after year, large shipments of timber were floated down the rivers to Bohemia and Thuringia as a considerable contribution to the abbey's economy.

The work of Cistercians in drainage was not restricted to fresh-water swamps; their activity was extended toward the Low Countries and the German coastland, where the reclaimed land was made fit for tillage or grazing, while the water stored between dams and walls was used for irrigation or milling purposes; the remaining lakes and reservoirs served also as fish ponds. By the end of the thirteenth century the abbey of Les Dunes (founded 1139) had converted some 25,000 acres of the sandy and marshy desert of Flanders' coastland into fertile soil while successively establishing on it 25 granges. Similar activity made famous the abbey of Dünamünde in East Prussia. The most spectacular Cistercian success on the largest scale, however, was the reclamation of the marshy bottom of the Thuringian Basin, the famous "Golden Meadows" (*Goldene Aue*). Until the middle of the twelfth century, this region was a wilderness of morasses. In 1144, Count Christian of Rothenburg donated a portion of this boggy area to the Cistercians of Walkenried, who within a matter of years turned their new property into a flourishing meadow. Learning of their wonderful accomplishment, Emperor Frederick Barbarossa authorized the abbey to extend the work along the whole region of the lower Rieth, where the new settlers, under expert direction, soon achieved similar results. An early example of the opposite activity of providing more water for certain crops in the Po valley was the irrigational canal at Chiaravalle near Milan, completed in 1138.

The grange was a characteristic innovation in Cistercian agriculture substituting for the feudal manor with much higher efficiency. As the territory expanded, the number of these granges increased proportionately. Large sections of the land, usually 500 to 700 acres, were organized into farming units, each developing to the full local advantages for special cultivation and proper types of produce. In the center of the grange, a building accommodated the necessary number of lay-brothers under the supervision of the *Grangiarius* or "master of granges," who kept a close contact with the monastery and its cellarer. The location of the original granges could not have been farther from the abbey than a day's walking distance.

Besides the rational administration of their growing estates, another factor of material success was the immunity of Cistercian property from the payment of the ecclesiastical tithes, the most common form of land taxation. This rare privilege was granted to the Order by Pope Innocent II in 1132, when it found its justification in the enormous financial stress weighing upon the Order as a result of the unexpectedly swift expansion during the lifetime of St. Bernard. Since, in early times, Cistercians themselves were working on lands put under cultivation for the first time, for which tithes had never been paid before, this privilege did not cause any change in the legal revenues of ecclesiastical tithe owners; however, the property of the Order soon began to increase through rich donations of previously taxed lands. Every such new acquisition deeply affected the episcopal incomes and the incredible speed of Cistercian expansion alarmed the bishops everywhere. This famous immunity became the target of bitter attacks; in 1156, Pope Adrian IV restricted the privilege to those lands cultivated for the first time by Cistercians. Eventually, under heavy pressure, Pope Alexander III, in a letter to the General Chapter of 1179, admonished the Order to refrain from acquiring new lands, especially in France and England, and to set a limit to the number of religious and material possessions of each house. As a result, the General Chapters in session between 1180-1206 passed various prohibitions against further accretions of property; moreover, in response to a strong demand of Pope Innocent III, the Chapter of 1214 prohibited new purchases altogether. The much-debated immunity from tithes was regulated by the Fourth Lateran Council (1215), which generally respected the privilege as far as the existing property of the Order was concerned, but subjected further acquisitions to the general rule. Nevertheless, as long as the Order preserved its initial vitality, formal legislation was scarcely able to keep within bounds its sweeping vigor. All these restrictive measures were many times revised and modified until the general economic crisis of the fourteenth century halted the expansion and forced the Order to change entirely the whole system of agrarian administration.

Commerce

The highly efficient Cistercian agriculture necessarily resulted in a certain amount of surplus production, thus promoting a gradual increase in commercial activity. Since the Order from the very beginning refused the acceptance of any ecclesiastical or feudal revenue, commerce presented the only way of obtaining the cash necessary to cover the unavoidable expenses; consequently, the exchange of goods took a far more significant place in Cistercian economy than in any other contemporary religious body. The earliest Cistercian legislation repeatedly regulated selling and buying. Only two brothers or monks were permitted to visit the nearest market-place for a determined time in order to sell their own farm products for a reasonable price and to buy whatever was absolutely necessary for the monastery. To accept goods as payment, with the purpose of selling them again for a higher price, was always strictly prohibited. The rules also opposed any business connection "overseas" i.e., crossing the English Channel. Any product which was not considered necessary for the monastery itself was to be used to support the poor, guests or the hired laborers.

The first and foremost business-like Cistercian enterprise was large scale sheep farming in England, especially in Yorkshire. It was not introduced by them, but the vast, desolate open spaces they possessed were especially appropriate for grazing sheep; furthermore the wool was necessary for their habits and cowls. While the wholesale production of wool remained outside the purview of the small village population, the organization and practically unlimited territory made it possible for the Cistercians to develop it into a great export trade with Italy and the Netherlands; during the time of its greatest expansion, the White Monks were the most considerable producers of wool in England. The larger houses were in direct contact with the agents of the great continental merchants, sometimes contracting their products for years ahead. The ports used chiefly by Cistercian wool exporters were Boston, York and Hull, where a number of Cistercian abbeys possessed houses and other properties. The same cities were also heavily populated by foreign merchants.

From the second half of the twelfth century until the fourteenth, Fountains, Rievaulx and Jervaulx usually led the list of exporters with 50 to 70 sacks of annual output (10-13 tons) which required about 10,000 sheep and secured an annual revenue of £400-500. On the other hand, the growing wealth of the

Cistercian houses became a constant menace for them because of the boundless avarice of the Crown. The exorbitant exactions sometimes meant financial ruin. Thus in 1198, Cistercians contributed more than one third of the total ransom of King Richard I, and continued pressure under King John brought many abbeys to the verge of annihilation. The almost permanent danger of wars and Scottish raids was another factor which made Cistercian prosperity in England anything but permanent. The heavy material burdens forced the abbeys into business activities, otherwise forbidden by the General Chapter. Thus, in some instances, lay-brothers bought up wool and other products in small quantities from the villagers and sold them wholesale to merchants, whereupon the traders of Lincolnshire in 1262 protested against it to the King, charging the Cistercians with unfair competition.

Direct figures on Cistercian sheep farming are not readily available, but the Abbey of Meaux in 1270 owned about 11,000 sheep and the abbot was bargaining at the same time with Italian merchants for 120 sacks of wool (24 tons). In 1318, its flock of sheep was reduced to 5406, but, in addition to them, the abbey possessed 606 cattle and 120 horses, amply proving that the Cistercians were by no means exclusively devoted to sheep farming; as a matter of fact, the profit from the wool trade amounted only to a fraction of the total incomes. During the fourteenth century, as everywhere else, the English economy underwent a number of changes, and the export of wool dropped considerably. Sheep farming, of course, was not restricted to England; on a smaller scale it was well established on the continent, too, e.g. Froidmont had in 1224, 5000 sheep in addition to 255 cows, 450 swine, 250 horses and mules; the same abbey sold in 1230, 7000 fleeces. Clairvaux owned during the thirteenth century, a herd of about 3000 sheep; the Austrian Zwettl in 1311 had 2000 sheep in one single grange.

The production of wine for liturgical purposes and also for the needs of the monastery was necessary everywhere, but it is clearly evident that, where local circumstances allowed Cistercian establishments produced wine in wholesale quantities for market. Thus the Abbey of Rein (Austria, founded 1129), as early as the middle of the twelfth century, operated a retail store in the city of Graz, "To the Gray Cowl," for the purpose of selling their agricultural products, primarily wines. The Bishop of Pécs (Hungary), in 1213, complained to Pope Innocent III that the neighboring Cistercian Abbey of Cikádor was buying many vineyards and while refusing to pay tithes, they produced the wine purely for profit; moreover, they exported it wholesale to other countries.

The cradle of the Order, Burgundy, was one of the best wine districts of France; Spain and Italy also excelled both in quality and quantity of their wines, but the most detailed records concern the flourishing Cistercian viticulture in the Rhineland. Baumgarten, Neuburg, Himmerod, and Heisterbach possessed the finest vineyards, and the Rhine and its tributaries offered the cheapest transportation to the great commercial centers of the country. However, the abbey of Eberbach surpassed them all and its wine cellars were famous throughout the whole continent. Although in that district the Cistercians were not the first wine producers, they were the first to discover the advantages of a terrace-like cultivation on steep hills, which formerly were left untouched. From the middle of the twelfth century, the abbey transported its wines, custom and tax-free, in its own ships, mostly to Cologne on an average of 200 *Fuder* (approx. 53,000 gallons) a year, where it was sold wholesale to local merchants. In 1566, well after the times of the real prosperity of the abbey, its cellars still contained 317 *Fuder* (84,000 gallons) wine. The greatest spectacle of the cellar was the world-famous "Giant Barrel of Eberbach" completed near the end of the fifteenth century. It was 28 feet long, 9 feet high, and had a capacity of 82 *Stück* (approx. 26,000 gallons), yet it was held together by only 14 hoops. The chronicle of the abbey preserved the classical distichs of the poet Vincentius Obsopaeus, comparing the huge cask to the "miracles" of Antiquity:

> Quid vetat Erpachium vas annumerare vetustis
> Miraclis, quo non vastius orbis habet.
> Dixeris hoc recte pelagus vinique paludem
> Nectare, quae Bacchi nocte dieque fluit.*

Wine played an important role almost everywhere in monastic economy. Thus, in 1204, Pforta in Saxony offered as purchase-price for a property 200 *Fuder* wine. The abbey of Walkenried in 1206 built a cellar and a store in the town of Würzburg for the sale of wine.

One of the oldest items of monastic economy, long before the Cistercians, was the pisciculture, which, in view of the dietary laws prohibiting the use of meat, always had a special importance wherever monks lived. Nevertheless, the Cistercians, experts in drainage and reclamation, had an excellent opportunity to develop fishery on an unusually large scale since water was plentiful in reservoirs, canals and behind the dams which stored the water for milling. There was scarcely a monastery without larger or smaller fishponds, and, where the geographical formations allowed, a long chain of connected ponds served for fish breeding on a commercial basis under the direction of an expert monk, the "master of fishes" (*magister piscium*). Such a territory was the Upper Pfalz in Germany with its mildly sloping Fichtel Mountains. There the abbey of Waldsassen (founded in 1133) developed its fish hatcheries from the twelfth century onwards into one of the largest known plants of its kind. Concerning its extension and production, reliable sources are available from the sixteenth century. In 1571, when the monastery already had lost a considerable

* What is there to prevent the cask of Eberbach, than which there is none larger in the world, from being included among the miracles of Antiquity? It may truthfully be said that it is a sea of wine and pool of Bacchus from which nectar flows day and night.

part of its former territory, there were still 159 ponds in operation. The select females were kept in 47 smaller ponds, the yearlings in 30 ponds while the two year olds, which needed more room and food, were maintained in 82 ponds. In the third year, the fish were sold wholesale in the neighboring cities, especially Eger (Bohemia). Here, as almost everywhere else, the main products were carp and in smaller amounts, trout and pike.

In addition to these fields of monastic economy, orchards and vegetable gardens were seldom missing from the vicinity of Cistercian houses, although their products, because of the difficulties of transportation, rarely equaled in commercial value grain, wool or wine. Nevertheless, Cistercian gardening, with its highly advanced methods and improved species, greatly influenced and forwarded horticulture among neighboring populations, especially in the northern and eastern regions of the continent. In 1273, Doberan had a glass-roofed house for purposes of plant experimentation. Fine fruits and rare vegetables were transplanted from France through the channels of the monastic affiliation. Thus, e.g., the apple known in France as "gray rennet" came from Morimond to Camp, and through the latter's numerous German affiliations had spread eastward. In Thuringia, apple-growing and cider-making were profitable activities of monasteries; Georgental and Pforta were especially well-known for their orchards. The latter possessed, besides 27 vineyards, orchards in nine different locations under the care of the "master of orchards." One of the former possessions of the abbey, Borsdorf, is still famous for its apples, originally transplanted from France.

In Norway, the country's largest abbey, Lyse (founded 1146, by Fountains), possessed in the district of Hardanger the finest orchards; this region is still famous for its fruit culture. The same monastery maintained a popular inn in the city of Bergen with the privilege of selling there its agricultural produce. The commercial connections of the abbey reached as far as England, exchanging the goods of the two countries in the monastery's own ships. King John Lackland granted these vessels the unique privilege of tax-free exportation in 1212. In Sweden, according to the testimony of contemporary documents, fishing was one of the most important items of monastic economy, all the more because the climate greatly limited the agricultural production. However, the Abbey of Gutvalla, situated on the island of Gotland, possessed rich lands in Estonia, and established a warehouse with a cellar in Reval. Its busy commercial activity presupposes also the maintenance of a considerable fleet.

Apart from the widely flourishing sheep farming, various other fields of stock farming contributed essentially to the Cistercian agrarian economy. Jervaulx (England) was always famous for breeding horses; the Abbey of Otterberg (Germany) sold 80 wild horses to Prince Louis of Pfalz in 1426. In the thirteenth century Clairvaux possessed 800 swine, apparently for commercial purposes. Milk products were important in the monks' diet and early documents testify to the great efforts made to improve the stock. In the year of St. Bernard's death (1153), lay-brothers were sent from Clairvaux to Italy in order to purchase animals; the brothers returned from the difficult trip across the Alps with 10 magnificent cattle. About a century later, the same abbey possessed a herd of 900 cattle. The Abbey of Kirkstall in England, although never one of the wealthiest, had at the end of the thirteenth century 216 oxen, 160 cows, 152 yearlings and bullocks, and 90 calves, in addition to 4000 sheep. Morimond owned 700 cattle and 2000 swine. Also worthy of mention was the bee-keeping in many houses carried on under the care of a monk, called *apiarius*. Honey during the Middle Ages was far more important than it is in our days, since honey was the principal substitute for sugar.

Industry

Following St. Benedict's Rule, Cistercian monasteries everywhere endeavored to produce all things necessary within the walls of the monastery. Each establishment operated its own workshops, manufacturing clothing and footwear as well as all kinds of household and farming equipment. Although their products rarely reached the outside world, one branch of monastic industry, milling, often grew to be a commercial enterprise, especially in the second period of economic administration, when the estates, because of the scarcity of lay-brothers, were leased wholesale to the peasantry, who became necessarily customers of the mills owned by the abbeys. In some cases, milling developed into the main industry of the monastery, as happened at Zinna (Germany), which in 1480, operated 14 watermills within its vast domain. The abbey of Foigny (Aisne, France) owned the same number of mills in addition to a brewery, a glassworks, a fulling mill, 2 spinning mills, 3 forges and 3 press-sheds. In some locations in Germany milling developed into a monopolistic Cistercian industry. During the thirteenth century Reinfeld and Doberan bought all available mills in their neighborhood, both water and wind-mills. Elsewhere, if they could not control milling directly, they tried to achieve the same results indirectly, through their extensive water-rights, regulating the rivers by dams.

Although the Cistercian economy was basically of agrarian character, as a striking proof of its extremely practical-minded management and admirable flexibility exploiting local possibilities to the utmost, in some countries the monasteries of the Order were also pioneers in mining. Stone mines for building material and lime were operated where circumstances allowed; large scale mining of coal, iron ore, precious metals and especially salt was well developed in Scotland, Germany and Austria. One of the earliest Cistercian settlements in Scotland, the abbey of Newbattle (founded 1140) opened one of the first coal mines of the region. At the beginning they confined their work to the coal on the surface but later followed the seams wherever the level allowed. In the same country extensive coal mines were operated by Culross (founded 1217) in combination with a large export trade. At the neighboring port, some 170 ships were engaged in transporting abroad the monastery's produce. Both abbeys also exported salt. Fountaines, in England, shortly after its foundation, started to work the surrounding ancient lead-mines, established smelting works, and had full mineral rights in their whole district.

The first Cistercian salt mine, opened in 1147 at Aussee (Austria), operated by the abbey of Rein, was also the first significant salt mine in Styria. Northern Germany with its vast salt deposits presented a challenge for all Cistercian houses in those districts. During the twelfth century the salt works of Magdeburg and Marlow were operated largely by the surrounding monasteries; moreover, the salt industry around Luneburg developed into a strictly Cistercian enterprise of the largest dimensions. From the middle of the thirteenth century Doberan and Reinfeld were mostly interested in mining, but as the plant expanded, more and more houses joined the undertaking and eventually, between 1375-1383, no less than 13 abbeys participated in the apparently profitable industry. The monastery of Walkenried possessed mines in the Harz Mountains, while Sedlitz, an affiliation of Waldsassen, undertook the mining of silver at Kuttenberg, near Prague; these mines were fully developed around 1300. Waldsassen itself obtained extensive privileges for mining within its own domain in 1230; however, effective work was not begun until the fifteenth century, when iron ore, gold, silver and copper were the main products.

The growing monastic industry and commerce indirectly promoted also the prosperity of those cities, where its products were sold to local merchants, usually wholesale. Nevertheless, the privileged status of the monasteries regarding tax and custom, frequently aroused the jealousy of the rival cities and skirmishes more than once forced the abbeys to sell their goods elsewhere, or even within the borders of their own territory. Such a typical feud between Waldsassen and the city of Eger led at the beginning of the fourteenth century to the foundation of two new commercial centers on the abbey's land which owed their existence wholly to the flourishing monastic economy. The selling of wine caused a long-lasting fight between Eberbach and Cologne and between Bebenhausen and Ulm. In their respective city each abbey built a cellar and a store and, since their wine was retailed free of taxes, the local merchants charged them with unfair competition. Eventually the monks were ousted from both places.

It is rather difficult to give a correct picture of the wealth of the Order and the extension of its property at the zenith of its rise, since local circumstances varied considerably; while in some countries the original system of Cistercian agrarian economy was already in full decline, elsewhere it was still expanding. Nevertheless, the century which elapsed between 1150-1250 certainly included an era of admirable success almost everywhere, although the last decades of even that period exhibited some signs of the approaching crisis.

The territorial expansion of monastic estates was especially rapid during the twelfth century, though where the original scheme of direct cultivation was retained in full vigor, the number of lay-brother vocations limited the growth. Villers in Brabant (founded 1146) possessed 15 granges at the end of the twelfth century; Himmerod in the Rhineland (founded 1138), in 1184 operated 10 granges; Meaux in England (founded 1151) within the first nineteen years founded 7 granges; Wardon (founded 1136), in the same country, operated 12 granges toward the end of the twelfth century. Accepting Henry Pirenne's estimate of 500-700 acres for a grange, an average Cistercian house in France, England, the Low Countries and in western Germany cultivated approximately 5000 acres of arable land in addition to pastures and forests; in view of the state of medieval agricultural methods, such holdings were certainly necessary for the stable maintenance of the establishment. The abbey of Foigny (France) may serve as a characteristic example; the total extent of the property amounted to 30,000 acres divided among 14 granges, but apparently only less than one third of the whole land was under actual cultivation.

The picture of Cistercian domains east of the Elbe and especially in Spain, differed greatly from that in the West. These monasteries, established during the second half of the twelfth century, never had a sufficient number of brothers for direct cultivation, while the land-lease system adopted by them left the door wide open for practically unlimited expansion since uncultivated land was still available there wholesale. As for size of property, the mighty Silesian abbey of Leubus (founded 1175) led the list with 950,000 *Morgen* (approx. 600,000 acres) and 65 villages, accumulated mostly during the first half of the thirteenth century as donations. Other Cistercian abbeys of the north-eastern German provinces were not too far from these figures; Zinna, near Jüterbog, far from being the largest among them, possessed around the year 1500 some 75,000 acres and 39 villages. Territorial extension of the western houses, even that of the wealthiest ones, was considerably smaller. Thus Morimond, although possessed of vast forests and pastures, maintained only about 4000 acres under actual cultivation. Eberbach had only about 11,000 acres under tillage, though the balance was restored by its precious vineyards in different locations numbering no less than a hundred. Bronnbach, in the diocese of Würzburg, possessed about 10,000 acres altogether; half of the land was forest.

In the face of such rapid territorial expansion and success, it was no wonder that the wealth of the Order became widely envied, and the earliest critics lacking material for comment, accused the Cistercians of avarice. As early as 1188, Gerald of Wales, while paying tribute to the work and discipline of the White Monks, observed their anxiety to acquire more and more land. Around the turn of the century, in the bitter attacks against the English Cistercians in the works of Walter Map, the principal subject was always the shameless and remorseless avarice, a crime frequently depicted in the satirical literature of the following century concerning Cistercians. On the other hand, Gerald of Wales offered as a significant apology for Cistercian avarice their unbound charity. "A good intention," he wrote, "I suppose, is the occasion of this greed of theirs which is denounced throughout the world; it arises from the hospitality which the members of this order, although in themselves the most abstemious of all others, indefatigably exercise, in their unbounded charity to the poor and to strangers. And because they have no revenues, like others, they greedily seek for lands with so much effort, in order that they may provide sufficient for these purposes, and so they strive to get farms and broad pastures with unabated perseverance." And elsewhere: "Their gate is never closed; but at morning, noon and evening, it stands open to all comers, and in their hospitality to strangers they excel all other religious orders."

The Collapse of Traditional Economy

In the thirteenth century, however, there were already cases in increasing number of impoverished monasteries deeply submerged in debts. The General Chapter of 1227 complained that "many houses of the Order in various countries but especially in the Kingdom of France are oppressed by accumulated debts." Strict measures were applied to avoid further deterioration of the financial crisis; however, the efforts could hardly halt the process of economic dissolution. In 1318, the General Chapter stated pessimistically that "the Order is tending toward the very depth of poverty." Not only the smaller and less significant establishments were afflicted by grave financial difficulties but also such prominent abbeys as Villers in Brabant. The house was found hampered with many debts, as early as 1271. In 1329 the capital debt amounted to £3,200 and 1,300 bushels of wheat due yearly to the creditors. The abler abbots still managed to ease the burden from time to time but general collapse seemed inevitable. In 1433, the debt amounted again to more than £12,000. During the fourteenth century, the same sad eventuality became a quite common phenomenon throughout the West in the whole field of monastic economy, without, however, having any direct connection with the moral decline of monasticism. Its origin coincided with the essential changes of the social and economic order of western Europe, and its final outcome corresponded with the new grouping of economic factors, being but one sector of the general evolution.

The fallen state of the peasantry and rural economy, characteristic of the eleventh century, was considerably improved during the following era and reached its climax during the middle of the thirteenth century. Refined methods of agriculture, the cities with their growing markets, better and faster transportation of agricultural products, consolidated the status of the rural population, and consequently raised the value of arable property, promoted the increase of villages by increasing also the proportion of land in the hands of peasant farmers at the expense of the declining feudal domain. The rising standard of living among the rural population was followed by a partial emancipation of the peasantry, and, while the servile tenure and in particular the labor services gradually disappeared, the serfs were transformed into lease-holders with a remarkable degree of personal freedom, paying only a fixed annual rent for the land already held firmly in their own hands. The conditions and terms of these leases were of an infinite variety, but the effect of the evolution was invariably the same: the disruption of the manorial organization of feudal estates. The fate of ecclesiastical property was by no means an exception; bishops and abbots lost direct control over their own lands just as well as secular lords, and were compelled to accept the land-lease system with all its inevitable consequences leading to the ruin of the traditional order and causing a long-lasting financial crisis. The indebtedness of large estates grew rather general and the feudal owners never regained complete control over the land, while the peasantry enjoyed a hitherto unmatched prosperity. In the Rhineland, the value of farms increased seven times; meanwhile the customary rents remained the same with the consequence that the lion's share of the profit enriched the lease-holders and ruined the large abbatial estates.

The Cistercians never adopted the manorial system; on the contrary the key to their success was direct cultivation through lay-brothers. It might be presumed that the crisis sketched above left the Cistercian economy untouched; yet the Order proved to be far more exposed to the social consequences of the changing system than expected. This steady agrarian prosperity, with new and wide possibilities for the rising lower classes together with some other factors of the approaching Renaissance, caused the number of lay-brother vocations to drop at a tremendous rate, and the abbeys found themselves facing the same problems as the remainder of the large estate owners.

The General Chapters, as in all other matters involving sacred traditions, fought vigorously against any change in the original scheme of labor and cultivation. However, the spread of the Order towards the East, where social conditions were greatly different from those of France, soon made some concessions inevitable. Since in the eastern regions the number of lay-brothers always fell short of the minimum requirements, the Chapter of 1208 conceded that "less useful" lands might be leased to secular holders. During the course of the following years, this permission was made more and more flexible and in 1224 it was extended to any property if reasons of expediency demanded. At the end of the century, when the crisis began to spread throughout the West, the shift to the new rental system found scarcely any resistance and became just as general as it was in any other ecclesiastical property. The process can be followed by documentary evidence, as in the case of Eberbach, where it originated at the end of the thirteenth century and during the course of the fourteenth century almost every piece of the property went under the cultivation of leaseholders for longer or shorter terms or even perpetually, with legal precautions as to the conservation and proper use of the land. The rental was rarely money, but more frequently *naturalia,* a determined part of the property's produce. In the fifteenth century, when the whole process had already been concluded, the last traces of the once characteristically Cistercian agrarian economy vanished, and from then on, there was scarcely any conspicuous difference in the administration of monastic property, no matter which order claimed its ownership. Nevertheless, supposing that the Cistercians might have been able to avoid the consequences of the social and economic revolution, they certainly would have fallen victims of the commendatory system, which destroyed not only the lay-brotherhood and material prosperity, but also the religious life itself.

As stated frequently above, the differences between the evolution of West and East were considerable. Since the original system of direct cultivation never flourished in the central and eastern European foundations, these latter establishments felt much less the detrimental effects of the crucial changes than did those of the West. Furthermore, the emancipation of the peasantry was rather restricted in the East; moreover, the nobility soon managed to reverse the process and continued to hold a much firmer grip on their lands than the same class in the West. The commendatory system was also less disastrous in the East than it was in France and Italy; hence, many of the great Cistercian abbeys of Germany and Austria survived even the tempest of the Reformation with remarkable holdings and a sound economy. The official inventories taken up at the time of the secularization revealed that most of the remaining abbeys succeeded in preserving the bulk of their ancient possessions, which were, in some cases, of a fabulous capital value. Thus in 1802, Kaisersheim's holdings amounted to approximately 130 square miles (84,000 acres) with 18 whole and 14 half villages having a total population of 9,537 subjects. The abbey owned altogether 1,629 buildings, had 18 parishes, 14 missions, 8 other benefices, and supported 12 parochial schools.

When, during the past century, some of the suppressed abbeys were revived, besides the bare walls of the monasteries their former property never was recovered, and the material basis of their new life was other than land. However, those houses in Austria and Hungary which continued their existence without the drastic breach of the secularization, possessed until the latest times extensive farms, operated by hired labor. The last remnant of Cistercian farming on a large scale was the 50,000 acre estate of the abbey of Zirc in Hungary. Until its total confiscation, following the Russian occupation of the country in 1945, that property, under a highly efficient management and exemplary cultivation, supported not only the 200 members of the community, but 7 affiliated houses and a score of institutions, among them 5 high schools and 15 parishes, without any financial aid from the state or noticeable contribution of the people; even the schooling in their "Gymnasiums" was practically free, for only nominal tuitions were charged. Such enormous holdings in the background of the small, overpopulated European countries now may seem anachronistic and, one way or another, their partition was certainly impending; but as long as they existed, every acre served the intentions of the late pious donators.

17. Lay-Brotherhood

The institution of lay-brothers as a true religious body under strict monastic discipline in charge of the economic affairs of Cistercian establishments, in its full development, was certainly a distinctive feature of the Order, yet not without remarkable antecedents.

During St. Benedict's time, the majority of monastic personnel consisted of lay people; priests were only occasionally ordained or admitted, insofar as the spiritual and liturgical needs of the abbeys demanded. All the monks took equal parts in the necessary manual labor and if, at the harvest time, the work surpassed their capacity, hired laborers were called. However, from the seventh century onwards, monastic property grew enormously while the monks, already mostly priests and engaged in various missionary and cultural activities, were unable to fulfill the demands of their estates in the matter of manual labor. As a solution, the early medieval monasteries, including Cluny, accepted the system of the developing feudalism and shifted the agricultural duties to the rural population, thus freeing the monks' time and energy exclusively for their increasing liturgical, pastoral, scientific or educational activities.

This settlement, however, deeply involved the monasteries in worldly and merely political affairs; consequently, the reform movements of the eleventh century, in their endeavor for solitude and strict asceticism, though unable to change the basic principles of the established economic system, tried at least to impose upon their lay helpers some sort of monastic discipline. Lay servers were first organized by St. Romuald at Camaldoli after 1012, followed by St. Peter Damian at Fonte Avellana in the middle of the same century; but only St. John Gualbert, the founder of Vallombrosa called them *conversi,* the name given to lay-brothers by the Cistercians. Independently of the Italian movement, the German Reform-Congregation of Hirsau also gave its lay-servants a precise religious status and popularized the idea with such success that all other reformed orders or congregations, started shortly before or after the Cistercians, in one form or another, adopted the institution.

Thus, the Cistercian lay-brotherhood did not represent altogether a revolutionary innovation, although no other order employed them on such a large scale and with such great efficiency. In fact, for the Cistercians, who rejected the traditional manorial system of cultivation together with all sorts of incomes of feudal origin, there was certainly no other choice but to organize a group of lay religious for agricultural work because their settlements were established usually in a deserted wilderness, where no other labor was available and the choir monks themselves were incapable of working alone on their fields and also fulfilling their various liturgical and monastic obligations. Thus, the first document of Cistercian history, the *Exordium Parvum* speaks about the *conversi* as admitted at Cîteaux at the very beginning of the "New Monastery," "because without their help they were unable to observe the commandments of the Rule in its entirety, day and night." The lay-brothers' first regulation, the *Usus Conversorum* was composed by St. Stephen Harding, and was amply implemented later by the annual General Chapters.

Candidates for brotherhood were accepted for a one year novitiate, like choir monks. During that time, they were trained for their future duties and in monastic discipline, memorizing a few prayers, *Pater, Credo, Miserere,* with some short responsories. The use of books or any other particular studies were excluded. After the year of probation, they took perpetual vows and by that they became full-fledged religious, although without active or passive rights in voting for monastic officials; nor could they ever become choir monks or priests. Their habit was also distinct from the choir monks, being made of darker grayish or brown material. As a punishment, they even worked in civilian clothes.

The brothers' simple life was spent at the monastery in different workshops or at domestic duties, but the majority of them were put to work at the granges as farmers and herdsmen. Those living in the monastery had living quarters similar to the choir monks, but they were separated from them, having their own weekly chapters for spiritual guidance and further religious instructions. Except for Sundays and holydays they were not present at the Divine Office, but under the direction of the oldest of the group, they recited a certain number of *Pater Noster*s at the time of the canonical hours wherever they happened to be working. Those living in distant granges returned to the monastery only on Sundays and on greater feasts in order to take a part in the solemn services; otherwise, during the week, they were all by themselves, since the choir monks usually were not permitted to stay outside of the monastery. The reception of Holy Communion was compulsory only seven times a year. Their immediate superior was the cellarer or his subordinate, the *grangiarius,* usually a brother himself. They kept strict silence while working, but the rule of fasting was somewhat milder and they slept longer than the choir monks.

In addition to the daily routine occupations, the work of constructing and repairing buildings was also one of the important tasks of lay-brothers. They went to the market to sell surplus products and to make necessary purchases; they were employed as messengers and accompanied the abbots in official visitations. In some instances, Cistercian lay-brothers were in charge of charity organizations at royal courts as almoners, as at the end of the twelfth century in England. The highest office brothers ever obtained was certainly that of the papal *bullatores,* at Avignon, which seemed to be the privilege of Cistercians during the fourteenth century. The Curia employed them under the supposition that they, being unlettered, would keep secrecy while copying and handling papal documents, since they were unable to understand their contents.

The vast majority of lay-brothers came from the lower classes of contemporary peasantry and were accustomed to heavy work and hard living; however, in early times, there were among them nobles and clerics who, in their deep humility, concealed their status. The number of *conversi* grew even faster than that of the choir monks and until the end of the thirteenth century in the western countries they apparently made up the majority of monastic personnel, whose heroic labor was the key to the phenomenal economic success of the early Cistercian establishments. In the middle of the twelfth century, at Clairvaux, there were 200 choir monks and 300 *conversi;* at Vaucelles the brothers outnumbered the choir monks, 130 to 103; at Pontigny, 300 to 100. At Rievaulx (England), in 1165, there were 140 choir monks and 500 brothers; around the end of the thirteenth century at Villers in Brabant there were 100 monks and 300 *conversi;* at Les Dunes (Flanders), about the same time, 181 monks and 350 brothers; somewhat later at Froidmont near Beauvais, 50 monks and 100 brothers.

Decline

Nevertheless, the fourteenth century witnessed the rapid decline of Cistercian lay-brotherhood both in number and morals and a century later the whole institution, as an economic factor, disappeared completely, causing a dangerous crisis in the whole field of Cistercian agriculture.

For a deeper understanding of both the rapid success and the sudden decline we must consider the epochal changes of medieval society. The western countries of eleventh century

Europe, in view of the backward state of agricultural cultivation, were already overpopulated. The feudal classes were perfectly ignorant and disinterested in the ways of improving the insufficient production, while the poor, neglected and despised peasantry, without any large scale organization or direction, was also unable to change the traditional wasteful methods of a purely extensive cultivation. The growing rural populations made every effort to escape their hopelessly distressed state. They furnished the masses for the first crusades, swarmed into the prosperous cities, willingly joined large groups moving eastward, where land was still cheap and taxes lighter. Finally, thousands of them followed the call of the newly established Cistercians, where work was reasonably regulated and there was perfect security from the ill treatment of secular lords, and where they were free from taxation and manorial duties. On the other hand, on the monastic property their toil was always appreciated and they personally became brethren of a religious community of the highest reputation where the restored self-esteem and human dignity abundantly rewarded them for the sacrifices necessarily connected with the religious life. In addition to these merely natural and utilitarian aspects, the vocation for lay-brotherhood was greatly invigorated by a sincere religious enthusiasm, which deeply penetrated the lower classes of the twelfth century society.

However, the quick numerical growth of the uncultured *conversi* soon created a crucial disciplinary problem, more dangerous than the similar difficulties regarding choir monks, because a large proportion of the brothers, living permanently outside of the monastery, easily escaped the vigilance of their superiors. As a matter of fact, the vast majority of early disciplinary cases handled at the General Chapters concerned the behavior of lay-brothers. The situation became further aggravated, when, during the first half of the thirteenth century, the vocations for brotherhood decreased remarkably due to the vigorous start of the Mendicants, whose urban establishments were more appealing to prospective brother candidates than the Cistercian estates; moreover, a general and steadily increasing prosperity of rural economy resulted in a universal reduction in the number of vocations. Towards the end of the thirteenth century, the old manorial organization began to disintegrate; servile tenure and labor services gradually disappeared; the lords went over to the rental system, while serfs were transformed into prosperous free tenants, who, with improved means of cultivation soon achieved a considerable degree of wealth. Thus, the religious vocation lost its former natural appeal. This prosperity, particularly in France, was not of long duration, but the scarcity in labor caused by the Black Death and the Hundred Years' War increased also the ardent dearth of lay-brother vocations.

Some monasteries tried to acquire the number of needed working personnel by lowering the standards of admission; but such a procedure always met the vigorous opposition of the General Chapter. In some cases, as it was recorded at the Chapter of 1262, the abbots, in order to avoid continuous difficulties disciplining the brothers, confided the granges to the *conversi* with full responsibility, the only obligation being the return of a regular rent. Thus the grange became a purely agricultural unit, the brothers lease-holders, without religious character. In order to prevent a further decline in the already low average of vocations, the Chapter in 1220 ordered a six month period of probation (postulancy) for brothers, preceding the novitiate. There was an attempt made to develop the institution of *familiares*—an old form of intermediate status between hired workmen and lay-brothers—as a substitution for the missing labor. Sometimes called *donati* or *oblati,* they were in most cases devout laymen, who, for their labor, were supported by the abbey. They wore secular clothing, did not take vows, but simply promised obedience to the abbot and were treated as brothers. The General Chapters of the thirteenth century endeavored to transform them into lay-brothers without much success. Their number never became considerable.

Meanwhile, instances of revolt among the *conversi* steadily increased, involving intimidation of monks at abbatial elections, violent seizure of monastic property or even plots against the lives of abbots or other superiors. Simultaneously with these riotous incidents the wholesale apostasy of lay-brothers became a common phenomenon; in some places a shortage of clothing emerged, because the departing brethren left the monastery too well provided with garments. Under the pressure of necessity, the Chapter agreed as early as 1237 that monasteries having no more than eight brothers might hire lay-servants for the kitchen. The permission was soon extended to all fields of monastic labor and, as a result, ended in a complete change in the economic administration. From the beginning of the fourteenth century, the once admirably efficient Cistercian direct cultivation gave way to the new rental system, in which the monastic property came under the care of lease-holders for a regular rent. Thus, from the fifteenth century onwards, the characteristically Cistercian lay-brotherhood ceased to continue its former decisive role in the economic life of the Order; moreover, in some countries, e.g., in England, it vanished almost completely. Meaux, which had, in 1249, 60 monks and 90 lay-brothers, numbered a century later 42 monks and only 7 brothers. In the once overpopulated Rievaulx, by 1380, the number of brothers dropped to 3. Meaux, at the same time, already employed 57 lay-servants; elsewhere, the institution was kept alive but the brothers' activity was reduced to the duties of the monastic household; Froidmont in 1224 still had 100 brothers, but the abbey employed 227 hired servants. In Himmerod, where in 1224 there were 60 monks, and 200 brothers, the figures changed by 1438 to 33 monks and 9 brothers. If their number was not sufficient, their place was taken by lay-servants even within the walls of the monastery, as actually happened rather generally in the great abbeys during the seventeenth and eighteenth centuries. At Clairvaux, where there were 50 brothers in 1667, this number dwindled to 10 by the year 1790. In other houses, under the rule of commendatory abbots, the monks were deprived of the responsible administration of their goods, which made any attempt for a revival of lay-brotherhood impossible.

Since the fate of the Cistercian lay-brotherhood was so closely connected with the state of the contemporary economic and social system, which varied greatly from country to country, the evolution and importance of the institution was far from being uniform. The present sketch roughly covers the development in France, the Rhineland, the Low Countries and England. Elsewhere, lay-brothers were never employed in a decisive number; consequently, those abbeys were much less affected by the institution's general decline.

18. Cistercian Nuns

Unlike the well documented story of Cîteaux's foundation, the beginning of Cistercian convents is shrouded in obscurity. Contemporary sources are silent about the organization of the first nunneries, and late traditions preserved in the works of the seventeenth century Cistercian historians are contradictory.

The pious conjecture that the first convent was Jully, in the diocese of Langres, and was founded by St. Bernard for the women-relatives of his thirty companions, including his own sister, Humbelina, cannot be seriously contended. Jully was and remained always a Benedictine convent affiliated with Molesme and although Humbelina after her conversion did join this community, there is no evidence that either she or St. Bernard ever had any part in the foundation of the first Cistercian nunnery. Nevertheless, it was Jully, whence under the leadership of Elizabeth, daughter of the Count of Chalons, some zealous sisters departed and after establishing themselves at Tart, some eight miles north-east of Cîteaux, began a new life in imitation of the Cistercian example. Such a foundation scarcely could have been established without the knowledge and consent of Abbot St. Stephen, but it is very doubtful that the sisters received any noticeable moral or material assistance from Cîteaux in accomplishing their plans.

The time of the foundation is also ambiguous. The secession from Jully seems to have happened before 1125, yet the year 1132 was traditionally considered as the date of the foundation at Tart. During the first year the nuns faced the same difficulties as Cîteaux, but at Tart not only the hardships of life hampered their success, but also the repulsive attitude of the General Chapter. Any interference in the nuns' affairs was regarded as a dangerous breach in the principles of solitude and contemplation, involving the monks in pastoral duties which, during the course of the twelfth century, were always strongly opposed. The first impulse effectively promoting the divulgation of Cîteaux's ideals among women was the fusion of the Savigniac Congregation to the Cistercians, when not only the monks accepted Cîteaux's institutions but also a considerable number of convents affiliated with that group of monasteries. From the middle of the century, Cistercian nunneries grew with the same amazing rapidity as did the monasteries for men, although the General Chapter persistently ignored the movement and refused to establish any legal connection with them.

The greatest success awaited the Cistercian nuns in Spain, where Tulebras, in Navarre, was probably the first convent founded outside of France. With royal support the number of new settlements increased steadily. The King of Castile himself, Alfonso VIII, founded the famous Las Huelgas at Burgos in 1187, where his daughter, Constance, made her profession. The growing number of nunneries soon necessitated the creation of a central organization and knowing the General Chapter's forbidding attitude, the sisters themselves undertook the initiative. In France, the Abbess of Tart claimed the right of visitation over her affiliations; moreover, for the abbesses of a number of houses annual chapters were held, following the custom of Cîteaux. In Spain, independently from Tart, Las Huelgas exercised similar rights of holding chapters and visitation and in 1191 King Alfonso turned to the General Chapter with the request that it would urge all Spanish nunneries to attend the chapter at Las Huelgas. The Chapter praised the endeavor, declining, however, the issue of such an order, since the nuns were not under the Chapter's jurisdiction. This was the first time that Cîteaux had to act officially with regard to the nuns and the time was not too far off when the government of the Order gave serious consideration to the possibility of establishing a legal connection between the two groups of Cistercians. The annual chapters of both Tart and Las Huelgas united only a relatively small number of abbesses; Tart controlled some 18 convents, Las Huelgas only 13. At the chapters of Tart, the Abbot of Cîteaux or his delegate presided while the Spanish branch gradually loosened its connections with France. These gatherings were never too popular even among the nuns and, when later the General Chapter of Cîteaux took charge of Cistercian nunneries, these conventions lost their importance. The last records of the chapters of Tart are dated from the beginning of the fourteenth century; the similar institution of Las Huelgas lived longer.

In the administration of convents the abbesses enjoyed similar rights and privileges to those of abbots. There are indications that especially in Spain, in some instances, the abbesses claimed even the right to preach and to hear the confessions of the sisters. The existence of such abuses was corroborated by a prohibition of the latter practice passed at the General Chapter of 1228.

The Incorporation of Convents

Neither the exact time nor the motives for the move are known when the Chapter, reversing its former policy, gave assent to the incorporation of convents into the Order. Presumably the official action was preceded by arbitrary measures of individual abbots, who assisted at the foundation of the new nunneries without authorization. In 1213 the procedure had already begun under the auspices of the General Chapter, provided that the incorporated nunneries would be strictly cloistered. The decision was certainly a reluctant one but as in many other cases of evident innovations, there was hardly any alternative. The number of convents surpassed that of the monasteries, their popularity reached its climax, and since they used the same name and same Rule, the safeguard of their high reputation could no longer be a matter of indifference to Cîteaux. Instead of abandoning hundreds of flourishing convents to an uncertain future under the care of other orders or diocesan tutorship, it seemed to be more advisable to furnish the necessary assistance and guidance through the cooperation of neighboring monasteries.

The growing interest taken in the affairs of the nuns was most likely also stimulated by the successful start of the Second Order of the Mendicants, which enjoyed the full support and recognition of the Friars. The relationship between the Cistercians and the first Dominican convent was particularly close. The foundation (1206) was fully supported by the Cistercian Bishop of Toulouse, Fulco, one of the most active and influential prelates of the Order. At the beginning, the first Dominican sisters wore Cistercian habits and followed Cîteaux's institutions and customs; the fact that the group soon developed its own way of living was largely due to the General Chapter's reluctance in incorporating them into the Order.

The changed attitude of the Order evidently resulted in an even faster increase of membership than before. The Chapter of 1218 urged the visitors to set the maximum number of sisters for each convent, since their funds could not support an indefinite number of nuns. The visitation and spiritual care of the convents imposed such a heavy stress upon the abbots that in 1228 more drastic measures became necessary. In order to meet the existing obligations, the Chapter declared that no nunneries would be incorporated in the future, although it did not oppose the foundation of convents following the Cistercian institutions; these, however, could not rely in any respect upon the Order's assistance. Hence, from that time, two kinds of Cistercian convents must be distinguished; those, incorporated into the Order, under the jurisdiction of the General Chapter, and the independent communities, under the survey of the diocesan bishops.

Around the middle of the thirteenth century, according to conservative estimates, the total number of nunneries following Cistercian regulations was not far from 900. In some countries, Cistercian establishments for both sexes were so close to one another that the Chapter of 1218 passed regulations defining that monasteries and convents could not be nearer than six hours' walking distance, while houses of the same sexes must be separated by a distance of ten hours. Not even the number of incorporated convents was strictly closed by 1228; upon Papal intervention scores of new establishments were legally affiliated to the Order, until the Renaissance reduced the number of religious vocations in both sexes.

Through the act of incorporation the convents became full-fledged members of the Cistercian family and participated in its exemption and privileges. They were under the jurisdiction of the General Chapter just as the monasteries of men, and they also were under the direct survey of an appointed abbot, whose role was identical with that of the Father Abbot in a monastery. His duty was the annual visitation of the convent. He was to be consulted in cases of admission or dismissal; he was responsible for the general state of discipline and material administration; he presided at the election of abbesses and, after the ratification of the procedure, his right was the solemn benediction of the newly elected abbess. The internal life of these nunneries, the liturgy and daily schedule, with some slight but necessary differences, corresponded exactly to the life and customs of the monasteries of men. The Divine Office and labor occupied their time, but because of the strict enclosure the work in the fields was replaced by other occupations such as the making of church vestments and other ecclesiastical attire, copying and illuminating manuscripts, but most of all the education of girls. Their churches were always kept strictly closed to the public.

Besides supplying purely moral assistance, the monastery of the Father Abbot supported them with labor and other necessary personnel. In the first period of incorporations, the Order furnished the convents with confessors, chaplains and lay-brothers; however, in 1222, the Chapter petitioned the Holy See not to demand such services in the future, since they could not be continued without grave disadvantages for the Order. Shortly thereafter, to take the place of the missing labor, lay-sisters were admitted into the convents and they adhered to a rule which allowed them more time and freedom for working outside of the cloister.

Concerning spiritual and liturgical guidance, during the thirteenth century, a rather peculiar compromise had been reached. The abbeys in charge of Cistercian convents accepted for the novitiate clerics and priests who were willing to work in nunneries, and who, after having been trained in Cistercian liturgy and spirituality, made their vows at the convent in the presence of the abbess and promised obedience to her. Thus, these priests lived permanently in the service of the sisters' community, wore Cistercian habit, yet strictly speaking were not members of the Order because they did not belong to any monastery of men and their immediate superior was the abbess. This arrangement survived until the canons of the Council of Trent, which basically reformed the monastic life for both sexes. According to the decisions of the Chapter of 1601, elderly members of the Order were put in charge of the nuns' spiritual welfare. Also, the members of the Order or able and reliable laymen were given responsibility for the economic administration of the convent's possessions.

Since direct cultivation never flourished on the farms of Cistercian nuns, their economic accomplishments and role in agricultural development were far behind the great abbeys of men, although some of the convents were endowed with extensive possessions, e.g., the royal foundation of Las Huelgas near Burgos included the territory of 64 townships. Medieval nunneries, however, always took a prominent place in the structure of contemporary society. For widows and unmarried women of the higher classes there was scarcely any other acceptable state of life except the sisterhood; conceivably the majority of conventual personnel consisted of women in whose life the religious vocation was only a second choice. Nevertheless, as long as the vigor of medieval religious ideals remained intact, the mere fact of such an arrangement never impaired the atmosphere of a deep and sincerely devout spirituality. This social background was also responsible for the fact that in a large number of nunneries only members of the nobility were admitted to the rank of choir sisters, while the dignity of abbess in particular was reserved for the highest aristocracy, in some instances for royal princesses. Furthermore, for the girls belonging to the same class, the convent presented for a long time the only possibility of obtaining higher education, and while Cistercian monasteries refused the admission of boys Cistercian nuns always received girls for education. St. Mechtilde entered the Cistercian convent at the age of seven, St. Gertrude at the age of four. The curriculum was basically the same as in monastic or chapter-schools for boys, frequently including a full course of the *Trivium* and *Quadrivium,* since Latin was indispensable for the daily office and spiritual reading. Naturally, the higher grades of the convent-school were usually reserved for the girls who wanted to join the community. The regulations of the Chapter of 1601 explicitly decreed that above the age of twelve only those girls should be educated within the convents who had religious vocation.

The Cistercian convents of the thirteenth and fourteenth century were also the most influential centers of the new spirituality inaugurated by St. Bernard. Some of his congenial followers contributed essentially to the edifice of Christian mysticism and their writings have never ceased to inspire God loving souls ever since. Among many others, the convent of Helfta in Saxony, during the long regime of Abbess Gertrude of Hackeborn (1232-1292), developed into a school of mystics of the foremost importance, although the nunnery belonged to the large number of the non-incorporated ones. The Abbess' sister, St. Mechtilde of Hackeborn and St. Gertrude the Great, the latter living at the same time in the convent as a simple nun, were both illustrious for their revelations. Another great mystic of the era, St. Mechtilde of Magdeburg, also spent the last years of her life at Helfta.

The whole group of nuns belonged to the early promoters of the devotion to the Sacred Heart. Meanwhile, a circle of convents with the same type of spirituality was formed around the abbey of Villers in the Netherlands. Their chief glory was St. Lutgarde of Aywières (d.1246) whose visions of the Lord showing her His pierced Heart constituted the first recorded revelation of the Heart of Jesus. Other distinguished members of the same group were Blessed Ida of Louvain, who received the stigmata, and two others of the same name, both nuns of the convent of La Ramée in Brabant, a renowned center of sanctity and letters. Blessed Aleydis of Schaarbeck, a nun of La Cambre, near Brussels, suffered the martyrdom of leprosy while healing others with the same malady by her simple touch. At that glorious time there were many noble ladies who spent only their last years in the Cistercian convent, yet reached a high degree of perfection, such as Blessed Jeanne, daughter of Baldwin, first Latin Emperor of Constantinople, who ended her days at Marquette near Lille, and St. Hedwig, the patroness of Silesia, maternal aunt of St. Elizabeth of Hungary, who after the death of her husband, Duke Henry of Silesia, finished her life at the convent of Trebnitz, where her daughter was the abbess.

Reforms

The factors which resulted in a decline in materials, morals and personnel in the monasteries for men also affected the convents with similar consequences, although the nunneries remained free from the evil of the commendatory system. As early as 1339, the General Chapter dispensed all Cistercian convents from making contributions for the central administration of the Order, due to their universal financial distress. From the end of the fourteenth century the General Chapters found themselves frequently engaged in disciplinary measures against convents of lax or even scandalous conduct. Luxury in clothing, food and living quarters, and the violation of the enclosure were the most common charges, partly as a result of the practice whereby noble ladies moved into the convents with their maid servants, an example imitated by the sisters themselves. The measures applied against recalcitrant houses were more then once extremely drastic, including forcible unification of communities or dissolution of whole convents, when their property was taken over by a nearby monastery. Nevertheless, not even the severest reprisals could halt the general decline; moreover, in the process of deterioration, the Order of men was not entirely blameless either. The regular visitations of Father Abbots became more and more rare or ceased entirely, the spiritual care of convents was neglected or assumed by priests of other orders, and the example set by the neighboring monasteries was not always an edifying one. The climax of the general dissolution was reached by the Reformation, when the majority of Cistercian convents were secularized and the nuns dispersed. It is worth mentioning that Luther's wife, Catharine of Bora, had formerly been a Cistercian nun.

While the Reformation undermined the moral foundations of monastic life, the religious wars during the course of the subsequent century materially shattered the remaining convents. The nuns were even more helpless than the monks against the plague of enemy invasions; at the rumors of approaching troops they fled into the nearby cities, while their property was ransacked by the undisciplined hordes. The communities in almost continuous danger, especially in the Rhineland and the Low Countries, established themselves permanently in the cities with the full consent of the General Chapter. Under these circumstances most of the convents subsisted in great poverty; when the misery became unbearable, the sisters did not even shrink from begging like the Mendicants, although this practice was always opposed by the Chapter. The only steady sources of income were the educational institutions for girls, maintained by the convents; in some cases, as at Byloque à Gand (Flanders), the nuns also owned hospitals, operated by lay-sisters. However, the expensive building programs of some of the greater houses during the eighteenth century were always carried out by using the personal fortunes of the abbesses or through the support of those wealthy families whose members were living in convents. The membership of the communities during the same period exhibited a declining tendency; vocations were rare, and the convents which managed to survive without decrease in personnel belonged to the fortunate ones.

Efforts for a wholesome reform among the nuns were made simultaneously with similar activities among the men. The General Chapter of 1601 passed detailed legislation for convents, reemphasizing the duties of Father Abbots, chaplains and confessors, regulating the nuns' daily schedule, liturgy and spiritual exercises, the admission of new members, the administration of their goods, enforcing the strict enclosure and excluding lay personnel from the convents. These regulations, however, did not prevent the disintegration of the unity of Cistercian nuns on account of precipitated reformatory activities of individual houses or abbesses. Since such actions never obtained the approval of the General Chapter, the representatives of these movements severed their connection with the Order, abandoned Cistercian liturgy, placed themselves under episcopal jurisdiction and, under extraneous influences, embraced a discipline largely different from Cistercian traditions, most commonly changing the life term of the office of abbesses to a three year term. In most of the cases, the Holy See readily granted its approval for the organization of reform-congregations; hence, the General Chapter was not in a position to check the advancing dissolution.

First among the best known independent congregations of nuns may be mentioned that of the Conceptionists', founded in 1489 in Spain by Blessed Beatrix de Silva, and having a program of special devotion to Mary's Immaculate Conception. The Spanish spiritual renewal during the sixteenth century served as a background for the reform of the Recollects or Discalced Bernardines, whose rule was approved by Pope Paul V in 1606. As a female counterpart of the Feuillants' movement, the group of Feuillantines originated in 1588, under the auspices of Marguerite de Polastron and her daughter Jacqueline, in the convent of Montesquieu, near Toulouse. St. Francis de Sales became the spiritual father of another reform effected by Louise de Ballon, in Savoy, in 1622, known as the Bernardines of the Divine Providence, and closely resembling the Visitation Order. A branch of the same congregation, established at Paris, by Mother Baude, under the auspices of the Strict Observance, called themselves Bernardines of the Precious Blood. Their statutes were approved in 1661 by Jean Jouaud, the Vicar General of the "abstinents." The famed Cistercian nunnery of Port Royal des Champs was reformed by Angélique Arnauld during the early years of the seventeenth century, but under the guidance of Abbé Saint Cyran, the convent became a stronghold of Jansenism, although at that time they were already living under diocesan jurisdiction. In 1709, the house was dissolved by Papal authority; however, its affiliation, Port Royal de Paris, survived until the French Revolution, engaged in the perpetual adoration of the Blessed Sacrament. The Trappist Congregation did not incorporate convents until Dom Augustine de Lestrange gathered together some scattered Cistercian nuns of France in Switzerland, in

1795. From that time on, an increasing number of Cistercian convents accepted the jurisdiction of the Cistercians of the Strict Observance.

The waves of secularization in various countries throughout the nineteenth century closed the doors of many Cistercian convents although the procedure against them was generally more lenient than in the case of monasteries. Thus, in Spain, the anticlerical legislation of the 1830's abolished convents with less than 20 sisters, but the law was never fully enforced, and almost all Cistercian houses for women survived. This explains why Spain has the largest group of Cistercian convents, numbering altogether 62 houses and almost 1500 sisters, though most of them are under diocesan jurisdiction.

The majority of Cistercian nuns in other countries, too, are organized under episcopal authority, but a considerable number of houses have retained their allegiance to the Order under the jurisdiction of the General Chapter. At present, the Cistercians of the Common Observance control 15 convents with a total of 623 members, while 28 convents have placed themselves under the Rule of the Trappists with a membership of 1,548 nuns. The communities belonging to the Common Observance are engaged mostly in the education of girls; those affiliated to the Strict Observance are of a purely contemplative character. Concerning the state of Cistercian convents under diocesan jurisdiction, recent statistics are not available; there are approximately 75 such houses with a membership of nearly 2,000 sisters situated largely in Spain, France, Germany, Italy and Switzerland.

Appendices

APPENDIX I

The *EXORDIUM PARVUM**

A translation by
Robert E. Larkin, M.A.

THE BEGINNING OF THE CISTERCIAN COMMUNITY

Preamble to the Beginning of the Community of Cîteaux

We Cistercians, the original founders of this community, make known to our successors through this present writing by what canonical procedure, under what authority and by which persons as well as what time the community and their manner of living had its beginning. After the publication of this matter which has been written with sincere truthfulness may they love more tenaciously the place as well as the observance of the Holy Rule, which, with God's grace, we ourselves have somehow begun therein; and may they pray for us who have suffered indefatigably the burden and the heat of the day, and may they labor on the straight and narrow way prescribed by the Rule until the exaltation of their souls, so that after the burden of the flesh has been sloughed off, they may happily pause in eternal rest.

* The translation follows the critical edition of the Latin original published in the *Cistercienser-Chronik* (9), 1897.

The Commencement of the Community of Cîteaux

In the year 1098 of the Incarnation of our Lord, Robert of blessed memory, the first Abbot of the community of Molesme, in the diocese of Langres, and certain of the brethren from the same community appeared before the venerable Hugh, then Legate of the Apostolic See and Archbishop of the Church of Lyons. Before him they promised to arrange their life in the observance of the Holy Rule of Father Benedict, and begged therefore fervently that he give them his support as well as the strength of the Apostolic authority for the unhindered realization of this intention. The Legate gladly espoused their wish and laid down the foundations of their beginning with the following letter.

Letter of the Legate Hugh

Hugh, Archbishop of Lyons and Legate of the Apostolic See, to Robert, Abbot of Molesme, and to the brethren who together with him desire to serve God according to the Rule of Saint Benedict. Be it known to all those who rejoice in the advancement of our Holy Mother the Church that you and some of your sons, brethren of the community of Molesme, appeared before us at Lyons and pledged yourselves to follow from now on more strictly and more perfectly the Rule of the Most Holy Benedict, which so far in that monastery you have observed poorly and neglectfully. Since it has been proven that because of many hindering circumstances you could not accomplish your aim in the aforementioned place, we—keeping in view the spiritual welfare of both parties, namely of the departing and of the remaining—consider that it would be expedient for you to retire to another place which the Divine Munificence will point out to you, and there serve the Lord undisturbedly in a more wholesome manner. Therefore, to you who presented yourselves: Abbot Robert, and the brethren Alberic, Odo, John, Stephen, Letald and Peter as well as all others who properly and by unanimous consent have decided to join you, we advise and commend to persevere in this holy endeavor which we, through the impression of our seal corroborate forever by the Apostolic authority.

About the Departure of the Cistercian Monks from Molesme and about their Arrival at Cîteaux as well as about the Monastery which they Commenced

Supported by such an imposing authority, the above named Abbot and his followers returned to Molesme and there they chose from the monastic community as their companions brethren devoted to the Rule, so that those who had spoken before the Legate in Lyons and those who were chosen from the community, amounted to twenty-one monks. Surrounded by such a following they happily started on their way to the hermitage which was named Cîteaux. This area, situated in the diocese of Châlons, was inhabited only by wild animals, since it was a wilderness of dense woods and thorny thickets, impenetrable for humans. Here then came the men of God and the more they discovered it to be despised and unapproachable by worldly men the more they found this place suited for their religious life as they had first intended and for which reason they had come here. After they had cut down the woods and removed the dense thorny thickets, they began to build a monastery there under the approval of the bishop of Châlons and with the permission of the landlord. These men, while still living in Molesme and inspired by divine grace often spoke, complained and lamented among themselves over the transgression of the Rule of St. Benedict the Father of Monks. They realized that they themselves and the other monks had not at all observed it, even though they had promised by solemn vow to follow the Rule. That was the reason, as we mentioned above, why they came into this solitude by the authority of the Legate of the Apostolic See, namely to fulfill their vows through the observation of the holy Rule. Lord Odo, the duke of Burgundy, pleased with their holy fervor, and having been requested in a letter by the aforementioned Legate of the holy Roman Church, completed with his own means the wooden monastery which they had begun, and provided them there abundantly for a long time with every necessity, with land as well as with livestock.

How that Place Rose to an Abbey

At the same time, the Abbot who had come here, upon the command of the above mentioned Legate received from the Bishop of the diocese the shepherd's staff together with the charge of the monks, and made the brethren, who had come with him, to affirm in the proper manner their stability at the same place. Thus that growing monastery, through Apostolic authority, rose canonically to an abbey.

How those from Molesme Annoyed the Pope in the Matter of Abbot Robert's Return

Shortly afterwards, the monks of Molesme with the consent of their Abbot, Lord Godfrey, the successor of Robert, went to Rome to Pope Urban. They began to demand that the often cited Robert be reinstated in his former position. Moved to yield by their importunacy, the Pope ordered the Legate, namely the venerable Hugh, that the same Abbot, if it could be done, should return and the monks who loved the hermitage might stay there in peace.

Letter of the Pope regarding the Return of the Abbot

Urban, Bishop, Servant of the Servants of God, to the venerable brother and fellow-bishop Hugh, Vicar of the Apostolic See, greeting and Apostolic blessing. We have heard in council the great clamor of the brethren of Molesme who vehemently demanded the return of their Abbot. Namely, they have said that the regular life in their monastery has declined and that they have become hated by the princes and other neighbors, because of the absence of that Abbot. Compelled then by our brethren we commend Your Grace through our present script, the indication of our desire, that if it can be done, that Abbot be returned from the hermitage to the monastery. If you can not accomplish this, let it be your concern that those who love the hermitage may live in peace, and those who are in the monastery observe the regular discipline.—After the Legate had read this Apostolic letter, he assembled capable and God-fearing men and decided the matter in question in the following manner.

The Legate's Decision in the Whole Matter concerning the Monks of Molesme and Cîteaux

Hugh, servant of the church of Lyons, to the most beloved brother Robert, Bishop of Langres, greetings. We have considered it necessary to let Your Fraternity have knowledge of what we have decided in the recently held meeting at Portansille regarding the matter of the community of Molesme. There appeared before us monks from Molesme with your letter. They described to us the sad conditions and the ruin of their place which was caused through the removal of the Abbot Robert and begged emphatically that he might be given back to them as father. For, they had no hope that peace and quiet could return to the community of Molesme nor that the full vigor of the monastic discipline could be reinstated in its pristine state in any other way. Brother Godfrey, too, presented himself to us, whom you had placed as Abbot over the same community, stating that he would gladly relinquish his place to Robert as to his father if it should please us to return him to the community of Molesme.—Therefore, after considering your request and that of the monks of Molesme and having reread the letter of the lord Pope addressed to us in this matter, in which he left everything to our disposition and decision, and upon the advice of many pious men, bishops as well as others who were there with us in council, we have finally decided in compliance with your and their wishes, to give Robert back to the community of Molesme. This change should be transacted in such a manner, however, that before his return there, he should come to Châlons and deliver his crosier and the charge of the abbey into the hands of our brother the Bishop of Châlons, to whom, following the tradition of other abbots, he had vowed obedience. The monks of the New Monastery, who before him, as their Abbot, had professed and had promised obedience, he should release and declare free of the profession and obedience. Similarly, he shall then be released by the Bishop of the vows which he had made to him and to the church of Châlons. Also, we have given permission to return with him to Molesme all those brethren of the New Monastery who will follow him when he leaves it, provided that in the future neither side will attempt to convert or receive anyone of them to their side, except in the manner prescribed by Saint Benedict concerning the admission of monks of a known monastery. When he will have done the aforementioned, we shall send him to Your Grace, so that you shall reinstall him as the Abbot of the community of Molesme. However, this will only be done on the condition that if, in the future, he should in his usual fickleness leave the same community, no one during the lifetime of the named Abbot Godfrey shall be put in his place without our and yours, as well as Godfrey's approval. Be it understood that all this was arranged by virtue of the Apostolic authority. With regard to Abbot Robert's chapel and the other things which he took with him upon his departure from Molesme and with which he went to the bishop of Châlons and to the New Monastery, we have ordered that all remain safely with the brethren of the New Monastery. This is with the exception of a certain breviary which, upon the approval of the monks of Molesme, they may keep until the celebration of the feast of Saint John the Baptist, so that it may be copied. At this decision were present the bishops Norigaudus of Autun, Walter of Châlons, Barandus of Mâcon, Pontius of Belley and the abbots

Peter of Tournus, Jarento of Dijon, Jocerandus of Ainay, as well as Peter, chamberlain of the lord Pope, and many other honorable and esteemed men.—The Abbot praised all this and also executed it in releasing the Cistercians from the obedience which they had promised him at that place or in Molesme. Likewise, Bishop Walter of Châlons released the Abbot from the leadership of the said community. And so he returned with a few monks who did not find the hermitage to their liking. In this manner, due to Apostolic ruling, these two abbeys remained in peace and in complete freedom. The returning Abbot, however, brought to his bishop as a shield for his defense the following letter.

Commendation of Abbot Robert

To the most beloved brother and fellow-bishop Rodbert, Bishop of Langres, Walter, servant of the church of Châlons, sends greetings.—Be it known to you that brother Robert whom we had assigned to that abbey which is being called New Monastery, situated in our episcopate, due to the decision of Archbishop Hugh, has been released by us from the vows made to the church of Chalons as well as from the obedience promised us. He himself, too, has released and declared free those monks who have decided to remain in the aforesaid New Monastery, from their obedience they had promised him and from the tie of profession. Have, therefore, no hesitation to accept him and to treat him with honor from now on.—Farewell.

About the Election of Alberic the First Abbot of Cîteaux

Deprived of its shepherd, the community of Cîteaux assembled and through a regular election they elevated a certain brother by the name of Alberic to be their abbot. He was a man of letters, well versed in both divine and human sciences, and a lover of the Rule and the brethren. For a long time he had served as prior in the community of Molesme as well as here, and he had long urged the brethren to move from Molesme to this place, for which endeavors he had had to suffer many insults, prison and beatings.

About the Roman Privilege

After the above mentioned Alberic, although very reluctantly, had taken over the shepherd's position, he began, as a man of admirable wisdom, to weigh what storms of tribulations could shake and disturb the house delivered into his trust. Taking precaution beforehand, and after consulting the brethren, he sent two monks, John and Ilbodus to Rome, petitioning lord Pope Paschal through them that his community might forever remain quiet and safe under the wings of the Apostolic protection from the pressure of any person, ecclesiastical or secular. The two previously named brethren, furnished with sealed letters from Archbishop Hugh, from John and Benedict, Cardinals of the Roman Church, as well as from Bishop Walter of Châlons, safely arrived at Rome and from there back again. This was before Pope Paschal himself failed in the captivity of the Emperor, and the Apostolic privilege which they received from him was composed entirely according to the wishes of the Abbot and his associates. We consider it suitable to hand down in this little work these letters as well as the Roman privilege, so that our successors might realize with what great circumspection and authority their community has been founded.

Letter by the Cardinals John and Benedict

To our lord and father, the Pope Paschal, to whom everywhere distinguished praise is to be given, John and Benedict, remain in deepest devotion.—Since it is your office to care for the needs of all churches and to give a helping hand to the just wishes of the petitioners, and since the Christian religion shall receive its growth through leaning on the support of your justice, we beg Your Holiness, with all our strength, that you might lend merciful hearing to the carriers of this letter who, upon our advice, have been sent by certain religious brethren to Your Paternity. Namely, they ask that the decree which they received from your predecessor, our lord Pope Urban of blessed memory, be perpetuated. This is in regard to the peace and solidity of their monastic life and to those things which in accordance with the same decree the Archbishop of Lyons, then Legate, and other fellow-bishops and abbots had settled among themselves in order that the abbey of Molesme from which they had departed because of the religious life, might remain forever undisturbed through the privilege of your authority. We ourselves know them and vouch for their true religious life.

Letter of Hugh of Lyons

To his most reverend father and lord, Pope Paschal, Hugh, servant of the church of Lyons, in deepest devotion.—The brethren who are delivering the present letter, on their journey to the Highness of Your Paternity, have taken the road through (our town). Since they live in our province, namely in the diocese of Châlons, they asked our unworthy self for a letter of recommendation to Your Highness. You should know, however, that they come from a place which is called New Monastery, where they had settled after they left the community of Molesme with their abbot, in order to live there and to lead a more rigorous and secluded life following the Rule of St. Benedict. In the observance of this Rule they have resolved in abandoning the usages of certain monasteries where the monks maintain that in their weakness they are unfit to bear such a great burden. For that reason the brethren from Molesme and some other monks of the neighborhood do not cease to annoy and disturb them, thinking that in the eyes of the world they are valued less and are looked upon with contempt if the world will take notice what exceptional and new kind of monks are living in their midst. We, therefore, humbly and trustfully ask your fatherly benevolence, so dear to us, that in your usual kindness you welcome these brethren. Next to the Lord, they have placed all their trust in you. Therefore, they seek refuge in your Apostolic authority, so that they and their monastery may be delivered from this annoyance and disturbance and that you might protect them through a privilege of your authority; since the poor of Christ have no defence through riches or power against their enviers, but place their hope on God's and your mercy alone.

Letter of the Bishop of Chalons

To the Honorable Father, Pope Paschal, Walter, Bishop of Châlons, greeting and due subservience. As Your Holiness most ardently desires the advancement of the faithful in the true religion, so must these brethren not miss the shelter of your protection, the encouragement of your consolation. We, therefore, plead urgently that you might deign to corroborate through the privilege of your authority what has been ordered with regard to these brethren. They have longed for a more severe life, and upon the advice of holy men whom the Divine Mercy has placed in our diocese, departed from Molesme. The delegated bearers of this letter from these men stand before you. All has been done in accordance with your predecessor's order, corresponding to the decision and letter of the Archbishop of Lyons, then Legate of the Apostolic See, as well as other bishops and abbots. On this occasion we were present and acted together with others. We plead therefore that you confirm that the place might remain a free abbey forever, under the canonical subjection, however, due our person and our successors. Moreover, the Abbot whom we have installed in that place and the remaining brethren also ask your kindness most insistently for this confirmation to secure their peace.

The Roman Privilege

Paschal, Bishop, Servant of the Servants of God, to the Venerable Alberic, Abbot of the New Monastery, located in the episcopate of Châlons and to all his properly installed successors from this day forward. A petition which is obviously aimed at a religious purpose and the welfare of the souls is to be granted without any delay upon God's demand. Therefore, my sons, most beloved in the Lord, we comply with your petition without the least objection, because we congratulate you with paternal affection on your religious life. We decree, therefore, that the place which you have chosen in order to live in monastic tranquillity, be secure and free from any annoyance by all men and that an abbey may exist there forever and be particularly sheltered through the protection of the Apostolic See, not impairing the canonical reverence to the church of Châlons. By means of this present decree we, therefore, forbid that anyone permit himself to change your way of life or admit monks of your community which is called New Monastery, without the recommendation as demanded by the Rule, nor to disturb your community through any kind of annoyance or violence. Concerning the decision of the controversy between you and the monks of the monastery of Molesme, which has been reached by our brother, the Bishop of Lyons then Vicar of the Apostolic See, together with the bishops of his province and other religious men, by the commitment of our predecessor, Urban II of apostolic memory, we confirm it as a reasonable and laudable one. You must, therefore, remember, sons most beloved and dearest in Christ, that one part of you has left the broad roads of the world, another even the less strict paths of a laxer monastery. Consequently, in order that you may be considered always more and more deserving of this grace, you must strive to keep always in your hearts the fear and love of God, so that the more free you are of the noises and pleasures of the world, the more you aim to please God with all the powers of your mind and soul. Truly, should in the future an archbishop or bishop, an emperor or king, a prince or duke, a count or viscount, a judge or any other clerical or secular person knowingly dare to counteract this our constitution, and upon two or three reprimands not make amends for his mistake through an adequate satisfaction, he shall be deprived of the powers and honor of his dignity and it should be known that he is guilty before the divine judgment because of the committed iniquity and he shall be estranged from the Body and Blood of our God and our Lord Jesus Christ and undergo severe punishment at the Last Judgment. Upon all those, however, who respect the rights of this monastery, rest the peace of our Lord Jesus Christ, in order that already here on earth they may receive the fruit of their good deeds and before the strict Judge may find the award of eternal peace.

The Statutes of the Cistercian Monks who Departed from Molesme

Thereupon the Abbot and his brethren, mindful of their vows, unanimously decided to establish and keep the Rule of Saint Benedict in that place. They rejected what was contrary to the Rule, namely wide cucullas, furs, linen shirts, cowls and breeches, combs and blankets, mattresses, a wide variety of dishes in the refectory as well as fat and everything else which is opposed to the Rule. In thus taking the rectitude of the Rule as the norm of conduct for their whole way of life, they fully complied with its directions in ecclesiastical as well as in other observances and arranged themselves accordingly. In this way discarding the old man they enjoyed putting on the new one. And since they could not find either in the Rule or in the life of Saint Benedict that this teacher ever possessed churches, altars or offerings, burial places or tithes of other people, or bakeries or mills or farmhouses or serfs and that women ever had entered his monastery, nor was buried there anybody with the exception of his sister, they renounced all of that saying, where the holy father Benedict teaches that the monk stay aloof from the doings of the world, there he distinctly explains that those things should not have any place in the actions or in the hearts of the monks who, in fleeing the world, ought to live up to the etymology of their name. They also said that the tithes had been divided into four parts by the holy Fathers, who were the instruments of the Holy Ghost and whose instructions it was a sacrilege to transgress; namely, one part for the bishop, the second for the parish priest, the third for guests who came to the church concerned, or for the widows and orphans or for the poor who had nothing else to live on; the fourth for the maintenance of the church. And since in this distribution they did not find mention of the monk who owns his land for the purpose to live on it through his own work and of his animals, they therefore detested to usurp unjustly the rights of others. And behold, after the new soldiers of Christ, poor themselves as Christ was poor, had denounced the riches of this world, they began to consult with one another, how, with what work or occupation, they should provide in this world for themselves as well as for their arriving guests, rich and poor alike, who after the Rule were to be welcomed as Christ. Since they realized that without their help they would be unable to fulfill perfectly the precepts of the Rule day and night, they decided to admit unlettered men as lay-brothers with the approval of the bishop and to treat them in life and in death as their own, except for the rights reserved for choir monks. For the same reason they resolved to employ hired hands. They also wanted to take on landed properties which lay removed from human dwellings, as well as vineyards and meadows and woods and waters in order to install mills, but only for their own use, and because of the fishing, also to keep horses and cattle and various things that are needed and useful to men. They also decided that when they would have established farmhouses for the practice of agriculture, the said lay-brothers should manage those houses, and not monks, whose residence according the Rule should be within their cloister. Since it was also known to those holy men that Saint Benedict had built the monasteries not in towns or in fortified places or in villages, but in places removed from the traffic of men, they promised to follow the same, and as he installed twelve monks together with a father abbot in each of the newly erected monasteries, so they declared their wish to proceed in the same manner.

About their Sorrow

To the aforementioned man of God, the Abbot and those with him, it caused some sorrow that in those days only seldom did anyone come there in order to become their imitator. Namely, the holy men vehemently desired to hand down to their successors, for the benefit of many souls, this treasure of virtues found in such heavenly manner. Nevertheless, almost all those who saw or heard of the unusual and almost unprecedented rigor of their manner of life, instead of approaching them, tried anxiously to avoid and forget them, doubting always in their perseverance. But the mercy of God who had inspired his own for this kind of spiritual military service, continued to enlarge and complete it for the benefit of many, as the following will show.

About the Death of the First Abbot and the Election of the Second and about their Regulations and their Happiness

The man of God, Alberic, however, after he had practiced fruitfully regular discipline in the school of Christ for nine and a half years, went home to the Lord, glorious in his faith and virtues, therefore deservedly rewarded by God in the eternal life. His successor was a brother by the name of Stephen, an Englishman by nationality, who had also come here with the others from Molesme, a lover of the Rule and the new place. During his time, the brethren and this Abbot prohibited the duke of that country or any other sovereign should keep court at any time in that monastery as they used to do before at big feasts. Furthermore, in order that in the house of God, in which it was their desire to serve God devoutly day and night, nothing would remain that savored pride and superfluity or eventually corrupt poverty, the safeguard of virtues, which they had chosen out of their free will, they resolved not to keep golden or silver crosses but only painted wooden ones; no candelabra, but only one of iron; no thuribles, but only of copper or iron; no chasubles, except of wool or linen, without silk, gold or silver weave; no albs or amices but of linen, similarly without silk, gold or silver. They eliminated entirely the use of all kinds of palliums, copes, dalmatics and tunics. However, they retained siver chalices, not golden, but when it could be done, gold plated, as well as the communion tube of silver, gold plated if possible; stoles and maniples were of silk only, without gold and silver. They also ordered that the altar cloths be made of plain linen and without embroideries and that the cruets should have nothing in gold and silver on them.

In those days the monastery increased in its possessions of land, vineyards, meadows and farmhouses; they did not decrease, however, in monastic discipline. Therefore, God visited that place about this time in pouring out his deepest mercy over those who implored, cried and wept before him day and night, groaning long and deep and had almost come to the rim of despair because they had no successors. God's mercy had sent to that community so many literate clerics as well as laymen who were in the world as powerful as they were distinguished, that thirty all at once happily entered the cells of novices and by bravely combatting their own vices and the temptations of the evil spirits completed their course. Through their example old and young, men of every walk of life and from various parts of the world became encouraged since they saw through them that what they had feared impossible, the observance of the Rule, was possible. So they began to flock together there in order to bow their proud necks under the sweet yoke of Christ, and to love fervently the rigorous and burdensome precepts of the Rule, and they began to make that community wonderfully happy and strong.

About the Abbeys

From then on they established abbeys in the various episcopates, which under God's rich and powerful blessing prospered more from day to day, so that within eight years those who departed from Cîteaux and those who descended from them had altogether founded twelve monasteries.

APPENDIX II

The *CHARTER OF CHARITY**

A translation by
Denis Murphy, S.J.

Preface. Already before Cistercian abbeys had begun to spread Father Stephen and his brethren, with a view to avoid all difficulties between the bishop and the monks, ordained that no abbey should by any means be founded in any diocese before the bishop should approve and confirm the decree passed between the abbey of Cîteaux and its filiations. In this decree the aforesaid brethren, in the intention of obviating rupture of mutual concord explained and ordered and transmitted to those to come after, the bond and manner, or rather the charity whereby their monks divided in the body in abbeys in different parts of the world, should be indissolubly banded together in the spirit. They also considered this decree should be called Charter of Charity because putting aside the burden of any money contribution, it pursued only charity and the utility of souls in things human and divine.

Chap. 1. Because we are all servants, unprofitable indeed, of the one true King, Lord, and Master, therefore we demand no exaction of temporal profit or earthly goods from the abbots and the brethren whom the goodness of God has been

* This translation is reprinted from *Cistercienser-Chronik* (11) 1899. The original *Charter of Charity* composed by St. Stephen Harding, known as *Charta Caritatis Prior,* was repeatedly modified after 1152. This translation represents the text in its final, modified form, the so-called *Charta Caritatis Posterior.* The *italicized* print indicates the most significant additions proper to this final version.

pleased, through our unworthy instrumentality, to bring together in divers places, in the observance of regular discipline. For, desiring only to be of service to them and to the children of Holy Church, we will do nothing toward them that can be either a burden to them or a subtraction of their temporal substance, lest striving to be made wealthy from their poverty, we may incur the guilt of the vice of avarice, which the Apostle terms the "serving of idols." It is, however, our intention, for the sake of charity, to watch with care over their souls; so that if they should at any time decline from their good resolution and the observance of their holy rule, which misfortune may God in his mercy avert, we may be able by our constant solicitude to bring them back to the religious life.

Chap. 2. We wish henceforward and command them to observe the rule of St. Benedict in everything, as it is observed in the New Monastery, and to understand it in no other sense than that which our pious forefathers of Cîteaux have given to it and maintained, and which we ourselves now understand and hold after their example. And because we receive all monks coming from other monasteries into ours, and they in like manner receive ours, it seems proper to us, that all our monasteries should have the same usages in chanting, and the same books for the divine office day and night and the celebration of the holy sacrifice of the Mass, as we have in the New Monastery; that there may be no discord in our daily actions, but that we may all live together in the bond of charity under one rule, and in the practice of the same observances. *Let no monastery or person of our Order dare to ask for any privilege from anyone, or if already obtained, to make use of such privilege which is opposed to the established constitutions of the Order, in whatsoever way it may have been obtained.*

Chap. 3. When the abbot of the New Monastery shall go to any other monastery for the purpose of visitation, the abbot of the monastery so visited shall acknowledge the abbey of

Cîteaux to be the mother-house, and shall yield precedency to its abbot in every part of his monastery; so that the abbot of the New Monastery shall take and hold the place of this abbot as long as he remains in that monastery. However, he shall not eat in the guest apartments, but in the refectory with the community to maintain discipline, unless there should be no proper abbot at that time in the monastery. The same rule shall be observed, when several abbots shall come to any monastery. If the abbot of the monastery at the time be absent, then the one who is oldest in the abbatial dignity shall eat at the stranger's table. The abbot, however, in his own monastery will always, even in the presence of an abbot of superior dignity, profess his own novices at the end of their year of noviceship. Let the abbot of the New Monastery be careful not to touch anything, to ordain anything, or to dispose of anything, with reference to the possessions of the monastery which he visits, without the consent of the abbot and his brethren. If he shall perceive that any of the precepts of the rule or the institutions of the Order are violated in the monastery he is visiting, let him, with the advice and in the presence of the abbot, charitably endeavor to correct the brethren. But if the abbot of the monastery be not present, he shall, nevertheless, correct what he finds amiss.

Chap. 4. The abbot of a mother-house shall visit annually, *either in person or by one of his co-abbots,* all the filiations of his own monastery. And if he should visit the brethren more frequently than this, let it be to them a subject of joy. *The four abbots of La Ferté, Pontigny, Clairvaux and Morimond, shall visit in person unless prevented by sickness, once in the year, and on the day which they shall appoint, the monastery of Cîteaux, besides their attendance at the General Chapter, unless one of them is prevented by grave illness.*

Chap. 5. When any abbot shall come to the New Monastery, due respect shall be paid him. If the abbot be absent, he shall occupy his stall and eat in the guest apartments. But he shall not do these things if the abbot is present. The prior, in the abbot's absence, manages the business of the house. Let the following be the rule of abbeys that do not stand in the relationship of filiations or mother-houses. Every abbot shall yield precedency to an abbot paying him a visit, that this admonition of the Scripture may be fulfilled, "in honor preventing one another." If two or more pay a visit at the same time, he who is the senior in the abbatial dignity shall hold the first place. All of them shall take their food in the refectory, as we have said above, except the abbot of the monastery. But when they meet together, they shall take precedence according to the antiquity of their abbeys; so that the abbot of the most ancient house shall occupy the first place. And they shall all mutually pay each other the deference of a profound inclination when they take their seats.

Chap. 6. Whenever, by the mercy of God, any of our houses shall so increase as to be able to erect another foundation, let both the mother and the daughter follow the rule of charity which we adopt among our brethren; with this exception, that they shall not hold for themselves an annual chapter. But all the abbots of our Order shall meet each year in General Chapter, without excuse, except they are prevented by grievous sickness; and then they shall depute a proper representative. An exception is made also in the case of those who live in too distant countries, which shall be decided by the Chapter. If any abbot from any other cause shall presume upon leave of absence from the General Chapter, he shall ask pardon of the Chapter for his fault the following year, and receive a severe reprimand. In the General Chapter, the abbots shall consult upon matters that appertain to the salvation of souls, and shall ordain what is to be corrected, or what carried out in the observance of the rule and the institutions of the Order. They shall likewise mutually confirm each other in the bond of peace and charity. If any abbot be less zealous about the rule than he ought, or be too much intent upon secular business or be worthy of censure in any way, he shall be charitably reprimanded in the General Chapter; and when reprimanded, he shall ask pardon, and perform the penance imposed for his fault. No one but an abbot shall make this proclamation. *If any controversy shall arise among the abbots, or a fault so grievous shall be charged against any of them that he thereby deserves suspension or deposition, whatever is decreed by the General Chapter in this matter shall be observed. If through diversity of opinion there is engendered discord upon any subject, let that which the abbot of Cîteaux, with the more prudent and the more sagacious in council, shall decide with reference to the dispute be faithfully maintained. Neither of the interested parties shall be present during the discussion.*

Chap. 7. If any of our monasteries shall become extremely indigent, the abbot shall give notice to the General Chapter; then all the abbots assembled, animated by a lively charity, shall contribute to its relief, according to the means with which God may have blessed them.

Chap. 8. If any monastery of our Order be without an abbot, *the abbot of its mother-house shall take the charge of it until the election of a new abbot. If it is itself a mother-house, the abbots of the several filiations and* the monks of that house, being assembled *on the day appointed,* shall proceed by the advice and desire of the presiding abbot, to choose the new abbot.

Chap. 9. When Cîteaux, *the mother-house of all the monasteries of the Order,* is without an abbot, the abbots of La Ferté, *Pontigny, Clairvaux and Morimond,* shall provide for the election of a new abbot. And they shall have the charge of that house until such abbot has been duly elected and confirmed. Fifteen days' notice *at least* shall be given previous to the election of the Abbot of Cîteaux. Then *all the abbots whose monasteries are filiations of Cîteaux,* and such others as the *above-mentioned four abbots* of the greater houses and the brethren of Cîteaux shall judge proper, being together assembled in the name of the Lord, shall elect the new abbot. It is lawful for any mother-house to choose an abbot not only from the monks belonging to its filiations, *but likewise from any of the abbots of the said filiations,* if this be necessary. But no person of another Order shall ever be chosen abbot for one of our houses; nor shall any of our members be permitted to become an abbot in a monastery of another Order.

Chap. 10. *If any abbot, in consideration either of his extreme helplessness or extreme timidity, shall ask permission from the superior of a mother-house to be released from the burden of his abbatial office, let not the superior easily and without a just and necessary cause give his consent. But if the reason alleged be judged sufficient, then let him not do anything of himself; but having called together some other abbots of the Order and asked their advice, let him do what they think ought to be done.*

Chap. 11. If any abbot shall be known to despise the rule and prevaricate against the Order, or shall knowingly connive at the faults of his brethren, the abbot of the mother-house, as soon as convenient, shall either by himself or by his prior, exhort the delinquent, even to the fourth time, to an amendment of conduct. But if, in spite of these admonitions, he will neither correct his fault nor spontaneously abdicate, an assembly of abbots, though not numerous, of our institute shall remove the transgressor of the holy rule from his office; and another worthy of the dignity shall be forthwith elected by the chapter of the mother-house *and by the abbots of the filiations,* if any belong to it, and by the brethren of the monastery, in the manner above described. When an abbot who is deposed, and his religious become contumacious and rebellious (which may God forbid), so as not to acquiesce in the sentence which has been pronounced upon him, let them be excommunicated *by the abbot of the mother-house and his co-abbots, and afterward the abbot of the mother-house shall take the means apt and available to make them do their duty.* But if any of these disobedient members shall be sorry for his offense and wish to return to his mother, let him be received as a repentant son. Except in this case, no abbot of our Order shall retain the subject of another abbot without his consent. In like manner no abbot shall send members of his own community into the monastery of another without permission.

Chap. 12. If it happen (which may Heaven forfend) that the abbots of our Order learn that the abbot of Cîteaux becomes cold in the practice of his duties and departs from the observance of the holy rule and constitutions, the *four* abbots of La Ferté, Pontigny, Clairvaux *and Morimond,* shall, in the name of all the other abbots, admonish him to the fourth time, that he may correct himself and others. But if he prove incorrigible, then they must diligently carry out the instructions which we have given concerning the deposition of abbots, *with this proviso: if he does not abdicate of his own accord, they can neither depose him, nor pronounce against him anathema unless in General Chapter. But if it would be too long to wait for that, they must proceed with their censures in an assembly of abbots who have been taken from the filiations of Cîteaux, with others summoned for the occasion.* And when this unworthy superior has been deposed, they together with the brethren of Cîteaux shall choose a person with suitable qualifications to fill this vacancy. But if both the abbot and the brethren of Cîteaux conjointly prove contumacious, let them be solemnly excommunicated. If later any of these prevaricators repenting of his fault and desirious of saving his soul, shall seek refuge in one of these *four* houses, La Ferté, Pontigny, Clairvaux, *or Morimond,* let him be received, *after due satisfaction,* as one of the members of the house, until he shall be reconciled and return to his own monastery, as justice demands. During this time the General Chapter shall not be held at Cîteaux, but where the *four* abbots above-mentioned shall determine.

APPENDIX III

Historical Statistics

No. 1

PERSONNEL AND FINANCIAL STATUS OF CISTERCIAN MONASTERIES IN THE PAPAL STATES AND IN NAPLES AND SICILY ACCORDING TO THE VISITATION OF NICHOLAS BOUCHERAT IN 1561. (*Cistercienser-Chronik*, 1901, pp. 196-203.)

	Personnel	*Estimated annual income*
Fossa Nuova	5	?
Ponserto	deserted	200 Gold
Semprone	deserted	300 "
Real-Valle	deserted	1500 "
S. Pietro della Canonica	deserted	400 "
Sagittario	10	800 "
Acqua Formosa	6	2000 Scudo
Mattina	2 secular priests	3000 Ducat
Sambucina	deserted	1000 "
S. Angiolo in Frigido	2 secular priests	1200 Gold
Fonte Laureato	2 secular priests	?
Balnearia	8	?
S. Lucia	deserted	500 Ducat
Corazzo	6	1200 "
S. Laurentio	deserted	500 "
Altilia	secular priests	800 "
Maria Nova	2	?
S. Giovanni di Fiore	2	1200 Gold
S. Angiolo	deserted	300 "
SS. Trinita del Legno	4	?
S. Maria de Limachi	deserted	?
Galeso	deserted	800 Gold
S. Johannes in Lamis	deserted	2000 "
S. Maria Coronata	4 Augustinians	?
Ripalta	monks of other orders	3000 Ducat
Arabona	3 secular priests	2000 Gold
Casa Nova	8	?
Ferrara	3	500 Gold
Parco	deserted	?
S. Spirito	Benedictines	4000 Gold
Terrana	4	?
S. Maria dell'Arco	5	2000 Gold
Rocadia	4	1200 "
Nucharia	10	2000 "
Roccamadore	8	3000 "

No. 2

PERSONNEL OF CISTERCIAN MONASTERIES IN SWITZERLAND, TIROL AND GERMANY ACCORDING TO THE VISITATION OF NICHOLAS BOUCHERAT IN 1573-1574. (*Cistercienser-Chronik*, 1901, pp. 230-266.)

	Monks	*Lay-Brothers*	*Novices*	*Oblates*
Hauterive	22	—	—	—
St. Urban	24	—	—	12
Wettingen	19	—	2	—
Salem	56	12	4	—
Kaisersheim	38	—	2	—
Ebrach	22	1	5	12
Bildhausen	14	—	2	—
Langheim	18	—	6	—
Bronnbach	8	—	4	—
Fürstenfeld	18	—	4	—
Raitenhaslach	10	—	4	—
Stams	16	—	—	—
Aldersbach	6	—	—	—
Fürstenzell	4	—	—	—
Gotteszell	5	—	—	—
Thennenbach	4	—	2	—
Pairis	2	—	—	—
Lützel	27	—	6	2
Himmerod	34	3	3	—
Eberbach	27	—	3	—
Marienstatt	3	(living outside of the monastery)		
Heisterbach	13	—	—	—
Walberberg	5	—	—	—
Camp	20	4	5	4
Marienfeld	18	—	2	—
Bredelar	12	—	—	—
Hardehausen	14	—	—	—
Altenberg	40	—	4	—
Bottenbroich	14	1	1	—
Alna	?	—	—	—
Val-Saint-Lambert	22	—	—	—
Saint Rémy	19	—	—	—
Orval	25	—	3	—

No. 3

THE INCREASE IN PERSONNEL OF THE VICARIATE OF BOHEMIA, MORAVIA AND LAUSITZ, 1699-1780. (*Cistercienser-Chronik*, VOL. 21, 1909, p. 243, AND VOL. 40, 1928, p. 139)

	Priests		*Clerics*		*Novices*	*Brothers*		*Total*	
	1699	*1780*	*1699*	*1780*	*1699*	*1699*	*1780*	*1699*	*1780*
Goldenkron	24	32	3	3	—	1	4	28	39
Hohenfurt	41	53	5	3	4	3	2	53	58
Königssaal	30	41	9	4	—	1	—	42	45
Neuzelle	21	30	7	6	3	2	2	33	38
Ossegg	35	40	9	7	2	1	—	47	47
Plass	44	44	11	8	6	4	5	65	57
Saar	22	50	3	6	3	1	2	29	58
Sedlitz	15	20	6	—	3	—	—	24	20
Wellehrad	29	48	17	14	4	3	2	53	64
Totals	261	358	70	51	25	18	17	374	426

No. 4.

PERSONNEL AND FINANCIAL STATUS OF CISTERCIAN MONASTERIES IN FRANCE IN 1768, ACCORDING TO THE REPORT OF THE "COMMISSION OF REGULARS." (The houses belonging to the "Strict Observance" italicized.) (*Cistercienser-Chronik*, 33, 1921.)

	Number of Monks	*Net Annual Income*
Acey	5	7321 Livres
Aiguebelle	2	1756 "
André de Gouffre	7	10451 "
Ardorelle	6	5000 "
Aubepierres	2	1561 "
Auberive	6	8422 "
Aubignac	2	1400 "
Aubin du Bois	6	5500 "
Aulnay	6	1200 "
Aumône	8	9000 "
Balerne	4	5700 "
Barbeaux	10	18500 "
Barbery	15	18300 "
Barzelle	5	4400 "
Beaubec	13	28000 "
Beaugerais	4	3000 "
Beaulieu	5	5063 "
Beaupré (Lorraine)	14	13606 "
Beaupré (Ile-de-France)	7	10424 "
Bégard	10	12000 "
Bellaigue	8	8000 "
Belle-Branche	?	?
Belle-Eau	1	1700 "
Belle-Percke	11	14417 "
Bellevaux	7	11145 "
Belloc	3	3485 "
Benoît-en-Voivre	8	28178 "
Berdoues	6	5997 "
Beuil	2	1687 "
Billon	5	3000 "
Bithaine	4	9013 "
Bohértes	7	9819 "
Bois-Groland	4	3045 "
Boissière (la)	3	3588 "
Bolbone	13	17562 "
Bonlieu (Guyenne)	2	2301 "
Bonlieu (Marche)	?	?
Bonlieu (Dauphiné)	2	1800 "
Bonneaigue	7	8500 "
Bonnecombe	12	12000 "
Bonnefont	8	7400 "
Bonne-Fontaine	5	6130 "

No. 4. (*Continued*)

PERSONNEL AND FINANCIAL STATUS OF CISTERCIAN MONASTERIES IN FRANCE IN 1768, ACCORDING TO THE REPORT OF THE "COMMISSION OF REGULARS." (The houses belonging to the "Strict Observance" italicized.) (*Cistercienser-Chronik*, 33, 1921.) (*Continued*)

	Number of Monks	*Net Annual Income*
Bonneval	22	20000 Livres
Bonnevaux (Dauphiné)	7	7300 "
Bonnevaux (Poitou)	5	3853 "
Bonport	7	12000 "
Bonrepos	8	7200 "
Boquen	3	3000 "
Bouchaud	1	1254 "
Bouillas	9	5800 "
Boulancourt	5	5616 "
Bouras	3	2000 "
Breuil-Benoit	2	5388 "
Bussière(la)	9	5900 "
Buzay	8	28000 "
Cadouin	5	5757 "
Calers	8	4024 "
Candeil	5	7538 "
Cercamp	9	21533 "
Cercanceaux	4	3100 "
Chalade(la)	7	9611 "
Châlis	7	25000 "
Chalivoy	4	3461 "
Chaloché	6	6223 "
Chambons	9	13000 "
Champagne	7	4655 "
Charité(la) (Franche-Comté)	8	9690 "
Charité(la) (Champagne)	2	3000 "
Charmoye(la)	9	11700 "
Charon	4	2400 "
Chassagne	5	6000 "
Châtelliers(les)	5	9970 "
Chatillon	16	28000 "
Cheminon	12	14000 "
Cherlieu	10	8250 "
Chéry	4	8309 "
Chézery	5	6035 "
Cîteaux	60	70000 "
Calirefontaine	5	4757 "
Clairlieu	7	12191 "
Clairmarais	27	28689 "
Clairmont	7	8735 "
Clairvaux	54	78711 "
Clarté Dieu(la)	4	3600 "

No. 4. (*Continued*)

PERSONNEL AND FINANCIAL STATUS OF CISTERCIAN MONASTERIES IN FRANCE IN 1768, ACCORDING TO THE REPORT OF THE "COMMISSION OF REGULARS." (The houses belonging to the "Strict Observance" italicized.) (*Cistercienser-Chronik* 33, 1921.) (*Continued*)

	Number of Monks	*Net Annual Income*
Coëtmaloën	6	8600 Livres
Colombe(la)	3	4000 "
Cour Dieu(la)	9	7800 "
Crête(la)	5	6897 "
Dalon	6	8000 "
Eaunes	4	3848 "
Elant	6	9000 "
Epau(l')	7	6200 "
Escale-Dieu(l')	7	9000 "
Escharlis	4	4140 "
Escurey	6	12146 "
Etoile(l')	1	1761 "
Faise(la)	7	8166 "
Fenières	4	3128 "
Ferté(la)	12	39000 "
Flaran	4	3927 "
Foigny	7	7232 "
Fontaine-Daniel	8	9634 "
Fontaine-Jean	3	3090 "
Fontaines-les-Blanches	3	4954 "
Fontenay	5	8435 "
Fontfroide	10	14300 "
Font-Guillem	2	4175 "
Font-Morigny	7	7249 "
Foucarmont	13	16668 "
Franquevaux	3	5109 "
Freistorff	6	8000 "
Frénade(la)	2	1800 "
Froidmont	6	10863 "
Gard(le)	10	11000 "
Garde-Dieu(la)	3	3600 "
Gimont	9	10400 "
Gondon	2	3053 "
Gourdon	3	1800 "
Grâce-Dieu(la) (Poitou)	4	7438 "
Grâce-Dieu (Franche-Comté)	5	3942 "
Grandselve	15	25225 "
Grosbois	2	5000 "
Haute-Fontaine	7	4902 "
Haute-Seille	5	7803 "
Igny	6	10440 "
Jouy(la)	20	14200 "

No. 4. (*Continued*)

PERSONNEL AND FINANCIAL STATUS OF CISTERCIAN MONASTERIES IN FRANCE IN 1768, ACCORDING TO THE REPORT OF THE "COMMISSION OF REGULARS." (The houses belonging to the "Strict Observance" italicized.) (*Cistercienser-Chronik*, 33, 1921.) (*Continued*)

	Number of Monks	*Net Annual Income*
Ile-en-Barrois	8	10172 Livres
Ile-Dieu	6	8432 "
Landais	7	11000 "
Langonnet	8	10000 "
Lannoye	12	8000 "
Lanvaux	3	4000 "
Larrivour	6	8554 "
Léoncel	5	7000 "
Lieu-Dieu	8	6813 "
Lieu-Croissant	6	6374 "
Loc-Dieu	5	5000 "
Longpont	10	19121 "
Longuay	3	5390 "
Long-Villiers	5	7340 "
Loos	10	34900 "
Loroux	5	7300 "
Loroy	4	4100 "
Maizières	9	21000 "
Marcel S.	3	2250 "
Marcilly	1	2000 "
Mazan	11	9200 "
Mégemont	4	2700 "
Mellerray	3	6500 "
Merci-Dieu(la)	3	3065 "
Miroir	?	? "
Montier-en-Argonne	9	10059 "
Montpeiroux	6	7300 "
Mont-Sainte-Marie	7	7144 "
Moreilles	4	8355 "
Mores	3	2845 "
Morimond	30	20800 "
Mortemer	6	10270 "
Nizors	4	5200 "
Noë(la)	3	2744 "
Noirlac	6	6360 "
Obasine	6	4900 "
Olivet	6	3400 "
Ourscamp	29	27000 "
Palais (N.D.)	4	2048 "
Perseigne	7	11000 "
Peyrignac	2	4084 "
Peyrouse	4	2564 "

No. 4. (*Continued*)

PERSONNEL AND FINANCIAL STATUS OF CISTERCIAN MONASTERIES IN FRANCE IN 1768, ACCORDING TO THE REPORT OF THE "COMMISSION OF REGULARS." (The houses belonging to the "Strict Observance" italicized.) (*Cistercienser-Chronik*, 33, 1921.) (*Continued*)

	Number of Monks	*Net Annual Income*
Pierres (les)	4	7000 Livres
Piété-Dieu	5	3300 "
Pin(le)	9	7300 "
Pontaut	4	3257 "
Pontifroid	?	?
Pontigny	25	26831 "
Pontrond	6	6400 "
Pré-Benoît	2	1127 "
Prée(la)	5	12506 "
Preuilly	16	13500 "
Prières	16	8520 "
Quincy	4	7121 "
Reclus	4	7976 "
Relecq	12	9300 "
Rigny	7	9289 "
Rivet	3	5099 "
Roches	5	5109 "
Rosières	4	10159 "
Royaumont	17	18000 "
S. Léonard des Chaumes	3	1800 "
S. Maurice	7	6300 "
Sauvelade	2	2699 "
Savigny	18	16171 "
Sellières	2	2635 "
Sénanque	4	4000 "
Septfons	10	10000 "
Signy	9	26470 "
Silvanés	6	5200 "
Stürzelbronn	12	41070 "
S. Sulpice	11	13000 "
Theuley	7	9000 "
Tironneau	4	5552 "
Torigny	4	4082 "
Toronet	8	8900 "
Trappe(la)	67	17000 "
Trisay	3	2500 "
Trois-Fontaines	10	19502 "
Valasse	10	7670 "
Val-Benoîte	4	3000 "
Valcroissant	2	1800 "
Valence	3	3500 "
Valette	3	4000 "

No. 4. (*Continued*)

PERSONNEL AND FINANCIAL STATUS OF CISTERCIAN MONASTERIES IN FRANCE IN 1768, ACCORDING TO THE REPORT OF THE "COMMISSION OF REGULARS." (The houses belonging to the "Strict Observance" italicized.) (*Cistercienser-Chronik*, 33, 1921.) (*Continued*)

	Number of Monks	*Net Annual Income*
Valmagne	8	9000 Livres
Val-Richer	7	9763 "
Valloires	9	13400 "
Valroy	9	8624 "
Val-Sainte	3	2441 "
Varennes	2	3000 "
Vaucelles	27	29304 "
Vauclair	24	18900 "
Vauluisant	16	18600 "
Vauluisant-Bouchet	8	3859 "
Vaux-de-Cernay	11	14468 "
Vaux-en-Ornois	6	9897 "
Vaux-la-Douce	8	7000 "
Vieuville	6	5248 "
Ville-Longue	2	3983 "
Villeneuve	11	11100 "
Villers-Betnach	12	17900 "

No. 5.

THE INCREASE IN PERSONNEL OF THE CISTERCIAN ORDER OF THE COMMON OBSERVANCE, 1894-1950.

	Priests	*Clerics*	*Novices*	*Brothers*	*Total*
1894	602	177*	?	129	908
1898	644	133	46	146	969
1906	691	126	44	154	1015
1911	722	112	28	154	1016
1921	710	82	38	147	977
1925	720	121	40	185	1066
1931	770	176	66	331	1343
1938	855	262	57	439	1613
1950	957	216	103	448	1724

* This figure includes the novices too.

No. 6.

CONGREGATIONS AND MONASTERIES OF THE CISTERCIAN ORDER OF THE COMMON OBSERVANCE AND THEIR PERSONNEL IN 1950.

	Priests	*Clerics*	*Novices*	*Brothers*	*Total*
Congregation of the Sacred Heart (Austria)					
Rein	22	—	—	2	24
Heiligenkreuz / Neukloster	45	2	5	7	59
Zwettl	33	2	—	2	37
Wilhering	44	3	—	8	55
Lilienfeld	29	3	—	—	32
Schlierbach	32	3	1	23	59
Apolo (Bolivia)	2	—	—	—	2
Jequitibà (Brazil)	9	—	1	5	15
Total	216	13	7	47	283
Congregation of Mehrerau					
Mehrerau (Austria)	34	—	—	20	54
Marienstatt (Germany)	30	3	2	14	49
Stična (Yugoslavia)*	16	—	—	20	36
Seligenporten (Germany)	11	2	—	6	19
Stams (Austria)	13	1	—	3	17
Himmerod (Germany)	22	3	2	21	48
Mogila (Poland)	15	14	12	6	47
Hardehausen (Germany) / Itatinga (Brazil)	4	—	—	—	4
Untermais (Italy)	5	—	—	2	7
Hauterive (Switzerland)	7	—	1	6	14
Birnau (Germany)	6	—	—	5	11
Itaporanga (Brazil)	8	3	6	14	31
Total	171	26	23	117	337
Congregation of St. Bernard in Italy					
Chiaravalle	7	—	—	2	9
Santa Croce	13	10	—	4	27
S. Bernardo	6	—	—	2	8
S. Antonio	4	—	—	—	4
Foce di Amelia	4	—	2	2	8
S. Severino	7	—	—	2	9
S. Salvatore	4	—	—	1	5
San José (Brazil)	3	—	—	—	3
Total	48	10	2	13	73

* In dispersion

No. 6. (*Continued*)

CONGREGATIONS AND MONASTERIES OF THE CISTERCIAN ORDER OF THE COMMON OBSERVANCE AND THEIR PERSONNEL IN 1950. (*Continued*)

	Priests	*Clerics*	*Novices*	*Brothers*	*Total*
Congregation of Mary Mediatrix					
Val-Dieu (Belgium)	9	3	1	2	15
Bornhem (Belgium)	30	5	—	8	43
Marienkroon (Holland)	37	9	5	9	60
Total	76	17	6	19	118
Congregation of Senanque (France)					
Lérins	16	—	2	10	28
Senanque	2	—	—	3	5
St. Michel de Cuxa	6	—	—	3	9
Pont-Colbert	5	1	—	1	7
Rougemont (Canada)	14	1	4	14	33
My-Ca (Viet-Nam)	2	3	—	3	8
Total	45	5	6	34	90
Congregation of the Immaculate Heart of Mary (Czechoslovakia)*					
Ossegg	20	—	—	—	20
Hohenfurt	40	1	—	4	45
Total	60	1	—	4	65
Congregation of Zirc (Hungary)*					
Zirc	58	37	18	—	113
Pásztó	3	—	—	—	3
St. Gotthard	11	—	—	—	11
Eger	15	—	—	—	15
Székesfehérvár	16	—	—	—	16
Pécs	16	—	—	—	16
Baja	12	—	—	—	12
Budapest					
St. Emeric	19	—	—	—	19
St. Bernard	6	24	—	—	30
Elöszállás	6	—	—	—	6
Spring Bank (U.S.A.)	13	8	2	3	26
Gerowval (U.S.A.)	5	—	—	1	6
Buffalo (U.S.A.)	5	—	—	1	6
Total	185	69	20	5	279

* In dispersion

No. 6. (*Continued*)

Congregations and Monasteries of the Cistercian Order of the Common Observance and Their Personnel in 1950. (*Continued*)

	Priests	*Clerics*	*Novices*	*Brothers*	*Total*
Congregation of Casamari (Italy)					
Casamari	22	15	15	6	58
S. Domenico	8	—	—	2	10
Valvisciolo	6	—	—	3	9
Cotrino	8	—	—	2	10
S. Maria della Consolazione	3	—	—	1	4
S. Maria della Neve	3	—	—	1	4
SS. Vincenzo e Anastasio	4	6	—	2	12
Chiaravalle della Colomba	3	—	—	1	4
S. Nicola di Piona	4	—	—	1	5
S. Maria dell'Assunta (Ethiopia)	11	—	—	5	16
Trisulti	6	7	—	2	15
Garimpo (Brazil)	3	—	—	1	4
Total	81	28	15	27	151
Polish Congregation					
Szczyrzyc	8	12	—	6	26
Jedrejow	4	—	—	—	4
Oliva	3	—	—	—	3
Heinrichau	?	?	?	?	?
Total	15	12	—	6	33
Spanish Congregation					
Poblet	9	12	3	15	39
Monasteries outside of Congregations					
Phuoc-Són (Viet-Nam)	22	10	15	75	122
Châu-Són (Viet-Nam)	16	7	1	57	81
Queen of Peace (Hungary)*	8	6	1	28	43
Boquen (France)	5	—	4	1	10
Total	51	23	21	161	256
Totals	957	216	103	448	1,724

* In dispersion

Bibliographical Notes

General

The richest treasury of Cistercian history is a German language periodical, *Cistercienser-Chronik,* published monthly by the abbey of Mehrerau (Austria) since 1889, dedicated primarily to the history of the Order (*Cist.Chr.*). The *Collectanea Ordinis Cisterciensium Reformatorum,* published quarterly in Westmalle (Belgium) since 1934, is also rich in historical material; most of the articles are in the French language (*Coll.*). A yearbook, *Analecta Sacri Ordinis Cisterciensis,* is being published under the care of the Abbey General in Rome with articles of basic importance, mostly in the Latin language (*Anal.*). A considerable amount of Cistercian material was printed in the *Studien und Mitteilungen zur Geschichte des Benedictiner-Ordens un seiner Zweige,* a German language quarterly, started in 1880 by the Benedictine Academy of Bavaria, München.

A well documented list of Cistercian monasteries of men, *Originum Cisterciensium Tomus I.* (Wien, 1877), by Leopold Janauschek, is still indispensable for historians. The same is true regarding the collection of Statutes of the General Chapters, *Statuta Capitulorum Generalium Ordinis Cisterciensis, ab anno 1116 ad annum 1786,* 8 vols. (Louvain, 1933-41), by Josephus Canivez. Other useful collections of important documents are: Philippe Guignard, *Les monuments primitifs de la règle cistercienne* (Dijon, 1878); and Hugues Séjalon, *Nomasticon Cisterciense,* Editio nova (Solesmes, 1892).

Of the early attempts at a comprehensive presentation of the history of the Order the most significant, though incomplete (covers only the years up to 1236), was written by Angelus Manrique, *Cisterciensium seu verius Ecclesiasticorum Annalium a Condito Cistercio, Tom. IV* (Lyons, 1642-59). In any larger library available and still useful is: Hippolyte Hélyot, *Histoire des ordres mo-*

nastiques (Paris, 1714-19); the Cistercians are treated in vols. 5-6. Basically the same material was reprinted by Migne in his *Dictionnaire des ordres religieux* (Paris, 1847).

There is no modern scholarly survey covering the whole course of Cistercian history in any language. The nearest approach to it is a serial publication in *Cist.Chr.* 1925-27, by Gregor Müller, "Vom Cisterciense Orden," rich in dates and facts but unreadable and unavailable. Very recently the *Dictionnaire d'histoire et de géographie ecclésiastiques* (Paris, 1951-52), published a long article (Fasc. 70-71, *Cîteaux*) of similar nature by Joseph-Marie Canivez. Small booklets of summary information are: Anselme Le Bail, *L'Ordre de Cîteaux* (Paris, 1947), and Ailbe J. Luddy, *The Order of Cîteaux* (Dublin, 1932). The title of the *Compendium of the History of the Cistercian Order* (by Alberic Wulf, Gethsemani, 1944), is misleading; it contains only selected chapters on the history of the Order, presented in a rather amateurish fashion.

The notes which follow refer only to printed material consulted in the composition of the present study. For a more complete bibliography see the above mentioned article (*Cîteaux*) in *Dictionnaire d'histoire et de géographie ecclésiastiques,* and Anselme Dimier, *Recueil de plans d'églises cisterciennes* (Paris, 1949).

1. Western Monasticism

The most quoted work is Max Heimbucher, *Die Orden und Kongregationen de Katholischen Kirche* 3d ed. in 2 vols. (Paderborn, 1933-34). A book of similar nature, is Charles W. Courrier, *History of Religious Orders* (New York, 1894). There is a large number of shorter surveys, such as, Herbert B. Workman, *The Evolution of the Monastic Ideal* (London, 1913); J. C. Hannah, *Christian Monasticism* (London, 1924), and G. Ambroise, *Les moines du moyen âge* (Paris, 1942). A brief but brilliant chapter on the subject is contained in *The Cambridge Medieval History,* (1948) vol. 5, chapter XX. An excellent study on pre-Benedictine monasticism was written by Owen Chadwick, *John Cassian* (Cambridge, 1950). Concerning St. Benedict and his Rule a basic work is Cuthbert Butler, *Benedictine Monachism,* 2d ed. (London, 1924). A concise story of early Benedictine history is Ursmer Berlière, *L'ordre monastique, des origines au XIIe siècle,* 3d ed. (Paris,

1924). The same period is covered by the first three volumes of the recently completed compendium by Philibert Schmitz, *Histoire de l'Ordre de Saint-Benoît,* 6 vols. (Maredsous, 1948). These books deal extensively with the reform of Benedict of Aniane; cf. also, Watkin Williams, "St. Benedict of Aniane," *The Downside Review,* 1936. On Cluny, see André Chagny, *Cluny et son empire,* 4th ed. (Paris, 1949), and L. M. Smith, *Cluny in the Eleventh and Twelfth Centuries* (London, 1930). On the 11th and 12th century reforms there is the magistral work of David Knowles, *The Monastic Order in England,* 2d ed. (Cambridge, 1949), a rare masterpiece of historiography. Owen J. Blum, *St. Peter Damian* (Washington, 1947), is an intelligent dissertation. Other noteworthy contributions to this neglected subject are: two studies by H. F. Chettle, both in *The Downside Review,* "The English Houses of the Order of Fontevraud" (1942) and "Lesser Benedictine Groups in the British Isles" (serial, 1947-48). The same period is covered in the still incomplete monumental work of Fliche-Martin, *Histoire de l'Eglise,* vol. 7 (Paris, 1948), and in the first chapter of Jean-Berthold Mahn, *L'Ordre Cistercien et son gouvernement, des origines au milieu du XIIIe siècle,* 2d ed. (Paris, 1951). On medieval heresy the best concise study is Steven Runciman, *The Medieval Manichee* (Cambridge, 1947). Cf. the same in *The Cambridge Medieval History,* vol. 6, and the appropriate chapter in the *Oxford European Civilization,* vol. 3.

2. Cistercian Beginnings

A considerable number of 12th century sources deal with the foundation of Cîteaux; see their critical evaluation by Joseph Turk, "Cistercii Statuta Antiquissima," *Anal.* 1948. The most important of them is certainly the *Exordium Parvum,* frequently quoted in this and the following chapter. Its English translation in Appendix I, appears for the first time in printing. The most detailed analysis of the foundation is a long serial by Gregor Müller, in *Cist.Chr.,* 1908, 1909, 1916. Othon Ducourneau, *Les origines cisterciennes* (Ligugé, 1933), and the same in *Revue Mabillon,* 1932-33, is a lengthy and ultra-conservative essay. The best comprehensive presentation of the whole period is the above mentioned J. B. Mahn, *L'Ordre Cistercien.* See a short sketch in Fliche-

Martin, *Histoire de l'Eglise,* vol. 8. pp. 445-57. St. Robert's 13th century *Vita* was recently published by Kolumban Spahr, *Das Leben des hl. Robert von Molesme* (Freiburg [in Switzerland], 1944). Substantial contributions to the same are: Seraphin Lanssen, "Saint Robert, fondateur de Cîteaux," *Coll.* 1937; Fernand Delahaye, "Un moine, Saint Robert, fondateur de Cîteaux," *Coll.* 1952; Watkin Williams, "St. Robert of Molesme," *Journal of Theological Studies,* 1936. On St. Stephen Harding, see the century old (first published in 1844) but readable and frequently reprinted J. B. Dalgairns, *Life of St. Stephen Harding* (London, 1898). There is a modern essay by Alexis Presse, "Saint Etienne Harding," *Coll.* 1934.

3. Rule and Constitution

On the sources of early Cistercian history see the above mentioned Turk, "Cistercii Statuta Antiquissima;" about the *Charter of Charity,* Gregor Müller published a serial in *Cist.Chr.* 1897, and another study in the same periodical (1934-35) in serials by Karl Kreh. Cf. also, Watkin Williams, "The Charta Charitatis," *Dublin Review,* 1928, and by the same author, "The First Cistercian Era," *Journal of Theological Studies,* 1930. An able presentation of the whole complex question is Colomban Bock, "Les codifications du droit cistercien," *Coll.* 1947. Find a brief summary of the same in the previously mentioned, Mahn, *L'Ordre Cistercien.* A translation of the *Charter of Charity* is reprinted in the present work as Appendix II.

About the internal problems of Cluny, in addition to the above cited works of Chagny and Smith there is a good survey by Joan Evans, *Monastic Life at Cluny (910-1157)* (Oxford, 1931). The antagonism between Cluny and Cîteaux, combined with an endeavor to return to the pre-Benedictine asceticism, as a major factor in the development of a peculiar Cistercian monasticism, was seldom fully recognized. The first who called attention to it was Edmund Bishop, whose correspondence on the subject was published by David Knowles, "Cluniacs and Cistercians," *The Downside Review,* 1934. An excellent study with the same conclusion is Adrian Morey, "The Conflict of Clairvaux and Cluny," *The Downside Review,* 1932. See also on the same subject, André Wilmart, "Une reposte de l'ancien monachisme au manifeste de Saint Bernard," *Revue Béné-*

dictine, 1934, and the essay by Cabrol, *Cluny et Cîteaux,* published in *Saint Bernard et son temps,* vol. 1 (Dijon, 1928). A striking proof for the antiquarian tendencies of Cîteaux, the *Dialogus inter Cluniacensem Monachum et Cisterciensem de diversis utriusque Ordinis observantiis* (published in Martène-Durand, *Thesaurus Novus Anecdotarum,* vol. 5), in this respect, was never fully evaluated. A short analysis of the work is Watkin Williams, "A Dialogue between a Cluniac and a Cistercian," *Journal of Theological Studies,* 1930. The peculiar nature of the Cistercian interpretation of the Rule of St. Benedict is another subject, so far, largely neglected.

4. St. Bernard and the Expansion

E. Vacandard, *Vie de Saint Bernard, abbé de Clairvaux,* 2 vols. 4th ed. (Paris, 1927), is still regarded as the standard biography. Ailbe J. Luddy, *Life and Teaching of St. Bernard* (Dublin, 1927), outlines in detailed fashion the Saint's writings; Watkin Williams, *Saint Bernard of Clairvaux,* 2d ed. (Westminster, Md., 1952), is rich in details concerning the Saint's outside activities, but scarcely readable. See also G. G. Coulton, *Five Centuries of Religion,* vol. 1 (Cambridge, 1923). On the spirituality of St. Bernard there is an admirable study by Etienne Gilson, *The Mystical Theology of St. Bernard* (New York, 1940). On the 12th century problem of love see Alexander J. Denomy, *The Heresy of Courtly Love* (New York, 1947), and a number of excellent essays by the same author in the recent volumes of the *Medieval Studies.* On Cluniac spirituality as represented in art there are two fundamental books by Werner Weisbach, *Religiöse Reform und mittelalterliche Kunst* (Einsiedeln, 1945), and *Ausdruckgestaltung in mittelalterlicher Kunst* (Einsiedeln, 1948). The full evaluation of St. Bernard's influence over the primitive ideals of Cîteaux is still missing. François Kovács furnished a few interesting details in "A propos de la date de la rédaction de 'Instituta Generalis Capituli apud Cistercium.'" *Anal.* 1951. Concerning the revision of the *Charter of Charity* cf. Turk, *o.c.* To follow the expansion of the Order the best guide is Leopold Janauschek's *Originum Cisterciensium Tom. I.*

5. The Vanguard of the Church

Concerning the early Cistercian interest in the Holy Land see

Watkin Williams, "Arnold of Morimond," *Coll.* 1940. Cistercian crusading activity is well covered in *Cist.Chr.;* the most detailed study is a serial by Eberhard Pfeiffer, in vols. 1935, 1936, 1939. On Cistercian diplomates there are serial publications in the same periodical by Luzian Pfleger (1910), Sigisbert Mitterer (1922) and by Gregor Müller, "St. Peter Tarantaise," 1891. The Citation by Boniface VIII on p. 48, quoted in Wulf, *Compendium,* p. 154. About the Albigensian mission and especially on Henry Cardinal of Albano see a serial in *Cist.Chr.* 1909, by Stephan Steffen. Cistercian and Dominican cooperation is ably presented by Pierre Mandonnet, *St. Dominic and his Work,* 3d ed. (St. Louis, 1948). Cf. also on the same subject an article by Adolf Dietrich in *Cist.Chr.* 1917. The story of the Prussian and Baltic mission follows Franz Winter, *Die Cistercienser des nordöslichen Deutschlands,* 3 vols. (Gotha, 1868-71). See the other details in Müller, "Vom Cistercienser Orden."

On the question of exemption there is a basic study by George Schreiber, *Studien zur Exemptionsgeschichte der Zisterzienser,* reprinted as chapter VII in *Gemeinschaften des Mittelalters* (Regensburg, 1948). A short but clear exposition is chapter IV in Mahn, *o.c.* About the Fourth Lateran Council see Mandonnet, *o.c.* and F. A. Gasquet, *Monastic Life in the Middle Ages* (London, 1922), pp. 226-28.

6. The Impact of Scholasticism

The development, organization and work of the General Chapter as well as the whole machinery of the administration of the Order is ably presented in a long and dry but indispensable serial publication by the tireless Gregor Müller, "Studien über das Generalkapitel," *Cist.Chr.* 1900-1908. On the "Clementina" and the feud between Cîteaux and the Proto-Abbots see the serial in *Cist.Chr.* (1924) by Severin Grill. Cf. also Mahn, *o.c.* pp. 229-38. About the origin of the "Definitorium" consult Müller, "Studien," *Cist.Chr.* 1901. The text of the "Parvus Fons" was recently published in Canivez, *Statuta,* vol. 3. Concerning the office of the Procurator General see Müller, *o.c. Cist.Chr.* 1907, p. 361; on the Cardinal Protector, *ibid.* 1908, p. 106; about studies in general, *ibid.* 1907, p. 48. Dealing with the foundation of the "Bernardinum" there is an article by

Müller in *Cist.Chr.* 1908; and another by Edmund Kwanten, "Le college Saint-Bernard à Paris," *Revue d'histoire ecclésiastique,* 1948. About the studies in the College, Leonhard Peter published an article in *Cist.Chr.* 1922. The "Fulgens Sicut Stella" was published in Canivez, *Statuta,* vol. 3. About the same and studies in general see Jean-Berthold Mahn, *Le Pape Benoît XII et les Cisterciens* (Paris, 1949). Both the "Clementina" and "Benedictina" are analyzed by Colomban Bock, "Les codifications du droit cistercien," *Coll.* 1948.

7. Renaissance and Reformation

The influence of the Hundred Years' War is described by Dominicus Willi in a serial in *Cist.Chr.* 1906. G. Müller discussed the declining General Chapter in his "Studien," *Cist.Chr.* 1901, pp. 342 ff. Find the facts on Irish nationalism in Thompson-Clapham-Leask, "The Cistercian Order in Ireland," *The Archeological Journal,* 1931. On the effects of Western Schism, see Müller's article in *Cist.Chr.* 1924, and on the devastation caused by Hussites a serial by Valentin Schmidt, *Cist.Chr.* 1908. On the fifteenth century reforms, despite its manifest tendency, it is worth while to read the well documented stories of G. G. Coulton, *Five Centuries of Religion,* vol. 4 (Cambridge, 1950). Quotation on p. 70, taken from this work, p. 624. The best source of reform-efforts within the Order is Canivez, *Statuta,* vols. 4-5. The Bull of unification of Cîteaux and Clairvaux was published *ibid.* vol. 5, p. 663. See also on the same reforms Colomban Bock, "Les codifications du droit cistercien," *Coll.* 1949.

The fate of monasticism during the stormy decades of the Reformation nowhere had been so thoroughly analyzed as in England. The ablest exponent of the Protestant view was the prolific G. G. Coulton while the chief representative of the Catholic case was Cardinal Gasquet, especially through his great work, *Henry VIII and the English Monasteries,* 2 vols. 6th ed. (London, 1902). An excellent contribution to the subject is the first volume of Philip Hughes, *The Reformation in England* (New York, 1951). The fate of the English Cistercian martyrs was, so far, little known; see concerning this, Hugh Talbot, "The English Cistercian Martyrs," *Coll.* 1935; L. E. Whatmore, "George Lazenby," *The*

Downside Review, 1942, and an article by Anton Weis, *Cist.Chr.* 1902.

There is no comprehensive work about the history of Cistercian establishments during the same period elsewhere. See the story of Loccum by P. Delattre, "Une abbaye protestante en Allemagne," *Coll.* 1936. Reports of Visitors in Germany and Italy were published in serials by Aloys Postina, in *Cist.Chr.* 1901. (Cf. Appendix III.) Concerning Switzerland, there are two studies, one by Adalgott Benz, a serial in *Cist.Chr.* 1909, another by Leonhard Peter, in the "Festgabe" in honor of G. Müller (Bregenz, 1926), pp. 77-78.

The commendatory system in general is well covered in any standard history of the Renaissance Church. See a few enlightening incidents in G. G. Coulton, *Five Centuries of Religion,* vol. 3, pp. 425 ff. The facts concerning Cistercian houses were taken from Müller, "Studien," *Cist.Chr.* 1907, pp. 141 ff. On pastoral activity, see *ibid.* 1907, pp. 82 ff.

About academic studies, here is a list of studies published in *Cist.Chr.*: on Dillingen, by A. Dietrich, serial, 1933; on Frankfurt, by G. Müller, 1905; on Freiburg, by D. Willi, 1911; on Heidelberg, by A. Amrhein, 1906; on the College of St. Jacob, a serial by A. Arnold, 1936; on Ingolstadt, by L. Reindl, 1912; on Cologne, by A. Arnold, 1937; there are three serials by the same A. Dietrich, on Leipzig, 1914; on Paderborn, 1934; on Rome, 1912.

8. The Rise of the Congregations

The legal relation of the Congregations to Cîteaux is analyzed in a serial by Idesbald Eicheler, "Die Kongregationen des Zisterzienserordens," *Studien und Mitteilungen,* 1931, without, however, giving the details of the inner life or spirituality of the Congregations. The same is true concerning the otherwise conscientious work of Colomban Bock, "Les codifications du droit cistercien," a serial in *Coll.* 1949-50. Cf. also Müller, "Studien," *Cist.Chr.* 1907, pp. 113 ff.

The latest on Abbot Joachim is by Herbert Grundmann, *Neue Forschungen über Joachim von Fiore* (Marburg, 1950). There is a substantial serial about the Congregation of Upper Germany by Karl Becker in *Cist.Chr.* 1936, rich in details about the life of the abbeys and containing the Statutes of the Congregation. On Orval, see an article by Johann B. Kaiser, in *Studien und Mitteilungen,* 1914, pp. 114 ff. On the Guillelmites find some further information in Schmitz, *Histoire de l'ordre de Saint Benoît,* vol. 3, pp. 25 ff. On the Congregation of Corpus Christi, there is a short publication in *Coll.* 1952, pp. 52 ff. On Belgium, see a serial by Roger De Ganck, in *Coll.* 1939.

The changes in the function of the General Chapter and in the administration, such as the Intermediate Chapter, the Vicariates, Common Novitiate etc. were characterized after Müller, "Studien."

9. The War of Observances

The seventeenth century reform is still regarded as a controversial subject. Under the pretext of preserving peace, both parties refrained themselves from a thorough and objective investigation of the basic facts and issues. As a result, there is not a single modern study dealing in substance with the problem, not even a biography of Abbot Vaussin, the key figure of the most critical period. Almost the whole bulk of the material is still in manuscript.

The present chapter was based chiefly on Gregor Müller, "Vom Cistercienser Orden," serial in *Cist.Chr.* 1926-27. A fragmentary essay was published by Otto Grillenberger, "Beiträge zu inneren Geschichte des Zisterzienserordens in 17. Jahrhundert," serial in *Studien und Mitteilungen,* 1904. For a brief summary of the era see Joseph-Marie Canivez, *L'ordre de Cîteaux en Belgique* (Forges lez-Chimay, 1926), pp. 35-51. Henry de Warren presents a few more details in *La Bretagne Cistercienne* (Saint Wandrille, 1946), pp. 119 ff. The traditional Trappist point of view is restated by Wulf, *Compendium,* pp. 233 ff. On Richelieu, see Edmund Bishop, "Richelieu and the Benedictines," *The Downside Review,* 1911, and the appropriate chapter in Schmitz, *o.c.* vol. 4. On de Rancé, there is a brilliant though not unprejudiced modern work by Henry Bremond, *The Thundering Abbot* (London, 1930). Cf. the apology by Ailbe Luddy, *The Real de Rancé* (Dublin, 1931). On Jansenism and Quietism there are four readable chapters in Ronald A. Knox, *Enthusiasm* (Oxford, 1950). The best guide in print throughout the controversy is Canivez, *Statuta,* vol. 7. Find the full text of the "In Suprema" in the same volume, pp. 426 ff.

10. On the Verge of Extinction

About the conditions in Austria after the Reformation, there are two studies in *Cist.Chr.,* one by Aelred Pexa, 1928; another by

Gebhard Rath, 1933. The important records of the provincial chapters of Bohemia were published in a long serial by Philibert Panhölzl, *Cist.Chr.* 1910-13. (Cf. also Appendix III.) The general decline of religious orders in France is well characterized in Fliche-Martin, *Histoire de l'Eglise,* vol. 20, pp. 21 ff. On the work of the Commission of Regulars see Schmitz, *o.c.* vol. 4. pp. 73 ff. Look for the other details in Müller, "Vom Cistercienser Orden." Concerning the General Chapter of 1771 there is a serial published in *Cist.-Chr.* 1898. The Constitution of 1783, missing from the collection of Canivez, was published in *Cist.Chr.* 1941.

The position of the Church under Joseph II and during the French Revolution is well presented in any standard Church history. On the abbey of Rauden there is a serial by Stephen Steffen, *Cist.Chr.* 1920. The trials of the Order in Belgium are detailed in a serial by Benedict van Doninckh, *Cist.Chr.* 1898-99. About Spain, cf. Amédée Garcia, "L'ordre de Cîteaux en Espagne." *Coll.* 1934. Find the peculiar arrangement in Lithuania in *Cist.Chr.* 1890.

11-12. Reconstruction and Cistercians in the Twentieth Century

These two chapters were based almost entirely upon the material available in the volumes of the *Cistercienser-Chronik,* concerning the latest period, in the news section of the magazine. The correlation of the two observances was recently discussed in the last part of the long but always useful serial of Colomban Bock, "Les codifications du droit cistercien," *Coll.* 1952, pp. 191 ff. The spectacular development of the Strict Observance is being well publicized in this country; for general information consult the frequently quoted Wulf, *Compendium.*

13. Spirituality

Those few essays bearing the title of "Cistercian Spirituality" usually identify the subject with the spirituality of the primitive Cîteaux or with that of St. Bernard, consequently, any deviation from the mentality of the Founding Fathers is being labeled as "decline"; some of these authors date the beginning of "decline" as far back as the death of St. Bernard. A well written work ably representing this tendency is a booklet translated and published by the fathers of the abbey of Gethsemani, *The Spirit of Simplicity* (Trappist, 1948).

Thus far, no attempt has been made toward a full historical survey of the Cistercian spirituality as a living and acting reality in the framework of the changing centuries. The field for such a research is not only enormous but practically unexplored, hence the present chapter can not be either complete in material or conclusive in its results.

The best known Cistercian authors of the 12th and 13th centuries are briefly mentioned in the standard work of P. Pourrat, *Christian Spirituality in the Middle Ages,* 3 vols. (London, 1924) ; in Felix Vernet, *Medieval Spirituality* (London, 1930) ; and in Ursmer Berlière, *L'ascèse bénédictine* (Maredsous, 1927). As to the spirituality of the primitive Cîteaux, see bibliography listed under chapters 2 and 3. On St. Bernard, there is the unmatched masterpiece of Etienne Gilson, *The Mystical Theology of St. Bernard* (New York, 1940). Cf. also Jean Leclercq, *Saint Bernard Mystique* (Paris, 1948). On the influence of St. Bernard see the article under his name in *Dictionnaire de Spiritualité,* vol. 1 (Paris, 1937), by Anselme Le Bail, and by the same author, *L'influence de Saint Bernard sur les auteurs spirituels de son temps,* published in *St. Bernard et son temps,* vol. 1 (Dijon, 1928). All notable Cistercian authors of the 12th century are briefly evaluated in two excellent reference works, both by J. de Ghellinck, *L'essor de la littérature latine au XIIe siècle,* 2 vols. (Bruxelles, 1946) ; and *Le mouvement théologique du XIIe siècle* (Bruxelles, 1948). Concerning the most prominent personalities consult the following studies: A. W. Burridge, "The Spirituality of St. Aelred," *The Downside Review,* 1940; F. M. Powicke, *Ailred of Rievaulx,* published in *Ways of Medieval Life and Thought* (Boston, 1951) ; Walter Daniel, *The Life of Ailred of Rievaulx,* which is a contemporary *Vita,* translated with introduction by F. M. Powicke (London, 1950) ; J. Dechanet, *Guillaume de Saint-Thierry* (Paris, 1942). On Isaac of Stella there is an excellent chapter in G. B. Burch, *Early Medieval Philosophy* (New York, 1951) ; J. Leclercq, "Les écrits de Geoffroy d'Auxerre," *Revue Bénédictine,* 1952. (This Geoffroy is identical with Godfrey of Clairvaux.) There are two articles in *Coll.* both by Edmund Mikkers, one about Stephen of Salley (1946), another on Gerard of

Liége (1950). See Adam of Perseigne on novices in Berlière, *o.c.* p. 105. On the veneration of Mary see Vernet, *o.c.* pp. 98 ff. and a long serial by G. Müller, in *Cist.Chr.* 1889-91. Find the details about the feast of Corpus Christi in Villers in *Coll.* 1946, p. 218; the perpetual adoration in Kaisheim, *Cist.Chr.* 1911, p. 215.

On hagiography see a substantial serial by Bruno Griesser, in *Cist.Chr.* 1947. On the *Exordium Magnum,* there is an article by T. Hümpfner, in *Cist.Chr.* 1908. The Austrian collection of legends is mentioned in Ghellinck, *L'essor,* p. 168. About the 14th century mystics see Leo Schlegel's article in *Cist.Chr.* 1931. On St. Bridget consult Pourrat, *o.c.* vol. 2, pp. 92-95.

Cistercian historiography is relatively well covered in *Cist.Chr.* Quotation concerning Soroë on p. 156, taken from Janauschek, *Originum,* p. 145. The following articles all refer to *Cist.Chr.* written all by Cassian Haid: a serial on Otto of Freising, 1932-33; English-Scotch annalistic, 1907; Cistercian authors in Monumenta Germaniae Historica, 1919; Alberic of Troisfontaines, 1908; John of Victring, 1906; Peter of Zittau, 1931.—Annalistic in Alsace, by Luzian Pfleger, 1908. See the works of Otto of Freising published in translation by Charles Ch. Mierow, *The Two Cities* (New York, 1928), and *The Deeds of Frederick Barbarossa* (New York, 1953). Find a brief evaluation of the same in James W. Thompson, *A History of Historical Writing* (New York, 1942), vol. 1, p. 145. The other historians are covered by Ghellinck, *L'essor,* vol. 2, chapter 5.

Find the bibliography about organized studies under chapter 6 and 7. The quotation on p. 157, by Matthew Paris was taken from his *Chronicle, Monumenta Germaniae Historica, Scriptores,* vol. 28, p. 427. The known works of Parisian theologians of the Order are listed in P. Glorieux, *Repertoire des maitres en théologie de Paris au XIIIe siècle* (Paris, 1933), vol. 2, pp. 246-266. On Waarde, Keysere and Sindewint cf. August Pelzer, "Livres de philosophie et théologie de l'abbaye de Ter Doest," *Coll.* 1940. See the evaluation of Mirecourt's works in Etienne Gilson's *La philosophie au moyen âge,* 2d ed. (Paris, 1947), pp. 662-665. The works of Jean of Limoges were edited by Konstantin Horváth, *Opera Omnia,* 3 vols. (Budapest, 1933). On Thomas Cisterciensis see a serial by Bruno Griesser, in *Cist.Chr.* 1939. On Steynhus, cf.

the article by Adalrich Arnold, in *Cist.Chr.* 1936; on Vischel, by Severin Grill, *Cist.Chr.* 1937; on Konrad of Ebrach, by Adolar Zumkeller, *Cist.Chr.* 1949. On the study of law see G. Müller's article in *Cist.Chr.* 1908, pp. 135 ff. and Colomban Bock, "Les cisterciens et l'étude du droit," *Anal.* 1951.

On the library of Cîteaux see an article by T. Hümpfner in *Cist.Chr.* 1926. An exemplary study is André Wilmart, "L'ancienne bibliothèque de Clairvaux," *Coll.* 1949. An essay of similar value is, "Skriptorium und Bibliothek der Cisterzienserabtei Himmerod in Rheinland," by Ambrosius Schneider, published in *Bulletin of the John Rylands Library,* vol. 35, 1952. On Heilsbronn, there is an article by M. Wieland, in *Cist.Chr.* 1907, and another by Bruno Griesser in the "Festgabe" in honor of G. Müller (Bregenz, 1926), pp. 37-50. On Altzelle, see Ludwig Schmidt, *Beiträge zur Geschichte der wissenschaftlichen Studien in sächsischen Klöstern* (Dresden, 1897); and on Alcobaça, Camille Hontoir, "L'abbaye d'Alcobaça et sa bibliothèque au moyen-age," *Coll.* 1952.

Concerning the spiritual renewal in Austria and Bohemia in the 17th century, cf. the bibliography listed under chapter 10. On the Trappists, see bibliography under chapter 9. About the effect of Jansenism in Orval, consult J. M. Canivez, *L'ordre de Cîteaux en Belgique* (Scourmont, 1926), pp. 48-51. The textbook of ascetics in Fürstenfeld was published in serial in *Cist.Chr.* 1891-92. On Nucius, there is a serial by Bernhard Widmann, in *Cist.Chr.* 1920. Biesenberger's essay was published in serial in *Cist.Chr.* 1894; see the quotation on pp. 167-8, *ibid.* p. 90. On Raitenhaslach, cf. the article by Gabriel Meier, in *Cist.Chr.* 1918. The description of Salem was published in serial by Konstantin Horváth, *Cist.Chr.* 1931; find quotation on p. 169, *ibid.* p. 89. See the story of Ulrich Mayr in a serial by Luitpold Reindl, *Studien und Mitteilungen,* 1915; the quotation on p. 169, *ibid.* p. 264. About the "White Jesuits," cf. Wilhelm Foster, "Die kirchliche Aufklärung," *Studien und Mitteilungen,* 1951, p. 184.

14. Liturgy

For a general background and as a good reference work, R. Aigrain, *Liturgia* (Paris, 1947), is recommended. Regarding Cistercian liturgy, there is a comprehensive study by André Malet,

La liturgie cistercienne (Westmalle, 1921). On Cluniac liturgy, consult the works cited in the bibliography of chapter 1. Cf. also Knowles, *The Monastic Order,* pp. 148-150. The quotation from the *Exordium Magnum* on p. 172, was taken from the text pubished by T. Hümpfner, *Cist.Chr.* 1908, p. 103. About the problem of the Office of the Dead find a good article by François Kovács, *Anal.* 1951. Abelard's letter was published by Migne, *P.L.* vol. 178, cols. 339 ff. About the newly recovered Breviary of St. Stephen see an article by Konrad Koch, *Cist.Chr.* 1950.

Concerning the development of Cistercian liturgy, the following essays are of basic importance: Bernard Kaul, "Le Psautier Cistercien," *Coll.* 1950; a long serial by G. Müller, in *Cist.Chr.* 1917-18; D. P. Blanchard, "Un monument primitif de la règle cistercienne," *Revue Bénédictine,* 1914. On the Bible of St. Stephen, the latest is a serial by Augustin Lang, in *Cist.Chr.* 1939. On the development of Cistercian Gregorian chant, there is a substantial study by Solutor Marosszéki, "Les origines du chant cistercien," *Anal.* 1952. Cf. also about the same a long serial by "Cantor," in *Coll.* 1947-49. A comprehensive publication on all questions involved is a serial by Nivard Renaud, "Les livres liturgiques cisterciens," *Coll.* 1936-39. On the Cistercian Mass rite, there are two outstanding essays: a serial by Fulgentius Schneider, in *Cist.Chr.* 1925-28, and Lancelot C. Sheppard, "The Cistercian Ordo Missae," *The Downside Review,* 1949. On the development of the Cistercian calendar, see the serials by Leodegar Walter, *Cist.Chr.* 1948, and by Bernard Backaert, "L'évolution du calendrier cistercien," *Coll.* 1950-51. On the first printed liturgical books, read Müller's above basic work, in *Cist.Chr.* 1917. The 17th century liturgical reforms are discussed in Colomban Bock's "Les codifications du droit cistercien," *Coll.* 1952. Find St. Francis of Sales' criticism over the old Cistercian rite in Müller's above study, *Cist.Chr.* 1917, p. 182. On the survival of Cistercian rite in Spain, see a serial by Bernhard Kaul, in *Cist. Chr.* 1947-48.

15. Art

Architecture is the best known chapter of the Cistercian cultural bequest; the bibliography on its medieval period is extensive, while the proper evaluation of the Cistercian Baroque is still wanting.

See the most complete bibliography on Cistercian art in the outstanding publication of Anselme Dimier, *Recueil de plans d'églises cisterciennes* (Paris, 1949).

The basic work on Cluniac art is Emile Mâle, *L'art religieux du XIIe siècle en France,* 3d ed. (Paris, 1928). Joan Evans, *Cluniac Art of the Romanesque Period* (Cambridge, 1950), is an outstanding contribution to the subject. Consult also the excellent works of W. Weisbach, listed under chapter 4.

The most conclusive work on Cistercian architecture is written by Marcel Aubert, *L'architecture cistercienne en France,* 2 vols. (Paris, 1943). Hans Rose, *Die Baukunst der Cistercienser* (München, 1916), speaks only to experts. A short but still useful chapter is included in the large work of Dehio-Bezold, *Die kirchliche Baukunst des Abendlandes,* 2 vols. (Stuttgart, 1884-1901), vol. 1. pp. 517-537. There is a similarly clear and readable work dealing substantially with Cistercians: A. L. Frothingham, *A History of Architecture,* 3 vols. (Garden City, 1915). Cistercian architecture is well presented by Joan Evans, *Art in Medieval France* (Oxford, 1948), pp. 62-76. Unfortunately, this author, too, misunderstood St. Bernard's position on art. Concerning the attitude of the early Cistercians toward art, see the article by Augustin Lang, mentioned in the previous chapter; Anselme Dimier, "Saint Etienne Harding et ses idées sur l'art," *Coll.* 1937; W. J. M. A. Asselbergs, "Un paradoxe au douzieme siècle," *Coll.* 1949. See the right interpretation of St. Bernard's much quoted *Apology* in Ervin Panofsky, *Abbot Suger* (Princeton, 1946), p. 25.

There is a large number of pictorial publications of different size, scope and value in almost every European country representing Cistercian architecture. Cf. in this regard, de Ségogne–de Maillé, *Abbayes Cisterciennes* (Paris, 1943), and Knowles–St. Joseph, *Monastic Sites from the Air* (Cambridge, 1952), with 38 Cistercian abbeys. Regarding the various countries, besides the works above, the present chapter was based upon the following studies: Abbot Gasquet, *The Greater Abbeys of England* (New York, 1908); Bruno Brard, "L'ecosse cistercienne," *Coll.* 1948; Aelredus Murray, "Melrose," *Coll.* 1935; Thompson-Clapham-Leask, "The Cistercian Order in Ireland," *The Archeological Journal,* 1931; Georg Dehio, *Geschichte der Deutschen Kunst* (Berlin, 1923), vol. 1, pp. 249 ff; Gilbert Wellstein, "Die Kunst der Cistercienser in Mecklenburg und Pommern," *Cist.Chr.* 1929; Bernard Bevan, *History of Spanish Architecture* (New York, 1939); Walter Cram Watson, *Portuguese Architecture* (London, 1908); T. Hümpfner, "Chiaravalle Milanese," *Cist.Chr.* 1907; Ladislas Gál, *L'architecture religieuse en Hongrie* (Paris, 1929); T. Hümpfner, "Cistercienser Reise durch die Schweiz," *Cist.Chr.* 1915; Frithiof Hall, "Beiträge zur Geschichte der Cistercienser Klöster in Schweden," *Cist.Chr.* 1903.

16. Economy

The accomplishments of the Order in economy are usually recognized in any standard work on the subject, although, in their praise, they rarely exceed generalities. The first successful evaluation of the work of the White Monks is an essay by E. Hoffmann, "Die Entwicklung der Wirtschaftsprinzipien in Cisterzienserorden," *Historisches Jahrbuch der Görres-Gesellschaft,* vol. XXXI (1910). The best brief survey in English is a chapter in James W. Thompson, *Economic and Social History of the Middle Ages (300-1300)* (New York, 1928), pp. 603-646.

On the backward state of agriculture see P. Boissonade, *Life and Work in Medieval Europe* (London, 1949), pp. 132 ff. Find quotation on p. 211, by Gerald of Wales in Thompson, *o.c.* On Les Dunes, see a serial by Camille Hontoir, *Coll.* 1951. Concerning tax-immunity, cf. Mahn, *L'ordre cistercien,* pp. 102-118. Sheep farming is a well explored subject in English economic history. Cf. Eileen Power, *The Wool Trade in English Medieval History* (Oxford, 1949). On Cistercians in particular, there is a good dissertation by F. A. Mullin, *A History of the Work of the Cistercians in Yorkshire* (Washington, 1932). See also David Knowles, *The Religious Orders in England* (Cambridge, 1950), pp. 64-77. On Cistercian viticulture in Alsace, consult Luzian Pfleger's serial in *Studien und Mitteilungen,* 1903. There is an outstanding study concerning Eberbach by J. Söhn, *Geschichte des wirtschaftlichen Lebens der Abtei Eberbach in Rheingau* (Wiesbaden, 1914); quotation by Obsopaeus on p. 217, was taken from here, p. 70. On Rein, see an article by Leopold Grill in *Cist.Chr.* 1932. Pisciculture in Waldsassen is detailed in Hans Muggenthaler, *Kolonisatorische und wirtschaftliche Tätigkeit eines deutschen zisterzienser Klosters* (München, 1924). On milling see Willy Hoppe, *Kloster Zinna* (Leipzig, 1914). On mining, cf. Hugh Talbot, *The Cistercian Abbeys of Scotland* (London, 1939). Find the story of the saltworks around Lüneburg in Franz Winter, *o.c.* vol. 3, pp. 32 ff. Other essays with interesting details on the above mentioned subjects are: Ambrosius Schneider, *Cistercienserabtei Himmerod* (Trier, 1938); Heinrich Pauen, *Die Klostergrundherrschaft Heisterbach* (Münster, 1913); Karl Schoene, "Kloster Hardehausen," *Studien und Mitteilungen,* 1914; Theoderich Rössler, "Pforta," *Cist.Chr.* 1931. On the size of granges, cf. Henry Pirenne, *Economic and Social History of Medieval Europe* (London, 1947), pp. 68-70. On contemporary criticism of Cistercian greediness, there is a well documented chapter in Knowles, *The Monastic Order,* pp. 662-678. Find quotation on p. 224, by Gerald of Wales in Thompson, *o.c.*

As a background for the changing economic system consult the following works: Clapham-Power, *The Cambridge Economic History* (Cambridge, 1941), vol. 1; Baldwin Summerfield, *Business in the Middle Ages* (New York, 1937); *The Cambridge Medieval History,* vol. 7, pp. 723-739.—The facts concerning Villers were taken from Coulton, *o.c.* vol. 4, pp. 10-17. On the decline of prosperity in England, see R. H. Snape, *English Monastic Finances in the Later Middle Ages* (Cambridge, 1926). Find the figures on the wealth of Kaisheim in *Cist.Chr.* 1934, p. 283.

17. Lay-Brotherhood

Since lay-brotherhood was an institution strictly connected with Cistercian economy, as to the background of its flourishing period and decline, see the reference works listed under the previous chapter.—The first substantial contribution to the subject was published by Eberhard Hoffmann, *Das Konverseninstitut des Cistercienserordens in seinem Ursprung und seiner Organisation* (Freiburg [Switzerland], 1905). The best known regulation of lay-brothers was published in Guignard, *o.c.* pp. 276-287. For the early period of the institution cf. Othon Ducourneau, *De l'institution et des us des convers dans l'ordre de Cîteaux,* in *Saint Bernard et son temps*

(Dijon, 1929), vol. 2, pp. 139-201. Regarding the office of the Papal Bullatores, see an article in *Cist.Chr.* 1908, pp. 139 ff. by Florian Watzl.

The decline of the institution is ably presented in a dissertation by James S. Donnelly, *The Decline of the Medieval Cistercian Laybrotherhood* (New York, 1949). A few interesting stories of riotous brothers are related in Coulton, *o.c. vol.* 4 (e.g. pp. 108-109). On Familiares, see Ludwig Dolberg, "Cistercienser Mönche und Conversen als Landwirthe und Arbeiter," *Studien und Mitteilungen,* 1892. See the conditions in England in Snape, *English Monastic Finances,* especially in chapter 1.

18. Cistercian Nuns

There is no comprehensive study on the history of Cistercian nuns. The articles published in *Cist.Chr.* on the subject are the following: Benedikt Hene, "Einiges über Cistercienserinnen," serial, 1897; Gregor Müller, "Generalkapitel der Cistercienserinnen," serial, 1912; and another publication by the same author, 1915, pp. 33 ff. About the relation of Cistercian and Dominican nuns see Mandonnet, *o.c.* pp. 369-379. The only source for the correlation of Cîteaux and the nuns regarding spiritual care and guidance is Canivez, *Statuta,* especially vols. 2 and 3. On saints and mystics there is a long serial in *Cist.Chr.* 1939, "Heilige Frauengestalten unseres Ordens," by Robert Klopfer.

On the reforms of nuns, cf. Ailbe Luddy, *The Cistercian Nuns* (Dublin, 1931), and Alexis Presse, "Les moniales cisterciennes reformées," *Revue Mabillon,* 1934. There are two voluminous works, both dealing with the fate of these institutions in the Low Countries: Joseph-Marie Canivez, *L'ordre de Cîteaux en Belgique* (Scourmont, 1926), and Th. Ploegaerts, *Les moniales de l'ordre de Cîteaux dans les Pay-Bas meridionaux, de 1550 a 1800,* 3 vols. (Westmalle, 1936-37). Unfortunately, however, both authors, instead of presenting the available material concerning internal life, focus upon the description of disasters which frequently afflicted those communities. On Spain, see Amédée Garcia, "L'ordre de Cîteaux en Espagne. Les religieuses," *Coll.* 1935.

Index

Historical Maps

OF CISTERCIAN ESTABLISHMENTS
IN EUROPE

FRANCE
CLAIRMARAIS
LOOS
LONGVILLIERS
VALLOIRES
CERCAMP
LIEU DIEU
LE GARD
VAUCELLES
BOHÉRIES
FOIGNY
FOUCARMONT
BONNEFONTAINE
SIGNY
ELANT
BEAUBEC
LANNOYE
BEAUPRÉ
OURSCAMP
VALROY
LE HAVRE
LA VALASSE
VAUCLAIR
CHATILLON
FREISTROFF
VILLERS BETNACH
MORTEMER
FROIDMONT
BONPORT
LONGPONT
CHERI
STURZELBRONN
TORIGNY
VAL RICHER
ROYAUMONT
CHALIS
ST LAZARE
LA CHALADE
BARBERY
N.D. DU VAL
LA NOE
LA CHARMOYE
ST BENOIT EN VOIVRE
ST ANDRÉ DE GOUFFERN
MOUTIER EN ARGONNE
ISLE EN BARROIS
NEUBOURG
BREUIL BENOIT
PARIS
BELLE-EAU
LE RECLUS
CHEMINON
STRASBOURG
BEGARD
VIEUXVILLE
TROIS FONTAINES
CLAIRLIEU
HAUTE SEILLE
LE RELECQ
LA TRAPPE
VAUX DE CERNAY
HAUTE FONTAINE
VAUX EN ORNOIS
St AUBIN DES BOIS
SAVIGNY
SELLIÈRES
PIÉTÉ DIEU
ESCUREY
BEAUPRÉ
COETMALOEN
BARBEAUX
BOULANCOURT
BAUMGARTEN
BOQUEN
BON REPOS
FONTAINE DANIEL
PERSEIGNE
PREUILLY
LANGONNET
VAULUISANT
LARRIVOUR
TIRONNEAU
LA CRÊTE
PAIRIS
CLAIRMONT
CHAMPAGNE
CERCANCEAUX
CLAIRVAUX
MORES
MORIMOND
L'EPAU
ST MAURICE
LONGUAY
CLAIREFONTAINE
LA COUR DIEU
LANVAUX
BELLEBRANCHE
LES ESCHARLIS
PONTIGNY
VAUX LA DOUCE
AUMONE
QUINCY
CHERLIEU
BEAULIEU
FONTAINE JEAN
LA CHARITE
AUBERIVE
BITHAINE
LA CHARITE
PRIÈRES
MELLERAYE
CHALOCHE
LA CLARTÉ DIEU
RIGNY
FONTENAY
PONTROND
LA BOISSIERE
FONTAINE LES BLANCHES
THEULEY
LUCELLE
LIEU CROISSANT
LES ROCHES
LOROUX
BELLEVAUX
NANTES
OLIVET
LORROY
BOURAS
DIJON
BUZAY
ACEY
LA GRÂCE DIEU
VILLENEUVE
VARENNES
BARZELLE
CHALIVOY
LA BUSSIERE
BULLION
ILE DIEU
CITEAUX
LANDAIS
FONT MORIGNY
BEAUGERAIS
ROSIERES

BOIS GROLAND
MOREILLES
ILE DE RÉ
TRISAY
LES CHÂTELLIERS
CHARON
LA GRÂCE DIEU
ST LEONARD
LE PIN
BONNEVAUX
VALENCE
LA MERCI DIEU
L'ÉTOILE
AUBIGNAC
COLOMBE
AUBEPIERRES
LA PREE
NOIRLAC
LES PIERRES
PRÉ BENOIT
BELLAIGUE
BONLIEU
SEPT FONS
MONTPERIOUX
LA FERTÉ
BALERNE
MONT ST MARIE
LE MIROIR
CHÉZERY
ST. JEAN D'AULPS
CHASSAGNE
ST SULPICE
HAUTECOMBE
TAMIÉ
LYON
BEUIL
PALAIS N.D.
LA FRENADE
GROSBOIS
PEYROUSE
BOUSCHAUD
DALON
BONNE AIGUE
LE BOUCHET
MÉGEMONT
FENIÈRES
LA VALETTE
OBAZINE
VAL BENOITE
BONNEVAUX
LA FAISE
BORDEAUX
BONLIEU
CADOUIN
LÉONCEL
VALCROISSANT
MAZAN
CHAMBONS
BONLIEU
AIGUEBELLE
LE RIVET
GONDOM
FORT GUILLEM
BONNEVAL
PEYRIGNAC
LA GARDE DIEU
BELLOC
BONNECOMBE
ST MARCEL
BOUILLAS
BELLEPERCHE
FLARAN
GRANDSELVE
CANDEIL
SILVANES
LA BESSIÉRE
VAL SAINTE
SÉNANQUE
PONTAUT
GIMONT
FRANQUEVAUX
SILVACANE
SAUVELADE
BERDOUES
ARDORELLE
VALMAGNE
SAUVERIAL
TORONET
LES FEUILLANTS
EAUNES
BOLBONNE
NISORS
CALERS
MARSEILLE
ESCALE DIEU
BONNEFONT
FONTFROIDE
VILLELONGUE
ST ANDRE & N.D. DU JAU
VALBONNE

GREAT BRITAIN
IRELAND
KINLOSS
DEER
ABERDEEN
CUPAR
BALMERINO
CULLROSS
EDINBURGH
GLASGOW
NEWBOTTLE
MELROSE
SANDAL
NEWMINSTER
SWEETHEART
GLENLUCE
HOLMCULTRAM
DUNDRENNAN
MOYCOSQUIN
GRAY ABBEY
ASTRATH
INISCOURCEY
CUMBER
NEWRY
BOYLE
MELLIFONT
LERHA
BECTIVE
SHRULE
KILBEGGAN
DUBLIN
KNOCKMOY
ST MARY
MONASTEREVAN
CORCUMROE
ABBEYLEIX
BALTINGLASS
ABBINGTON
KILCOOLY
GRAIGUENAMANAGH
NENAY
HORE ABBEY
HOLY CROSS
JERPOINT
ODORNEY
KILSHANE
INISLOUNAGH
TINTERN
DUNBRODY
FERMOY
CHORE (MIDLETON)
MAURE
TRACTON
RIEVAULX
BYLAND
CALDER
JERVAULX
FURNESS
FOUNTAINS
SAWLEY
MEAUX
WHALLEY
KIRKSTALL
LIVERPOOL
ROCHE
LOUTH PARK
RUFFORD
VALE ROYAL
KIRKSTEAD
BASINGWERK
REVESBY
DIEULACRES
ABERCONWAY
COMBERMERE
SWINESHEAD
HULTON
VALLE CRUCIS
CROXDEN
VAUDEY
CARENDON
CYMMER
BUILDWAS
PIPEWELL
STRATA MARCELLA
MEREVALE
COMBE
SAWTRY
SIBTON
STONELEIGH
CWMHIR
BORDESLEY
WARDON
BITTLESDEN
TILTEY
STRATA FLORIDA
DORE
HAYLES
WOBURN
COGGESHALL
FLAXLEY
OXFORD
GRACEDIEU
BRUERN
THAME
STRATFORD LANGTHON
WHITLAND
REWLEY
NEATH
TINTERN
MEDMENHAM
LONDON
KINGSWOOD
BOXLEY
STANLEY
MARGAM
WAVERLEY
ROBERTSBRIDGE
CLEEVE
NETLEY
BEAULIEU
DUNKESWELL
FORD
QUARR
NEWENHAM
BINDON
BUCKFAST
BUCKLAND

MONFERO
VILLANUEVA
VALDEDIOS
OVIEDO
BELMONTE
MEIRA
SOBRADO
SANTIAGO
PENAMAYOR
OSERA
CARRACEDO
ARMENTERA
S. CLODIO
FRANQUEIRA
MELON
JUNGUEIRA
OYA
MONTEDERAMO
S. MARTIN
MORERUELA
BOURO
PORTO
TAROUCA
SALCEDAS
COIMBRA
MACEIRA
CEICA
ALCOBACA
LISBOA
AVIS
ALCANTARA
SANDOVAL
VEGA
NOGALES
BENAVIDES
MATALLANA
PALAZUELOS
S. ESPINA
VAL BUENA
VALLADOLID
SACRAMENIA
VAL PARAISO
SALAMANCA
RIOSECO
BURGOS
BUJEDO
S. PEDRO
HERRERA
IRANZU
LEIRE
LAOLIVA
MARCILLA
S. PRUDENCIO
FITERO
VERUELA
HUESCA
LABAIX
LERIDA
SANTA FE
RUEDA
POBLET
ESCARPE
BARCELONA
S. CREUS
S. SUSANA
HUERTA
PIEDRA
SOTOSALBOS
BONAVAL
OVILA
BENIFAZA
MADRID
MONSALUD
VALDEIGLESIAS
M. SION
TOLEDO
VALENCIA
LAREAL
PALMA
VALDIGNA
MONTESA
CALATRAVA
S. ISIDORO
SEVILLA
SPAIN-
PORTUGAL

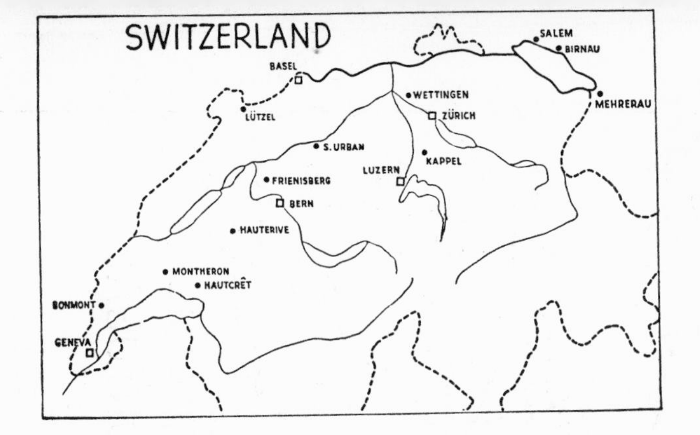
SWITZERLAND
SALEM
BIRNAU
BASEL
WETTINGEN
MEHRERAU
LÜTZEL
ZÜRICH
S. URBAN
KAPPEL
LUZERN
FRIENISBERG
BERN
HAUTERIVE
MONTHERON
HAUTCRÊT
BONMONT
GENEVA

MAIA BASSA
PIONA
ACQUAFREDDA
FOLLINA
CAPOLAGO
LE PIANE
SORDEVOLO
TORCELLO
CASALVOLONE
CHIARAVALLE
MAGUZZANO
LOCEDIO
CERREDO
MORIMONDO
LA CAVA
RIPALTA
ACQUALUNGA
S. STEFANO
BRONDOLO
BARONA
CASANOVA
QUARTAZZOLA
RIPALTA
VALSERENA
STAFFARDA
SEZZE
LA COLOMBA
FONTEVIVO
FERRARA
MT. BRAC
PREALLO
TIGLIETO
SESTRI
STRADA
JUBINO
BOLOGNE
S. SEVERO
CLASSE
LA CERVARA
MIRTETO
S. GODENZO
S. PANTALEONE
MONTE FAVALI
VERRUCA
BUONSOLAZZO
SETTIMO
SALA
CASTAGNOLA
MONTE ACUTO
QUARTO
S. M. DEI LUMI
S. ANTONIO
CLIENTE
S GALGANO
MONTECORONA
FIASTRA
MONTAMIATA
CASTRO
S. M. DELLE GRAZIE
S. SPIRITO
S. GIUSTO
S. MARTINO
CASANOVA
ARABONA
TREMITI
FALLERI
LA VITTORIA
SS. VITO E SALVO
S. SEBASTIANO
ROME
TRISULTI
RIPALTA
S. ANASTASIO
FRATOCCHIE
PALAZZUOLO
CASAMARI
VALVISCIOLO
MARMOSOGLIO
FOSSANOVA
SEMPRONE
STIRPETO
PONCIO
REALVALLE
S. M. DELLE PALUDI
CANONICA
S. SPIRITO
GALESO
COTRINO
L'INCORONATA
LA CARITA
CABUABBAS
S. M. DELLA
CONSOLAZIONE
SAGITTARIO
ACQUAFORMOSA
MATTINA
SS. TRINITA
SAMBUCINA
CORAZZO
S. ANGELO
USTICA
S. STEFANO
ITALY
PALERMO
ROCCAMADORE
ALTOFONTE
LA NUARA
SPANO
S^{T} NICOLAS
ROCCADIA
L'ARCO

GERMANY
RUHEKLOSTER
HIDDENSE
DOBERAN
NEUENKAMP
REINFELD
HAMBURG
DARGUN
ELDENA
STOLPE
HIMMELPFORTE
BUKOW
OLIVA
DANZIG
PELPLIN
HUDE
BREMEN
MARIENFLIESS
STETTIN
LOCCUM
COLBAZ
MARIENWALDE
BESSOW
BROMBERG
OSNABRÜCK
HANNOVER
CHORIN
HIMMELSTAEDT
LECKNO
MARIENFELD
RIDDAGSHAUSEN
BERLIN
KL.
GR.
BURIO
CAMP
MARIENRODA
MARIENTHAL
LEHNIN
MÜNSTER
DERNBURG
MAGDEBURG
NEU-DOBRILUGK
AMELUNGSBORN
PARADIES
HARDEHAUSEN
NEUZELLE
MARIENSEE
GREVENBROICH
OBRA
BREDELAR
CASSEL
ZINNA
BOTTENBROICH
ALTENBERG
WALKENRIED
MICHAELSTEIN
DOBRILUGK
AACHEN
KÖLN
HALLE
REIFENSTEIN
SITTICHENBACH
LEIPZIG
MARIAWALD
HEISTERBACH
VOLKERODE
PFORTA
HAINA
BUCH
WEIMAR
DRESDEN
MARIENSTATT
COBLENZ
ALTENZELL
BRESLAU
GEORGENTAL
LEUBUS
ARNSBURG
GRÜNHAIN
HIMMEROD
EBERBACH
GRÜSSAU
OSSEG
HEINRICHAU
MAINZ
TRIER
LANGHEIM
KAMENZ
HIMMELWITZ
DISIBODENBERG
EBRACH
EGER
FREISTORF
BRONNBACH
CASIMIR
WEILER
WERSCHWEILER
WÜRZBURG
BAMBERG
WALDSASSEN
METZ
OTTERBERG
SCHÖNAU
PRAGUE
RAUDEN
BILDHAUSEN
S. BENEDICTUS
STURCELBRONN
EUSSERTAL
NÜRNBERG
ESCUREY
SCHÖNTAL
HEILSBRONN
NEUBURG
MAULBRONN
HOHENFORST
HERRENALB
WALDERSBACH
STRASSBURG
STUTTGART
GOTTESZELL
BAUMGARTEN
KÖNIGSBRONN
BEBENHAUSEN
PAIRIS
KAISHEIM
THENNENBACH
ALDERSBACH
AUGSBURG
FREIBURG
FÜRSTENZELL
FÜRSTENFELD
SALEM
MÜNCHEN
REITENHASLACH
LÜTZEL
WIEN
BIRNAU
MEHRERAU

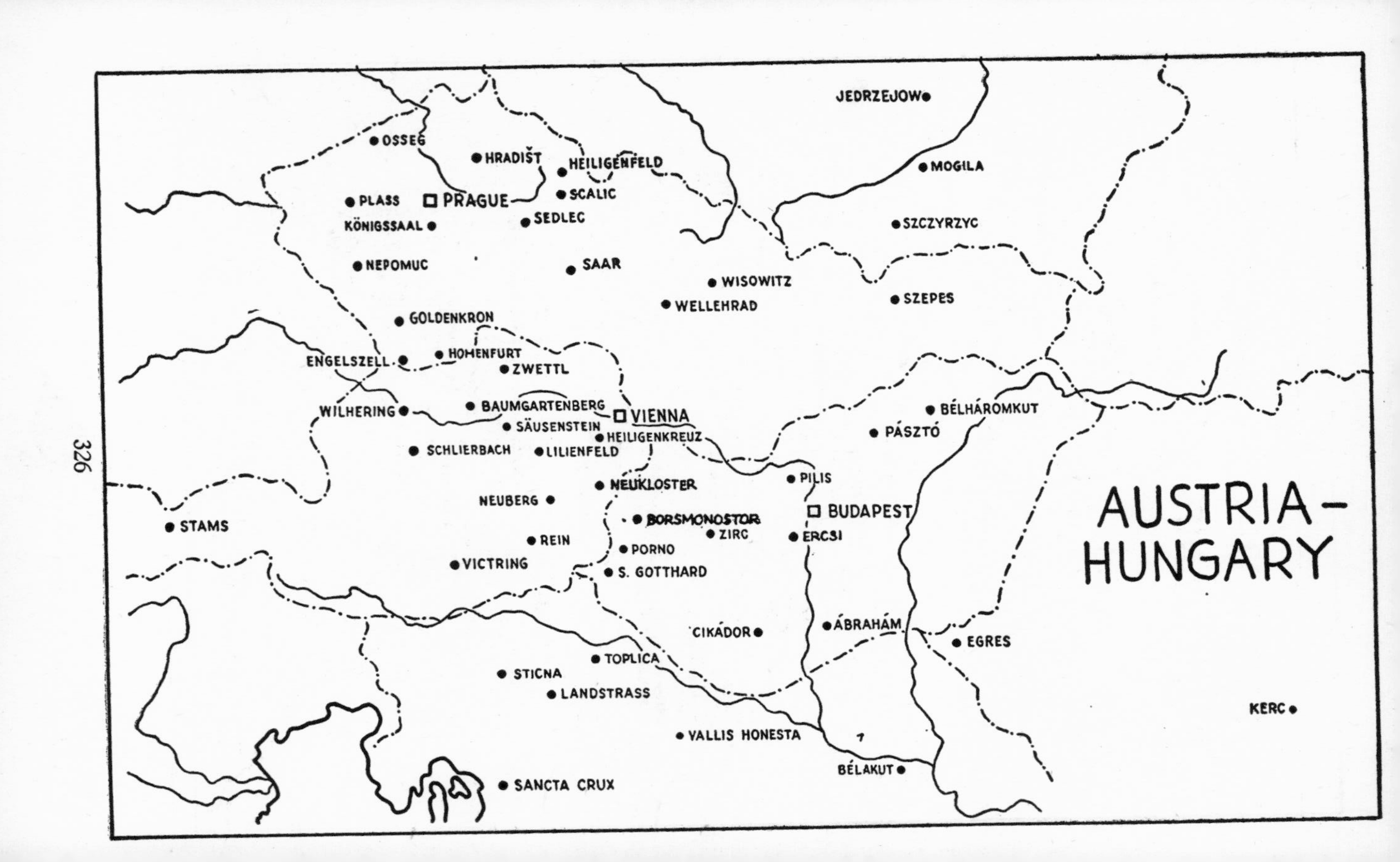
AUSTRIA–
HUNGARY
JEDRZEJOW
MOGILA
SZCZYRZYC
SZEPES
OSSEG
HRADIŠT
HEILIGENFELD
SCALIC
PLASS
PRAGUE
KÖNIGSSAAL
SEDLEC
NEPOMUC
SAAR
WISOWITZ
WELLEHRAD
GOLDENKRON
ENGELSZELL
HOHENFURT
ZWETTL
WILHERING
BAUMGARTENBERG
VIENNA
SÄUSENSTEIN
HEILIGENKREUZ
SCHLIERBACH
LILIENFELD
BÉLHÁROMKUT
PÁSZTÓ
PILIS
BUDAPEST
ERCSI
NEUKLOSTER
NEUBERG
BORSMONOSTOR
ZIRC
PORNO
S. GOTTHARD
STAMS
REIN
VICTRING
CIKÁDOR
ÁBRAHÁM
EGRES
TOPLICA
STICNA
LANDSTRASS
VALLIS HONESTA
BÉLAKUT
KERC
SANCTA CRUX

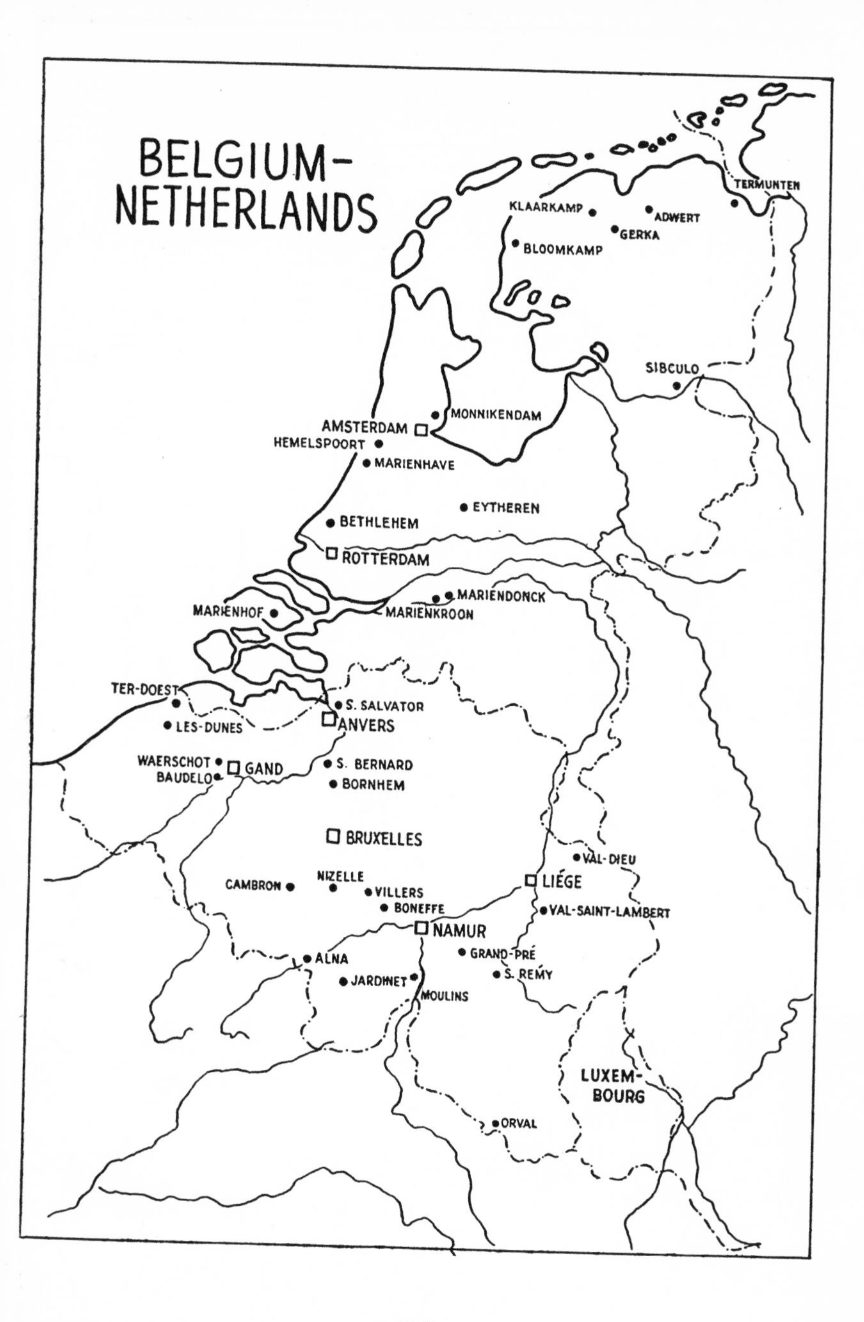
BELGIUM-
NETHERLANDS
TERMUNTEN
KLAARKAMP
ADWERT
GERKA
BLOOMKAMP
SIBCULO
MONNIKENDAM
AMSTERDAM
HEMELSPOORT
MARIENHAVE
EYTHEREN
BETHLEHEM
ROTTERDAM
MARIENDONCK
MARIENHOF
MARIENKROON
TER-DOEST
S. SALVATOR
LES-DUNES
ANVERS
WAERSCHOT
GAND
BAUDELO
S. BERNARD
BORNHEM
BRUXELLES
VAL-DIEU
LIÉGE
CAMBRON
NIZELLE
VILLERS
BONEFFE
VAL-SAINT-LAMBERT
NAMUR
ALNA
GRAND-PRÉ
JARDINET
S. REMY
MOULINS
LUXEM-
BOURG
ORVAL

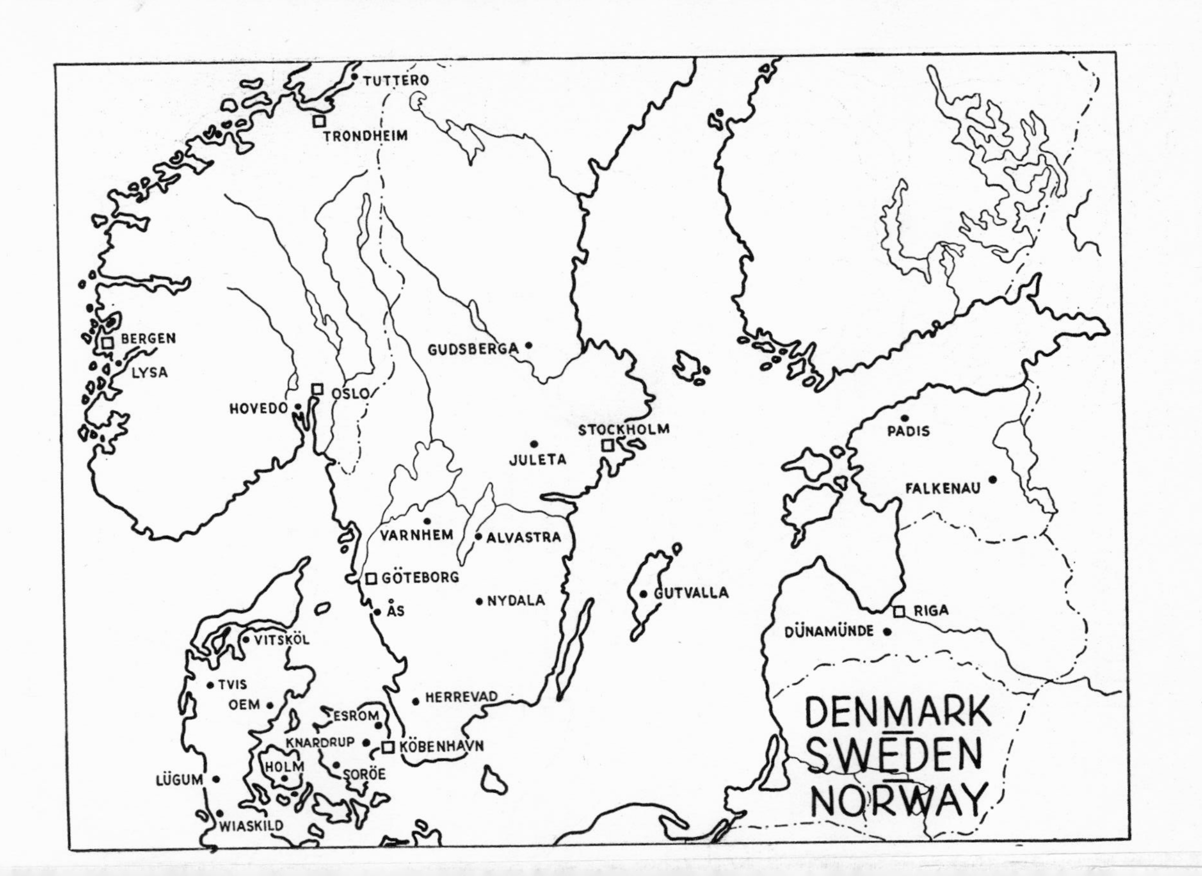
TUTTERO
TRONDHEIM
BERGEN
LYSA
HOVEDO
OSLO
GUDSBERGA
STOCKHOLM
JULETA
VARNHEM
ALVASTRA
GÖTEBORG
NYDALA
ÅS
GUTVALLA
PADIS
FALKENAU
RIGA
DÜNAMÜNDE
VITSKÖL
TVIS
OEM
HERREVAD
ESROM
KNARDRUP
KÖBENHAVN
HOLM
SORÖE
LÜGUM
WIASKILD
DENMARK
SWEDEN
NORWAY

1. The Bible of St. Stephen Harding. The beginning of the Book of Esther.

2. Washing-fountain in Heiligenkreuz.

3. Chapter-house in Maulbronn. 14th century.

Caisse Nationale des Monuments Historiques. Paris.

4. Dining-hall in Royaumont. 13th century.

5. Cloister in Hauterive. 12th century.

Caisse Nationale des Monuments Historiques. Paris.

6. The church of Fontenay. 1147

7. Senanque.

Courtesy of Office of Works. London.

8. FOUNTAINS. 13TH CENTURY.

Courtesy of Office of Works. London.

9. RIEVAULX. 13TH CENTURY.

Courtesy of Office of Works. London.

10. Melrose. 15th century

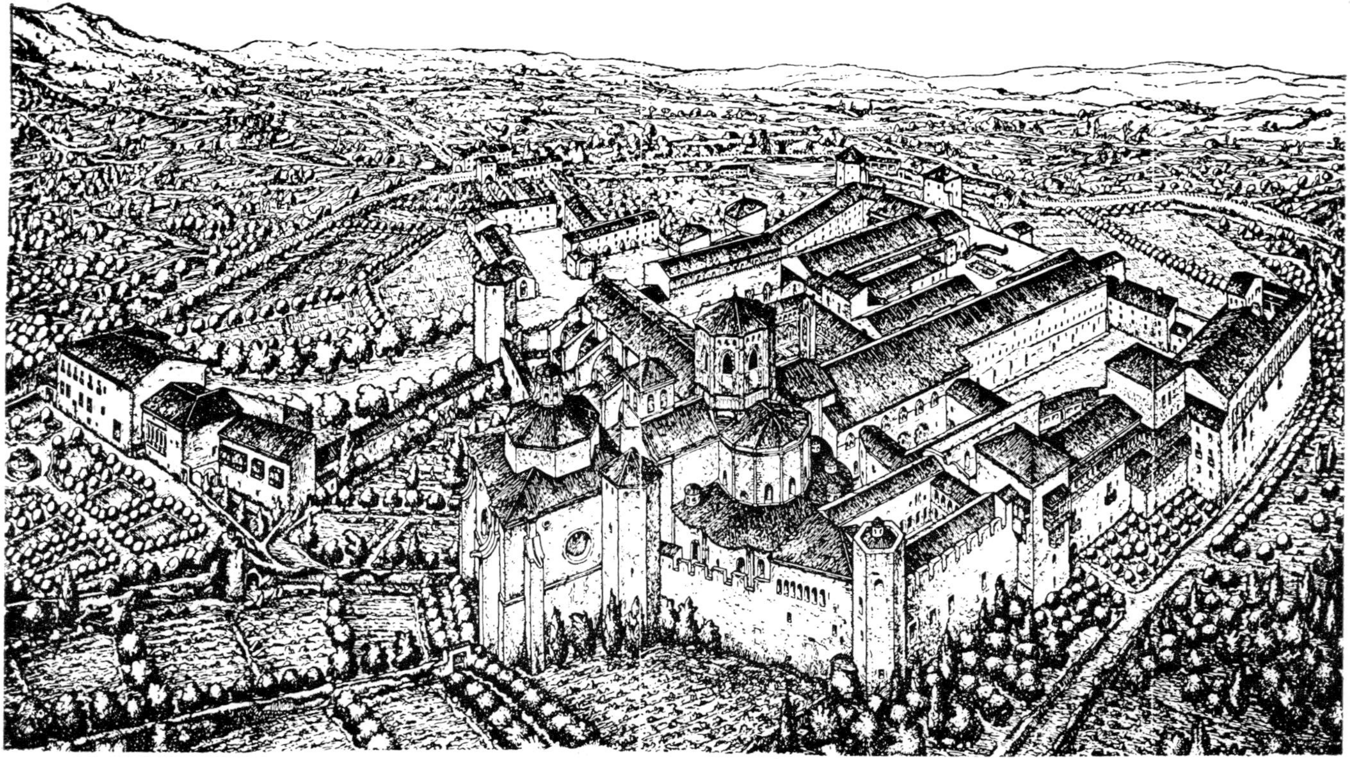

11. Poblet in 1830

12. Alcobaça. The tombs of Pedro I and his wife, Inez. 14th century.

13. Chiaravalle della Colomba. 13th century

14. THE CHURCH OF ALTENBERG. 13TH CENTURY.

15. Interior of the church of Altenberg. 13th century.

16. Western façade of the church of Chorin. 1334.

17. Façade of the church of Heiligenkreuz. 12th century.

18. Lilienfeld.

19. Zwettl. High altar. 14-18th centuries.

20. HAUTERIVE. 12TH CENTURY.

21. Choir stalls of St. Urban. 18th century.

22. Zirc from the air.

23. The old and the new Himmerod.

Reprinted from "Das Münster zu Salem" by the courtesy of Hirmer Verlag, München.

24. SALEM. THE ABBOTS' MONUMENT. 18TH CENTURY

25. Staircase in Ebrach. 1716.

Reprinted from "Vierzehnheiligen," by the courtesy of K.R. Langewiesche. Königstein.

26. Vierzehnheiligen. 1743.

27. Grüssau. 1735

28. INTERIOR OF THE CHURCH OF STAMS. 18TH CENTURY

29. The Baroque Rein. 18th century.

30. Choir stalls in Heiligenkreuz. 1707.

31. ZIRC. HIGH ALTAR. 1755.

32. The library in Schlierbach. 18th century.